ROBERT CANTWELL

AND

THE LITERARY LEFT

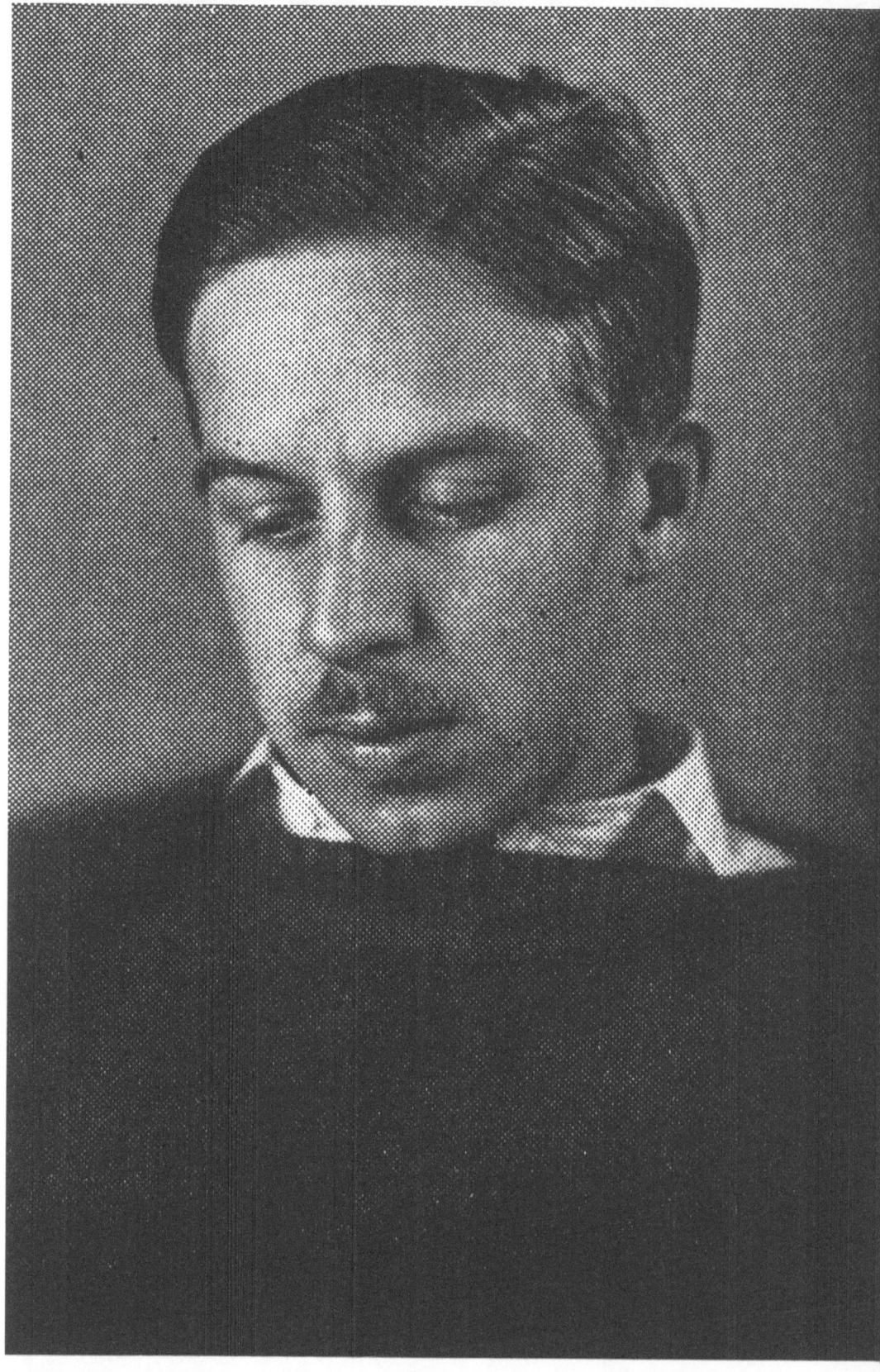

ROBERT CANTWELL AND THE LITERARY LEFT

A NORTHWEST WRITER REWORKS AMERICAN FICTION

T. V. REED

A ROBERT B. HEILMAN BOOK
UNIVERSITY OF WASHINGTON PRESS
SEATTLE AND LONDON

Robert Cantwell and the Literary Left: A Northwest Writer Reworks American Fiction is published with support from a generous bequest established by Robert B. Heilman, distinguished scholar and chair of the University of Washington English Department from 1948 to 1971. The Heilman Book Fund assists in the publication of books in the humanities.

© 2015 by the University of Washington Press
Printed and bound in the USA
Design: Dustin Kilgore
Composed in Minion, a typeface designed by Robert Slimbach
First paperback edition 2015
19 18 17 16 15   5 4 3 2 1

All rights reserved. No part of this publication may be reproduced or transmitted in any form or by any means, electronic or mechanical, including photocopy, recording, or any information storage or retrieval system, without permission in writing from the publisher.

University of Washington Press
www.washington.edu/uwpress

Library of Congress Cataloging-in-Publication Data

Reed, T. V. (Thomas Vernon)
Robert Cantwell and the literary left : a northwest writer reworks american fiction / T.V. Reed.
    pages   cm
Includes bibliographical references and index.
ISBN 978-0-295-99363-8 (paperback)
1. Cantwell, Robert, 1908–1978. 2. Authors, American—20th century—Biography I. Title.
PS3505.A58Z88 2014
813'.52—dc23
                    2014010609

The paper used in this publication is acid-free and meets the minimum requirements of American National Standard for Information Sciences—Permanence of Paper for Printed Library Materials, ANSI Z39.48-1984.∞

For Alan Wald, consummate chronicler of the US cultural left

CONTENTS

Preface ix

Acknowledgments xix

1 Rewriting the Left: Critical Contexts   3

2 Mill Towns, Blue Collar Work, and Literary Ambitions: Cantwell's Childhood and Adolescence   20

3 A Student of Karl Marx and Henry James: Cantwell and the Literary Wars of the Early 1930s   35

4 A Portrait of the Artist as Propagandist: Cantwell as Proletarian Novelist   64

5 The Revolutionist Meets the Capitalist: Cantwell as Biographer and Nonfiction Novelist   97

6 *Time,* Doubt, and the Popular Front: Cantwell and the Ideological Storms of the Late 1930s   118

7 Breaking Down, Moving On, Looking Back: Cantwell in the Wake of the 1930s   142

CONCLUSION: Lessons, Legacies, Literary Lefts: Cantwell and the Reworking of American Literature   159

AFTERWORD: A Working-Class Hero Is Something to Be   178

Notes 179

Bibliography 208

Index 222

PREFACE

He was Ernest Hemingway's "best bet" for a fiction writer of his generation. F. Scott Fitzgerald said he "had a destiny as [a literary] star." Who elicited such praise from these literary lights? Robert Cantwell (1908–1978), a novelist and critic born near Centralia and raised in Aberdeen, Washington. Cantwell was a writer who rose to prominence in New York left literary circles in the 1930s, but whose accomplishments were buried by post–World War II anticommunism and McCarthyism. Cantwell was among the two or three most widely read and widely praised "proletarian" fiction writers in 1930s America. His two novels and several short stories were lionized not only by Hemingway and Fitzgerald but also by the foremost cultural critic of the era, Edmund Wilson, as well as by such central literary figures as Malcolm Cowley, James T. Farrell, John Dos Passos, and Mary McCarthy (who worked for Cantwell as his editorial assistant at one point, and later used him as the basis for the main character in one of her more important stories). Cantwell was also very highly regarded by his peers as a literary critic, writing for the most prominent journals of the era, including the *New Republic*, the *Nation*, the *New York Times Book Review*, and the *Saturday Review*.

Yet, today few people outside of the circle of academic specialists on the 1930s know of Robert Cantwell. This book aims to help remedy that situation. But my goal is not simply to rescue one talented fiction writer and critic from oblivion. Rather my goal is to help draw greater attention to a much larger gap in popular knowledge about American literature and culture. For Cantwell was at the heart of a large-scale transformation that occurred in mid-twentieth-century US culture, a transformation that Michael Denning has called "the laboring of American culture."[1]

Cantwell's story matters both on its own merits and also because it gives insight into this larger mid-twentieth-century cultural process that moved millions of working-class US citizens from the margins to the center of the society, only to subtly and not-so-subtly remarginalize them during and after the Cold War era. Failure to acknowledge this cultural project has meant that millions of everyday American workers have remained largely absent from the story of American literature and the wider story of US culture.

Cantwell's particular life history illuminates this larger cultural transformation, and we can read his life history as being shaped by, but also in turn shaping, this larger social process. Cantwell's literary and personal trajectory proved to be almost wholly entangled with this process of putting the working class at the heart of American culture. In the midthirties Cantwell wrote that his key role as critic and fiction writer was "to give workers a sense of their own dignity."[2] This aim remains a worthy one, in which cultural historians and literary critics have a substantial part to play. It matters because exaggerated reaction to the "politicizing" of literature in the form of postthirties anticommunist hysteria continues to limit our understanding of the political nature of all literary and critical activity.

Robert Cantwell is an ideal subject for such a study because his career as a fiction writer and literary critic nearly perfectly coincides with that twelve-year period from 1929 to 1941 that we too conveniently label "the thirties." Those years forged the main contours of a restructuring of American culture around the reality and the image of the "worker," and Cantwell was at the very heart of that process. While Cantwell's novel *Land of Plenty* has received a modest amount of attention, even it has never been studied carefully in context, and his criticism and his career as a whole have never before been subjected to systematic sympathetic analysis. Cantwell is thus one key figure that, while not newly discovered, is ripe for renewed consideration.[3]

Emerging from western Washington as the thirties began, Cantwell was soon thrown into the center of the struggle to develop a Marxist literary criticism and a proletarian literature in the New York of that decade. But his fictional world remained centered in the Northwest, and his accomplishments have regional importance too. Bruce Barcott, editor of *Northwest Passages: A Literary Anthology of the Pacific Northwest*, has called *The Land of Plenty* "the first modern novel to come out of the Northwest ... innovative and brutal and gripping at the same time. If it had been set in New York or Chicago it would still be on college reading lists. It's just a shame that it's lost in the musty stacks instead."[4] Work on figures such as Cantwell is part of an emerging effort to view thirties literary and political radicalism as far more than the exclusive territory of a couple of large cities.[5]

Cantwell's story deserves telling for its intrinsic interest as he wends his way through such literary and critical influences as Henry James, James Joyce, John Dos Passos, Edmund Wilson, Ernest Hemingway, James T. Farrell, and Malcolm Cowley; builds a solid career as a literary radical; then abandons both literature and politics at the end of the decade. But his story also takes on wider import in that it is in many respects the story of a whole generation of writers who took up the literary vocation just as its traditional definitions were being challenged. Thus by focusing on Cantwell's criticism and fiction, I hope to illuminate key questions raised by the various scholars of thirties culture, examining how the forces and counterforces of the Depression decade played themselves out in the life of one writer attempting to follow, challenge, and embody in his fiction aspects of a revolutionary agenda.

My goal will not be to offer a full-scale biographical study of Cantwell, but rather to use him as a case study in the intellectual and cultural history of America in the thirties.[6] Indeed, I would say that Cantwell was so much a creature of his time that he was forced to entirely remake himself when the decade came to an end. Some scholars have rightly pointed to continuities with earlier and later periods that make the category "the thirties" an artificially contained and constrained time period.[7] But in Cantwell's case the thirties was in fact a discrete era, and that fact too must be acknowledged, not only in regard to his career but as a reminder that many figures of the literary left also thought of the thirties as a distinct, bounded time. While Cantwell continued writing after the thirties, he never again published fiction, and turned mostly to politically safe sports and nature writing.[8] I will not follow this part of his career in depth except to trace the fascinating ways in which, through the influence of people such as the infamous Whittaker Chambers, Cantwell came to distance himself from the positions he articulated amid the discursive struggles of the Depression era, even as Cantwell's thirties persona continued to haunt him until his death.

When I say that I am not offering a full-scale biography, I mean that despite basing my work in deep immersion in Cantwell's personal papers,[9] I am interested in his personal life primarily when it directly impinges upon or broadly illuminates his professional roles as fiction writer and literary critic. There are no doubt aspects of Cantwell's life that show continuity over the divide of 1939, but his life as a public figure, the part that concerns us here, shows a radical discontinuity. I am interested in Cantwell as an "individual" in so far as his particularities and idiosyncrasies shape his cultural role, but I want to view him also as a "discursive site," as a point of confluence for various cultural rhetorics and material processes. I aim neither to deny nor to exaggerate subjective factors, but to read Cantwell's career as exemplary in showing how a particular life was mediated through the larger historical forces of the era. My interest is in tracing how one talented young writer who came of age in the thirties was shaped by, and also shaped to his own skills and interests, the cultural formations of the decade. In doing so, I share the attitude and goals expressed by Alan Wald in these terms: "To reintroduce the individualized [context] of the writer's singular being and consciousness is not to become a biographer but to restore the self-activity of left cultural workers as well as supply some neglected mediations in the creative act—especially the mentality of the artist and the force field of the institutions within which he or she worked."[10]

My book seeks to play a small part in this larger, ongoing attempt to revise the Cold War–generated representation of Marxist-influenced American writers as "artists in uniform" marching in step to Moscow-manipulated Communist Party USA (CPUSA) bureaucrats with no interest in literary quality or historical truth. My study of Cantwell makes clear that neither he nor his cohorts fit these stereotyped images of the mid-century US literary left. The term "fellow traveler" in the thirties was often used disparagingly to name someone on the left who did not have the courage or conviction to join the most prominent leftist organization of the era, the CPUSA. But, as Michael Denning has argued, in a sense the "fellow travelers" were the heart of the radical movement of the decade, while the Party, crucially important as it was, represented only the tip of a much larger social movement.[11] Cantwell's position is an example of what might be called "critical fellow traveling," by which I mean to suggest that Cantwell and his peers were very much a part of the Marxist literary movement, but that involvement took the form of a critically engaged, independent approach committed to revolutionary change. This undogmatic approach was far more typical of writers during this era than critics allege.

Much important work in recent decades has sought to get beyond the image of the radical novelist as an angry young white male. Work informed by feminist, critical race, and queer theory has revolutionized our view of the thirties, as with much of US literary and cultural history. Unfortunately, one of the ironies of this revisionist work is that it has largely passed over Cantwell's case, presumably because he appears to be too close to the limited, earlier image of the dogmatic proletarian. This study will complicate that picture by looking at him as being class conscious in psychologically subtle ways, and as a writer engaged with issues of race, ethnicity, and gender as well.

In the spirit of the scholarly literature seeking to get beyond stereotyped reductions of the "Red decade," this examination of Cantwell will seek to answer questions such as these: In what specific ways do Cantwell's literary and political ideas suggest allegiance to any Communist "Party line" on literature, and to what extent do they suggest significant independence of judgment? In "The Intellectuals Turn Left," the main culture chapter of Irving Howe and Lewis Coser's widely influential Cold War study *The American Communist Party* (1957), Howe and Coser cite Cantwell as an exemplar of a writer whose closeness to the alleged "Party line" negatively affected his fiction. Were they right? To what extent and in what ways was Cantwell's talent aided or hindered by his association with the left? Were his fiction and criticism blunted or distorted by his association with Marxist ideas? Or did that association in some way help develop his writing in positive ways? Or did it do both? Does Cantwell's critical output confirm or challenge notions about the reductive nature of thirties Marxist criticism generally? How does Cantwell situate himself in regard to debates about the nature and purposes of "proletarian" writing? To what extent do his ideas remain constant or change in relation to political shifts in the era? To what extent does his fiction embody or extend his ideas about proletarian literature, and what generally does it reveal about relations between various critical and literary currents, and the particulars of one writer's literary production? How does that literary production look through lenses provided by more recent theoretical perspectives? What attitudes and beliefs about race and gender, for example, are embodied in his fiction and criticism? How does his work view class—as independent from or as embedded with gendered and racialized structures? Most broadly, how does Cantwell's career at once reflect and show reflection upon the "cultural front" that was so central to the wider "laboring of American culture" in the mid-twentieth-century?

Chapter 1 provides a set of critical contexts for situating the larger issues that this case study addresses. I comment on the scholarly literature that over several generations has sought to undo stereotypes and make more realistic and complicated sense of the 1930s as a period in our literary and political history. Particularly for those new to this field, I offer a set of arguments meant to locate my case study of Cantwell's career in terms of wider cultural issues regarding the 1930s that remain crucial today. Experts in the field may find this review useful too, or they may choose to skip it and jump directly into the material on Cantwell.

Chapter 2 dives into Cantwell's life, offering a brief sketch of his childhood and young adulthood as it helped form his sensibility, and as it provides a backdrop against which to measure the effect of the East Coast literary culture he encountered as he reached maturity in the 1930s. This chapter is also meant to give a general sense of the Northwest mill-town environment that is the setting for much of Cantwell's later fiction and to suggest sources from which he drew in linking Marxist ideas to his personal experience. I also clarify Cantwell's class origins, a subject of some confusion among historians and critics writing on the thirties. The bulk of the chapter, by examining Cantwell's pre-Marxist attitudes and preproletarian fiction, especially his first novel, *Laugh and Lie Down* (1931), will help pinpoint the ways in which the encounter with literary and other radicals in New York led him to revise his literary strategies, recode his personal history, and retell his region's social history.

The middle chapters employ a chronotopical approach to the explication of Cantwell's criticism and fiction from the thirties. Chapter 3 describes the cultural and political position Cantwell carved for himself in the "literary class wars" of the early thirties when the "proletarian novel" and "revolutionary criticism" were being defined amid lively debate. Here I analyze various ways in which Cantwell absorbed, rejected, argued with, and transformed the main radical critical positions prevalent at the time. My guiding questions are two: what kinds of intellectual forces and constraints was he under, and how did he maneuver within those force fields? I address Cantwell's relationship to literary "modernism," an area of much discussion among scholars who now question the assumption that the Great Depression brought a total break with modernist ideas and practices. I also address related questions about the tensions between older, humanist literary and critical traditions and emerging Marxist ones, testing some positions put forth by revisionists regarding the extent to which the radicals were drawn back, "boats against the current," to "bourgeois" literary forms from earlier eras.

Chapter 4 describes and analyzes Cantwell's major contribution to the proletarian literary movement, *The Land of Plenty* (1934), a novel based on his experiences as a mill worker in Aberdeen, Washington, that subtly explores the social psychology of class during a dramatic strike. That novel represents Cantwell's attempt to put into practice the literary and political values found in his criticism and implicitly carries on the discussion of the theory of proletarian fiction. Again I am interested in viewing this work with enough detail to get beyond a set of formulaic abstractions about the putatively formulaic nature of the proletarian novel. I also attend to issues of race, ethnicity, and gender that are more visible in the light of recent political and critical developments. In addition, I use the novel's publication as an occasion to examine the dynamics of literary reception in the thirties, analyzing reactions to the novel not only in reviews by prominent thirties critics but also by looking at sources revealing previously undocumented responses by workers in the factory depicted in the novel.

This fourth chapter also offers a brief excursus to situate Cantwell's most successful novel by placing it into two larger contexts. I sketch the wider Northwest literary left and labor culture of the twenties, thirties, and forties, and I look at two other novelists who, before and after Cantwell, wrote radical labor novels based upon their experiences in the lumber town of Aberdeen, Washington. I analyze and provide context for Louis Colman's *Lumber* (1931), and Clara Weatherwax's *Marching! Marching!* (1934). Looking at these two novels (and briefly noting several others) in the context of the specific history of the labor movement and of labor culture in the region is meant to open up a wider discussion of the extent to which a distinctive Northwest regional radical literary culture evolved during the thirties.

Chapter 5 traces a little-known, rather bizarre moment in Cantwell's career, his attempt to ghostwrite the autobiography of Boston Progressive millionaire department-store magnate E. A. Filene. Cantwell was commissioned to do the work in conjunction with an ailing friend, muckraker Lincoln Steffens. Cantwell turned the biography project into a fascinating, never-completed nonfiction novel detailing his horror and fascination as a young Marxist attempting to make sense of the life of a famous capitalist merchandiser deluded into believing that he could reform capitalism from within. This episode offers a vivid look into relations between reformism and radicalism in thirties literary-political culture, and clarifies the evolution of Cantwell's political views in the middle years of the decade, when key shifts were beginning to occur in the wider political landscape.

Chapter 6 traces Cantwell's career through the turmoil that shook the literary left in the latter part of the thirties, culminating in his disillusionment with the left following the Hitler-Stalin pact of 1939. During this period Cantwell was in correspondence and dialogue with a number of left literary figures, such as James T. Farrell and John Dos Passos, contending with their increasing distaste for Communist Party cultural policies. The Party's ideological shifts during this period, from uncompromising revolutionism to the broad antifascist coalitions of the Popular Front, are reflected in Cantwell's inability to give final shape to a planned third novel about the San Francisco general strike of 1934. This section allows me to assess the effects of the People's Front era on Cantwell's critical and literary production; to examine his assessment of the strategies and tactics of liberals, the CPUSA, Trostskyists, and independent radicals during these years; and to analyze his positions in the context of Michael Denning's reconceptualization of the Popular Front as a broader social movement of longer duration.

These central chapters offer a close reading of Cantwell's literary and critical work that attempts to locate it generally within and as a reflection upon the left literary debates of the thirties. By concentrating on the concrete particulars of his work, I have attempted to present this work as much as possible within the terms Cantwell set for himself, not to isolate him from his context but to show how general literary currents were modified in and mediated by his particular life history. I've tried to avoid the righteousness of retrospection that arose in Cold War–shaped studies stressing the aesthetic and moral flaws of thirties Communism in general and literary radicalism in particular. Where lines of influence seem important I have noted them, but I have resisted the hasty assimilation of Cantwell to his alleged influences, whether they be political parties or other writers and critics, in order to keep alive certain nuances that have tended to fall away in the collective literary histories written previously.

Chapter 7 traces Cantwell in the wake of the 1930s, including his disillusionment with the left, his mental breakdown in the early forties, and his subsequent career as a freelance author and mainstream journalist who made only sporadic, unsuccessful attempts to return to fiction writing. What accounts for Cantwell's abandonment of a promising career as a novelist? Was he a victim of ideology? If so, whose, the left's or the right's? Did he simply sell out or get caught up in the journalistic empire of Henry Luce, for whom he worked, with some significant breaks, from the late thirties to the seventies? Were personal factors more important than broadly sociohistorical ones in his inability to finish more fiction? These questions are important because Cantwell, more than most, may seem to fit the picture painted by the Cold War critics of a writer of promise destroyed by involvement with the Communist-led literary movement.

Cantwell's career in the late 1930s and early 1940s at *Time* magazine embroiled him in a very intense period of anti-Communism that climaxed with a mental breakdown in 1941–42. Cantwell had become involved in a small circle of extreme anti-Communists, led by his former Communist friend turned anti-Communist crusader, Whittaker Chambers. Following his breakdown, which he later attributed in part to his association with Chambers, Cantwell attempted to flee from all political involvement, writing primarily about sports and nature. His association with Chambers, however, drew him ineluctably into McCarthyism generally and the case of alleged spy Alger Hiss in particular in the late forties and fifties. I examine Cantwell's role in the Hiss-Chambers imbroglio, including offering new light on the long-held suspicion that Cantwell became a Federal Bureau of Investigation or House Un-American Activities Committee informer on his former comrades. At the end of his life, Cantwell turned once again to his thirties experience, working until his death on a nonfiction novel centered on a highly dubious character named Whittaker Chambers, suggesting that while he sought to cordon off the thirties, the era continued to shape his life to the very end.

By way of conclusion I look at Cantwell's career in the wider context of the thirties, and as part of the call for the continued "reworking" of American literature. I suggest some ways in which this particular study illuminates, modifies, and argues with perspectives raised by both Cold War anticommunist critics and certain revisionist critics regarding the politics of literature and the role of class in US literary studies. Without discounting ways in which Cantwell's history may be idiosyncratic at points, I point out the ways in which his particular intellectual odyssey reveals a good deal about the strengths, weaknesses, and contradictions of mid-twentieth-century literary politics, and about the strengths, weaknesses, and contradictions of the literary and cultural history that has been written about the period. Cantwell does not easily fit the simplifying categories used to generalize about this era and its writers, and the reexamined legacy of the thirties can cast light on the problems and prospects of literary/cultural theory and practice in our own time. The fact that the working class has never received the kind of sustained and institutionalized literary representation won through hard struggle in recent decades by literary movements based in gender, ethnicity, and sexuality needs to be remedied. Driven partly by these reconsiderations of the thirties left, a "reworking" of American literature is underway that is a crucial addition to our understanding of our literary and cultural history. This reworking will not isolate class as a force but rather will deepen its specific qualities as entangled with these other categories of social difference that are now recognized as such profound influences on US literature and culture.

ACKNOWLEDGMENTS

My greatest intellectual debt during the years of composition for this book is to Alan Wald, for whom a mere dedication is far from enough of an acknowledgement of his unparalleled contribution to the study of the US cultural left, or for the generosity he has always shown toward me and this project. Brilliant Paula Rabinowitz likewise offered crucial support at several junctures along the way, and has been an exemplary friend from our mellon fellowing (mellow feloning) days to this day. I am also grateful to the anonymous reviewers for the UW Press. Many other fine scholars, met and unmet, will find acknowledgement in footnotes and my bibliography. None of these, of course, is to blame for the lame parts of this book, or for errors of fact, judgment, sentiment, interpretation, or editing that are no doubt strewn about in hopefully not too obvious places in the text.

My deepest personal and intellectual debt is as ever to Noël Sturgeon, who has continued to push this project to conclusion over far too many years, and who is a stellar partner in every way that matters. Likewise for Hart Sturgeon-Reed, great companion and my best hope for the next generation of world makers.

At the University of Washington Press I want especially to thank Ranjit Arab, an unfailingly patient, compassionate, and thoughtful editor, Kerrie Maynes for her astute copyediting, and Mary Ribesky, Jacqueline Volin, Dustin Kilgore, and all the other folks at the press who worked to bring this book out to the world.

Many thanks to Mary Cantwell Nelson and the Knight Library Special Collections staff for permission to quote from the Cantwell Papers. And, appropriately last but not least, thanks to Amanda Paxton for her excellent indexing.

Portions of chapter 4 appeared in different form in Michael Steiner, ed., *Regionalists on the Left* (University of Oklahoma Press, 2013).

ROBERT CANTWELL
AND
THE LITERARY LEFT

1   REWRITING THE LEFT

Critical Contexts

To fully understand the stakes involved in rethinking the career of a writer such as Robert Cantwell, it is crucial to know something of the critical context in which radical writers of the 1930s have been evaluated. A caricature of the left-leaning writers of the mid-twentieth century as Communist dupes and party hacks came to dominate the American imagination during the height of Cold War hysteria in the 1940s and 1950s, and unfortunately continues to obscure perceptions of many writers of that era, despite more than five decades of brilliant revisionist scholarship.[1] Because few periods in American literary history have been as subject to vilification and distortion as the 1930s, it has taken an inordinately long time for scholars to bring us closer to the variegated truths about the body of writing produced by literary leftists during the Depression era and its wake. These distortions matter both for understanding this period and because they continue to taint any notion of "political literature" in the United States, suggesting that political commitment and literary quality are mutually exclusive.

Attacks on the dogmatic excesses of some of the writers and critics in and around the Communist Party USA began within the thirties left itself, a fact that belies reductive notions that all literary leftists were "artists in uniform" marching to the same Stalinist beat. I am alluding to the title of Max Eastman's deeply disillusioned portrait of Soviet culture, *Artists in Uniform* (1934), which later provided a label used by less careful critics to discredit US literary radicalism in toto. Eastman's foray was among the first sustained volleys in an intense set of literary left debates driven especially by anti-Stalinist Marxists close to Leon Trotsky. Two years after Eastman, James T. Farrell, a close friend to Cantwell, published *A Note on Literary Criticism* (1936), a work that richly critiqued some dimensions of the Communist literary left while remaining very much within a left tradition, signaling a more intense period of intraleft literary debate that was soon extended by a group of anti-Stalinist Marxist writers and critics clustered around the journal *Partisan Review*.

One atypically blunt essay, *Review* cofounder Philip Rahv's "Proletarian Literature: A Political Autopsy," has been cited incessantly as the true story of the Communist-led literary movement. The essay's most oft-quoted line, that revolutionary or "proletarian" writing in the thirties was "the literature of a party disguised as the literature of a class," is effectively wrong on both counts.[2] When radical writers in the thirties were forced into "disguise," it was most often to hide their Communist Party attachments from hostile anti-Marxists, and, while their productions were in no simple sense "the literature of a class," authors identified with the proletarian literary movement, working class or otherwise, did a great deal to bring the neglected experiences of the working-class majority in US society into our literature for the first time.

Rahv's essay notwithstanding, the intraleft debates about literature and politics in the late thirties were carried out on a relatively high plane compared to what would occur in subsequent years. In later decades attacks on the Stalinist literary left were put forward on a number of different levels, from the sophisticated plane of the "New York intellectuals" around *Partisan Review* to the rabid right-wing writings of sensationalist popular accounts such as Eugene Lyons's *The Red Decade* (1940). But even the best of these seldom reached much beyond stereotype, with reductive attacks proliferating, and growing shriller during the intellectual cold warfare of the McCarthy era of the late forties and fifties.[3]

One of the key things that the anticommunist witch hunts did was obscure the fact that only a small minority of the membership of the Communist Party USA (CPUSA) had any idea of the dictatorial and criminal nature of Stalin's regime in the Soviet Union. To the vast majority of members and fellow travelers (sympathetic nonmembers), the CPUSA was the organization doing most to challenge economic, racial, and gender inequality in America. At a time when capitalism's flaws were deeply visible, in a nation where more than one in three people were unemployed, thousands of people with a progressive vision saw the Party as the best hope for the country. The profound disillusionment that came with the revelations, beginning with the Soviet's pact with Nazi Germany in 1939, that Communism under Stalin had become a hideous, repressive distortion of Marxist ideals, led many to utterly dismiss what the Party actually meant in the US context. But in fact, many of the subsequent developments in the US labor movement, civil rights and ethnic rights movements, and women's liberation and gay liberation were driven by former Communists who were able to separate their progressive values from betrayal by Party leadership. Other former members, however, reacted to disclosure of Stalinist horrors by joining right-wing attacks on their former friends and on all who had been part of or close to the CPUSA.

Much of the shape of historical accounts of thirties radicalism was given initially by these participants on the left who later swung to the right (sometimes the far right) and thus sought fully to repudiate their "youthful follies" (Cantwell is among that group.) While this former involvement lent authority to these accounts, one may surely ask whether, having declared themselves to have been so thoroughly wrong in their youth, these recanting authors can be believed to have been so thoroughly right (correct) in their later years. Indeed, it is these writers who might best be described as revisionists, since they radically revised their own histories and those of their colleagues in memoirs deeply colored by Cold War hindsight. Even the best of these writings were too deeply colored by guilt over revelations of Stalinist atrocities and fear of McCarthy era reprisals to be capable of balanced discussions of their own cultural productions or those of other writers once close to the Communist Party USA. As we will see, Cantwell too went to considerable lengths to move away from his political positioning from the 1930s, and to disguise or repudiate much of his work from that era.

The process of undoing deeply distorted views of the Great Depression US cultural left began in earnest with two painstaking, still useful books, Walter Rideout's *The Radical Novel in America* (1956) and Daniel Aaron's *Writers on the Left* (1961).[4] The carefully crafted, calmly presented arguments in these books were the first major attempts to look dispassionately at particular writers and particular works, rather than generalize about the whole corpus of writing from the thirties left. Both authors acknowledged a range of more and less successful literary efforts, and noted a range of political positions that never simply echoed the views of the CPUSA or any other organization. This "liberal paradigm" of revision inaugurated by Rideout and Aaron, while immensely valuable, also had its limits in terms of openness to the radical ideas it chronicled; it remained anchored in certain Cold War assumptions about the United States, but these works opened the way for a rich array of equally thoughtful reassessments.

Revisionary works on the thirties continued apace through the sixties, seventies, and early eighties, until the growing momentum in the nineties, the first post–Cold War decade, ushered in still more sweeping changes in perspective on the literary old left. The telling of the story of thirties radicalism passed from the generation of the thirties itself to younger generations of scholars who were free of the need to excoriate or justify their own past actions, and generally less ensnared in particular, narrowly partisan positions.

With regard to the alleged control or manipulation of writers by the Communist Party USA, as revisionist critic Paula Rabinowitz was among the first to point out, one of the ironies of the literary history of the 1930s has been the way in which anti-Marxist critics of the allegedly mechanical materialism of much thirties literary theory have in fact subscribed to an actually mechanistically determinist model by portraying all thirties literary production as if it unproblematically reflected the ideas of Communist Party functionaries.[5] While some of those figures certainly did at times proffer dogmatic prescriptions for how to write, what to write, and for whom to write, subsequent critics themselves have been in many respects more slavish servants of these reductions than were the writers of the thirties. Especially by attending to the more complex, variegated, even contradictory, *practices* of thirties writers and critics, as opposed to relying simply on their most programmatic statements, a rather different picture of the decade's writing emerges.

The ongoing work of revolutionary revision is multifaceted and complex. Let me sketch some of the main aspects of this new body of work that have shaped my efforts to rethink Cantwell's contribution to the tradition of left letters. My division of the work into the following categories is somewhat artificial. In practice, the various elements outlined often work together in mutually reinforcing or cross-complicating ways. But I think it clarifying to treat each element distinctly, while along the way suggesting some of the many ways in which revisionist scholars have been recombining these elements.

GENDER

Much writing during the thirties, and much subsequent criticism, focused far too much on the worker and the worker-writer as white, male, and presumptively heterosexual. All three of these assumptions about gender, race, and sexuality have been challenged by recent work. Work on gender has proceeded on three main planes. First, there has been work of rediscovery and reassessment. Charlotte Nekola and Paula Rabinowitz's edited collection, *Writing Red: An Anthology of Women Writers, 1930–1940*, did much to set in motion this recovery of a wider range of women writers on the left. Certain of these women, including Muriel Rukeyser, Meridel LeSueur, Josephine Herbst, and Tillie Lerner Olsen (against whose trumped-up arrest in 1934 Cantwell worked), have been the subjects of extended study. But only a handful of the many other interesting female authors have received attention, and there is much further analysis to be done of both recovered and still undiscovered women writers on the left.[6]

A second, more controversial arena concerns the policy toward women and women writers adopted by the central organization of the old left, the Communist Party USA. Barbara Foley is no doubt the critic who has made the most positive case for the enlightened, feminist nature of CPUSA policy. Foley finds little fault with the Party's policies and sees them as a major step toward women's liberation. Paula Rabinowitz offers what is to me a more balanced and convincing portrait of the limitations of CPUSA gender policies and practices. And here the split between policy and practice seems important. Foley correctly cites a number of positive positions regarding "male chauvinism" taken by the Party. But Rabinowitz more forcefully shows how the assumptions and practices of many critics, particularly as reflected in the experiences of women writers themselves, were often far more riddled with sexism. Thus, while the Party was more progressive on gender issues than most political organizations of the era, it was still sexist in certain respects.[7]

Third, and finally, Rabinowitz's important book *Labor and Desire* incorporates and goes beyond both of these other levels by raising additional questions about the gendered nature of all left literary practice. That is, she moves beyond the ghettoizing of gender to mean women and looks instead at the various ways in which a male-centered, "phallocentric" discourse characterized much radical literary discourse during the thirties and beyond. She sees in both male and female writing from the thirties much celebration of the worker in terms that privilege the male body and maleness as the measure of radicalism. Rabinowitz's key insights remain too little considered by many later feminist critics who continue to limit themselves to the mode of rediscovery and revaluation. In addition to exploring this vein, the rich body of recent work conceptualizing and historicizing various modes and styles of masculinity might be more fruitfully brought to bear on the literary left as well such that monolithic images of the heroic white male worker are replaced by more nuanced analysis. As we will see, Cantwell, for example, had a fairly nuanced understanding of gender, particularly as entwined with questions of class.

RACE, ETHNICITY, AND ETHNO-RACIALIZATION

If all literary leftists have been portrayed as dupes, then radical writers of color, especially African American Communists, have often been portrayed as doubly duped. Work on race and ethnicity that challenges this stereotype is proceeding, like that on gender, primarily on three levels: rediscovery and reassessment of writers and texts, new analyses of Communist race policies, and new perspectives from cultural theory. Rediscovery and reassessment has meant both recovering "disappeared" writers of color and rethinking the effect of the radical affiliations of many well-known writers of color, including Claude McKay, Countee Cullen, Alain Locke, Richard Wright, Langston Hughes, Lorraine Hansberry, Ralph Ellison, Margaret Walker, Carlos Bulosan, and many other African American, Latino/a, Asian-Pacific American, and American Indian writers.

Rediscovery and reassessment have been very deeply tied to reevaluations of Communist Party race policies. Important overview essays and book chapters by Alan Wald and Barbara Foley, and book-length studies by James Smethurst, William Maxwell, and Bill Mullen have greatly enriched our understanding of Communist Party policies on race and culture, and have added depth to our understanding of the roles played by black politicos, critics, and writers in shaping and reshaping those policies.[8]

In *New Negro, Old Left*, for example, Maxwell has carefully documented the limits of claims to Communist manipulation of black cultural workers, offering a much more nuanced and convincing portrait of both CPUSA policy and practice. Maxwell seeks in particular to restore a sense of agency to African American Marxists who have often been treated condescendingly as political naïfs and dupes. Most importantly, Maxwell shows how black Marxist intellectuals of the twenties did much to shape the positions adopted by the Party in the thirties. He makes clear that African Americans were makers, not just victims of, Communist racial and literary policy over the course of several decades. While their experiences with the racism of the "white" left were certainly significant ones, there was also quite positive, nurturing involvement in the literary left by virtually all of the major African American writers of the era.

Comparable work on Latino/a, American Indian, and Asian-Pacific American writers is far less developed, and much needed, but a new paradigm is in play to view the relationship between the left and racial subalterns in a more dialectical light. Filipino writer Carlos Bulosan has received renewed consideration in relation to the literary left from E. San Juan, Jr. And Michael Denning has drawn attention to a cluster of Cultural Front representations of Mexican Americans, partly inspired by the Sleepy Lagoon case, a trial that was in many respects the Latino version of the famous Scottsboro rape case. Important work by San Juan on Filipino/a writing, by Lisa Lowe on Asian American writing, by Ramón Saldívar and José David Saldívar on Chicano/a writing, and by Robert Warrior on American Indian writing has greatly expanded the base from which to look at various racialized representations in fiction and criticism.[9]

Ethnicity and race have a long history as complicated and interwoven but distinct concepts. Recently the terms "race" and "ethnicity" have been given a greater nuance and complexity that are reopening a number of key questions about the literary left. Much of this work grows from a rethinking of the concept of "whiteness." This has worked in two directions. First, by racializing whiteness, critics have moved the discussion of race beyond an implicit assumption that talking race means talking of nonwhites. Racializing whiteness has also redounded back on questions of ethnicity. In particular, theorists have shown how groups such as the Irish, Italians, Slavs, and Jews had to "become white" through a complicated historical process still very much in play in the 1930s and beyond. That is, various Euro-American ethnicities were not immediately assimilated into the category "white," as many critics looking backward have assumed. These complications have led to renewed considerations of what were once labeled "white ethnics," as well as raising new questions about ethnic, racial and ethnoracial characterizations produced by "white" writers, "ethnic" and otherwise. In Cantwell's world, for example, the term "American" really meant white and Anglo, excluding other European ethnic groups only later assimilated to whiteness. Suzanne Sowinska models a complex race-gender analysis of this kind in "Writing Across the Color Line: White Women Writers and the 'Negro Question' in the Gastonia Novels."[10] Wald has likewise examined the process of "racial cross-dressing" in thirties writing, as found, for example, in the writing of Guy Endore.[11] It has also meant renewed consideration of Anglo writers such as Carey McWilliams of California, who exhibited a deep interest in the conjuncture of class and race in the context of the cultural left.[12]

SEXUALITY

Discussion and analysis of gay, lesbian, bisexual, and other "queer" forms of sexuality had become increasingly important to left literary studies by the turn of the twenty-first century. As he has in the areas of gender and race, Alan Wald has done a good deal of the recovery work entailed by this project, making it clear that a very significant number of radical writers were far from straight. Work on this terrain will entail both further rediscoveries of gay, lesbian, and bisexual writers, motifs, and subtexts, as well as a broader examination of sexuality as a structuring force in writing from the left.[13]

What role did their sexuality play in the politics of various left writers and critics? In their aesthetics? In their lives? Did experience in the gay closet make the move into a closeted Communist stance easier, or more difficult? In the case of one prominent left critic, F. O. Matthiessen, we have speculation on connections between his sexuality and his politics in both critical and fictional form.[14] Cantwell's story would certainly seem to confirm a significant gay left presence. Just in his immediate circle, at least three of his closest comrades, F. W. Dupee, Newton Arvin, and Whittaker Chambers, were gay or bisexual. These particular lives clearly suggest the difficulty of being gay in thirties America, since all three were deeply conflicted about their homosexual experiences and sought to "overcome" them. In the case of Chambers it seems plausible to suggest a linkage between his clandestine sex life and his proclivity for a clandestine, underground life in espionage—his break with Communism and his break with homosexuality were simultaneous. Surely in some other cases living a life of sexual nonconformity amid heteronormative oppression no doubt fostered sympathy for those suffering economic, racial, and other forms of oppression. At the same time, there can be little doubt but that the hypermasculine, tough-guy proletarian stance adopted by some in the era must have deepened a sense of oppression for those taught to associate gayness with effeminacy.

Research on sexuality may prove particularly significant with regard to African American authors. The Harlem Renaissance, for example, might almost as easily be called the Gay Black Renaissance, given that so many key figures, including Claude McKay, Langston Hughes, Countee Cullen, and Alain Locke, among others, were gay or bisexual. Since many of these writers joined the literary left in the thirties, they may well have felt a sense of triple jeopardy in being black, gay, and Marxist.

From a more theoretically informed angle, William Maxwell has used queer theorist Eve Sedgwick's work instructively to discuss the cross-racial homosocial (and at times homosexual) relations among male literary leftists. He also shows how these male-bonding cross-racial relationships tended to doubly marginalize black women writers, both straight and lesbian. While we are far from anything resembling a "queering" of the literary left, the basis for such an assessment is beginning to emerge.[15] Gary Holcomb's brilliant work on Claude McKay's complex transnational bisexuality is likewise highly suggestive of new territory to be explored in linking queerness and left politics in the thirties and beyond.[16]

DOGMA, COMMITMENT, AND AESTHETIC VALUE

The harshest, most often reiterated, and in some respects most challenging element of the left literary stereotype centers around questions of literary value, and the allegedly negative effect of political ideology on creative writing and criticism. Even the best of recent revisionist work has inadequately addressed these questions.

Arguments about aesthetics and politics were complicated in the thirties and have become far more entangled since. There is no space to tackle fully that incredibly complicated terrain here, but there is one general principle that theorists as distinct as Leon Trotsky, Raymond Williams, and Pierre Bourdieu agree upon: the logic of politics and the logic of aesthetic objects seldom, if ever, perfectly coincide. In Bourdieu's terms, the economies of culture and the economies of politics overlap and interact in a variety of ways but are never simply coextensive. Each "field," as Bourdieu calls them, is subject to its own particular internal rules and regularities. The fields meet in that overarching terrain he names the "field of power," but the meeting points in the field of power never exhaust the meaning of the work of art, and political meanings are always also in excess of aesthetic ones on their own terms. Put differently, any aesthetic text can be put to political ends, and all aesthetic texts have political implications, but no aesthetic text is reducible to its political meanings. Clearly some texts are born political, while others have their politics thrust upon them. Some texts wear their politics more overtly than others, but all texts have political tendencies that differing interpreters will engage. No text is ever exhausted by interpretation—a fact that, incidentally, guarantees that we literary critical types will never run out of work to do!

Much of the problem in thinking about literary left textual production resides in a confusion of genres and level of discourse. The argument made against the literature in the thirties, that overtly political forms of literary production are inherently inferior and reductive, stems from a twofold misdirection. First, these critics failed to acknowledge the relative newness of some of the forms that arose in the thirties. Second, they fail to recognize that putting a literary text to one kind of (political) use does not preclude it from being used in other (for example, "aesthetic") contexts. Attempting to find one universal aesthetic standard, a long-held goal in much Western philosophy, does violence to generically particular and otherwise variable aesthetic ideologies. In this regard, some of the works labeled "proletarian" in the thirties should be judged as (1) an "emergent literature,"[17] and thus subject to the underdevelopment any emerging form faces; and (2) seen as parts of a genre with particular social ends that distinguish it from other genres.

Similarly, a range of kinds of Marxist or leftist literary critical practices characterized the era, and those modes may have been more or less appropriately applied to understanding and judging any particular work. Cantwell, for example, was always careful to cite the most aesthetically rich authors of modern literature (most often Henry James and James Joyce) as a standard that leftist writers might aspire to, while also pointing out the relative newness of working-class literary genres and taking care to nourish this writing without exaggerating its accomplishments to that point in time.

As Williams and Bourdieu make clear, and as I have argued elsewhere,[18] understanding the nonidentity of the logics of aesthetics and politics, or the fields of art and the social, does not preclude locating aesthetic texts in relation to the larger social formation that shapes all representations in a given period. In my work, including this book, this has often meant concentrating on social movements as sites of cultural production and reception. Critic Lisa Lowe has articulated a related position in a different context. Lowe writes that comparing disparate texts, from reportage to testimony to literature, need not be aesthetically reductive,

> need not level the differences between evidential forms that gain meaning on the horizon of the "empirical" and literary or art forms that are more commonly interpreted on the horizon of the "aesthetic." . . . This mode of reading and reception seeks to situate different cultural forms in relation to shared social and historical processes and to make active the dialectic that necessarily exists between those forms because of their common imbrication in those processes. . . . While specifying the differences between forms, this understanding of cultural production troubles both the strictly empirical foundations of social science and the universalizing tendencies of aesthetic discourse. In this mode, we can read testimony as more than neopositivist "truth," as a complex mediating genre that selects, conveys and connects "facts" in particular ways without reducing social contradiction or compartmentalizing the individual as a site of resolution. Likewise, we can read literary texts like the novel not merely as the aesthetic framing of a "private" transcendence but as a form that may narrate the dissolution or impossibility of the "private" domain in the context of the material conditions of work, geography, gender, and race. In this sense, cultural forms of many kinds are important media in the formation of oppositional [and hegemonic] narratives and are crucial to the imagination and rearticulation of new forms of political subjectivity, collectivity, and practice.[19]

This observation about disparate kinds of texts ("empirical" and "aesthetic") is equally true of different kinds of literary texts. Various genres, styles, and forms carry with them differing "aesthetic ideologies" and need to be judged as being more or less successful in terms of those varied aesthetic ideologies, rather than held to some abstract universal standard.

Michael Denning has made some of the most astute observations on these questions, with specific reference to the era in question. Denning distinguishes theoretically between "aesthetic ideologies" and "cultural politics." Denning suggests that we use the latter term to name "the politics of allegiances and affiliations," at the level of "letterheads and petitions, the stances taken by artists and intellectuals that depend upon their understanding of the ground on which they work." In contrast, he uses the concept "aesthetic ideology" to name the embodied politics of form, a partly unconscious process shaping literary production, and a set of evaluative criteria, emerging through critical dialogues with these literary productions, that identifies the particular qualities typifying the works deemed most valuable.[20]

The best recent work on politically charged aesthetic ideologies wisely addresses questions of literary value in the thirties from two opposite but interrelated directions. First, some works aim primarily to show how some radical work reached the level of quality set by now canonical modernisms. Second, other works show that this modernist benchmark is itself but one aesthetic ideology operative in the era, and that there were other ideologies precisely aimed to challenge modernist assumptions. Cantwell himself generally negotiated these issues quite well. For example, as I will show in some detail, he was consistently interested in questions of literary value but also consistently showed a complicated, nuanced understanding of the relation between modernisms and emergent forms of radical writing that worked outside of or directly challenged modernist aesthetic assumptions.

Much revisionary work has treated the related aesthetic question of genre. For many years the key genres favored both for attack and for defense by those interested in the literary left were documentaries, reportage, and works of "social realism." Without displacing these undoubtedly important forms of left literary production, the range of genres deemed relevant to an understanding of the nature and extent of the literary left's effect has been expanding in several directions. One form of this expansion has been the uncovering and analysis of works by radicals in various genres of popular or pulp fiction, including mysteries, science fiction, historical novels, popular biographies, and even putatively trashier genres such as horror and romance. Alan Wald has been particularly productive in uncovering popular genre works by writers with deep connections to the Communist movement. Stepping beyond written work, others have made parallel efforts to recover the radical roots of thirties and forties jazz, folk, and country music. George Lipsitz has likewise illuminated the working-class, Cultural Front political roots of rock 'n' roll,[21] and Julia Mickenberg has shown the role of thirties left writing in keeping alive a progressive vision via children's literature during the Cold War.[22]

Working in something of the opposite direction, other critics have been examining certain relatively neglected "high" cultural genres from the era, such as poetry. Cary Nelson has played a particularly important role in the resurrection and revaluing of a number of forgotten radical poets. He has also recontextualized as leftists a number of other poets not usually identified with the left. In several splendid works he has offered a spirited demonstration of the variety and high quality of left poetry previously assumed to be rhymed sloganeering.[23] Denning has done similar reclamation work on drama and film, re-placing the early theatrical and cinematic work of Orson Welles, for example, in its Popular Front cultural context.[24]

Some critics have successfully linked these "high" and "popular" genres, noting that modernism and mass culture are related, mutually influencing forces, rather than simple opposites. In differing ways, both Rita Barnard and Denning show how the Old Left challenged the simple dichotomy between "mass culture" and "high culture." Much of this work refutes charges that Popular Front culture can be best characterized as "kitsch," "middlebrow," or "sentimental." Barnard examines the critique of commodity culture by left artists such as Kenneth Fearing and Nathaniel West, while Denning radically revises the Popular Front as entailing in part the formation of a mass culture rooted in the emergent laboring classes.[25]

Attention to other genres will no doubt also cast a new light back on those that have been the traditional focus. In that regard, more sophisticated theoretical tools for talking about forms of putative "realism" as manifested in fiction and documentary are also important to the revisioning process. For some time, theoretical approaches have challenged the assumption that "realist" and "naturalist" texts should be examined primarily in mimetic terms. But this latter point has been a slow one to gain adherents among literary left analysis due mostly to two opposite but interacting forces. On the one hand, there has been a clear preference among literary theorists, including leftist theorists, for high modernist and postmodernist texts. On the other hand, there is a lingering nostalgia, sometimes from these same theorists, for the thirties as a time of "real" as opposed to "merely textual" politics. This curious conjuncture has meant that the powerful new demonstrations by literary theorists of the last few decades that all literary and critical acts are ineluctably political have only slowly and unevenly redounded back favorably on this earlier period of openly political criticism. But there is also important work that offers a basis for challenging this pattern. Examples include June Howard's important rethinking of literary "naturalism," Amy Kaplan's parallel reconceptualization of "realism," and Paula Rabinowitz's rich reworking of the history of the documentary form.[26]

Of particular relevance in this regard is an understanding that the thirties was a period of "emergent literatures." Retrospectively treating the "proletarian novel" as an emergent genre helps to clarify its relation to aesthetic-political questions. At least some versions of proletarian literature were designed to bring a new class (in both senses of the word) into literary production. And any time a new group seeks literary representation, the struggle to find voice and to find a form to match that voice takes time. To a large extent, the proletarian literary experiment was shut down before it had time to really gather momentum. In his criticism, Cantwell clearly understood that an emergent literature is unfairly compared to great works of the past that have been nurtured for generations, and in that spirit his critiques of the limits of much proletarian fiction was generally matched by encouragement. And his own bright but tragically short literary career exemplifies what might have been had a working-class-oriented literature been allowed to achieve fruition.

WHITHER THE STATE OF THE ART?

Such a summary can of course not do justice to the richness and variety of the revisionary ideas about the mid-twentieth-century literary left and its wider Cultural Front. Some parts of this revolutionary repositioning are well under way; other parts constitute mostly an agenda of work to be done. Some parts entail finding and analyzing texts and authors "disappeared" by anticommunism and/or literary elitism. Some parts, including this book, involve taking a fresh look in greater detail and from different perspectives at figures long considered important to radical writing.[27] Much of this important radically revisionist revaluing work has rightly displaced the figure of the white, male worker as cultural producer and cultural icon. This book supports that project of displacement, but also seeks to (re)place the dominant white male worker image by looking differently at a writer, Robert Cantwell, who phenotypically but not stereotypically occupies that particular social location.[28]

Two of the most broad-ranging and important revisionist cultural historians of the left, Alan Wald and Michael Denning, were particularly important in shaping this book. Wald is inarguably the single most important figure driving the rewriting of US literary radicalism. Over several decades now he has produced a rich and varied body of work, has made signal contributions in all of the revisioning areas noted above, and has guided the work of countless other radical revisionists.

The chapters that follow seek to address Wald's cogently argued point that what is most needed now are more works that weigh competing revisionist claims, and test some of the general arguments and speculative insights in the most wide-ranging of these new studies, by looking closely at specific texts and authors in context.[29] Such more specialized work, which Wald suggests should eventually involve study of several hundred writers who seriously engaged Marxism in the middle decades of the twentieth century, is necessary partly because of a problem of methodology. Even the best of the general studies tend to suffer in clarity due to two types of decontextualization. First, they can seldom evaluate given statements or works in the context of the writer's entire, evolving career. Especially in surveying a time of rapidly changing perspectives this can lead to considerable distortion. Second, the survey approach seldom has space to consider generic context or the specific occasion of a given utterance. Whether a comment is uttered in a book review, a manifesto, a polemic, a letter to an editor, or a piece of private correspondence often matters considerably in specifying meaning. Thus works aimed as studies of particular authors, texts, journals, and topics are important additions and correctives to equally important general studies. That is the spirit in which I offer this book, one that I hope can serve both to introduce new readers to this field and offer a specific case study of interest to thirties scholars.

If this book has been shaped in its search for specificity and context by Wald's work, it has also been shaped by some brilliant reconceptualizations of the literary left in Denning's *The Cultural Front: The Laboring of American*

Culture in the Twentieth Century (1996). Two of the many conceptual innovations in Denning's book are particularly relevant to Cantwell's career. First, and most broadly, Denning argues that the "Popular Front" that peaked in the latter half of the 1930s was far more than a "front" (façade) for CPUSA policy, as its critics allege. Rather he gives the name "Popular Front social movement" to a widespread, left-liberal wave of social movement activity arising from the great industrial union organizing in the "era of the CIO" and centering around "a social democratic electoral politics; a politics of antifascism and anti-imperialist solidarity; and a civil liberties campaign against lynching and labor repression."[30] Where a focus on the Communist Party has generally portrayed the "proletarian" literary movement as declining in the latter half of the thirties, Denning's perspective argues that an expansion of the movement's principles, if not its precise rhetoric, occurred in the later thirties and beyond. While some have seen this argument as giving insufficient credit to the centrality of the Party as a force, Denning's notion that the literary left was riding atop a far wider Popular Front movement strikes me as accurate and crucially important in countering the Cold War notion that the Party was exaggerating and manipulating a less significant amount of social discontent.[31] Certainly, as I will show, Cantwell, from a position often very close to the CPUSA, was a popular front writer *avant la lettre*, and was among many who sought a broader radical culture more carefully attuned to the specificities of US history and politics long before it became official Party policy.

Second, as part of this larger argument, Denning attempts to rehabilitate the concept of the "fellow traveler." Where fellow travelers have often been seen as the insufficiently committed periphery of the truly radical Party, Denning reverses this image, arguing that "the periphery was in many cases the center, the 'fellow travelers' *were* the Popular Front."[32] Here too Denning's argument is clearly borne out not only by the particular career of Cantwell, but also by the stances of many in his circle. The distinction between Party members and nonmembers was far more important to the House Un-American Activities Committee of the fifties than it ever was at the height of Party influence in the thirties. As we will see, Cantwell's reason for not joining the Party had as much or more to do with fear of losing work than with ideological differences, although he clearly had those at times as well.

The various arguments of the radical revisionists matter not just out of historical interest, but also because the issues of the 1930s have shaped our present and because they are recurring ones facing any radically dissenting group. Questions first articulated amid the politics of the midcentury literary left are very much alive today. Issues debated in the thirties about centralized authority versus democratic autonomy, populism versus vanguardism, accessibility versus avant-gardism, and reformism versus revolutionism continue to be relevant, as do questions about the best representational strategies for expressing group views and values, and inquiries into the relations between aesthetic form and political content. These issues and questions recur in the Civil Rights, New Left, and Black Power movements of the 1960s; in the Women's Liberation movement of the late 1960s and early 1970s; and in the debates in the 1980s and 1990s among gay/lesbian/queer activists. Issues about "proper" representation swirl around feminist debates about pornography, about the sexual politics of music videos, and about the racial/sexual politics of rap music. Questions of ideological purity or consistency versus forming "popular fronts" with liberals and moderates continue to be debated by scholars, activists, and activists-scholars in various oppositional groups today. Knowledge of the tradition of the literary left will not provide definitive answers to these questions, but it may help avert some of the most dangerous answers. And it will certainly enrich the context of discussion, especially given the tendency, addressed in recent years by the Occupy Wall Street movement, to marginalize economic class in favor of other axes of difference. It is in that spirit of questioning that I offer this case study of one talented young writer's struggle to find his place as a critical, engaged, "fellow traveler" on the literary left.

2 MILL TOWNS, BLUE COLLAR WORK, AND LITERARY AMBITIONS

Cantwell's Childhood and Adolescence

At the turn of the twentieth century, the southwestern quadrant of Washington State was timber country, a region with dozens of logging camps in its hills, and dotted with mill towns lining the railway lines and rivers that carried lumber to cities and the sea. Robert Cantwell entered the world in one of these small mill towns, Little Falls, on January 8, 1908. The third generation of Cantwells to live in southwestern Washington, his family remained in the region throughout his childhood and adolescence. But the stability and class status that these facts might seem to imply were undermined by the turbulence that the lumber industry brought to social life in the Northwest in the first two decades of the twentieth century. The early twentieth century was an era in which cycles of economic boom and bust rocked all but the largest lumber companies, and these cycles, often combined with violent labor wars, wreaked havoc in and around the Cantwell family.[1]

Robert's birth name was Lloyd Emmett Cantwell, but he started calling himself "Bob" when he found he had difficulty writing a double "l" that did not look like a "z," and the name stuck. When later in life Robert had revolutionary views of his own, he delighted in what was in fact an accidental self-naming after an Irish revolutionary martyr, Robert Emmet. Lloyd "Bob" was the second of four children born to Charles and Nina Cantwell: an elder brother, James Leroy, a younger sister, Frances Dorothy, and a younger brother, Charles Harry, rounded out the clan.

Cantwell's paternal grandmother was among the first settlers in western Washington. His great grandfather was Michael Troutman Simmons, second-in-command of one of the first great wagon trains to make it over the Oregon Trail in 1844. The wagon train divided when it reached the Columbia River valley, and Simmons led a party of settlers to Puget Sound. At the town of Tumwater, close to the site of the current state capitol of Olympia, Simmons built a sawmill, a gristmill, and a store. He became US president Franklin Pierce's Indian commissioner for Washington Territory, and was eventually a member of the convention that drew up the territorial constitution.

Robert's birthplace, Little Falls (now Vader), was built and named by his grandfather, Charles James Cantwell. Charles Cantwell, Sr., was born in Ireland, and settled originally in Minnesota. He served during the Civil War as a private in Company One, Third Minnesota Infantry. After the war he was commissioned to serve in Arizona and New Mexico in command of the 57th Regiment of the United States Colored Infantry. Upon receiving his discharge, he headed further west, where he helped build the Northern Pacific rail line. In Washington he met and married Katherine Simmons, one of Michael Troutman Simmons's six children.

Little Falls became something of a boomtown in the 1880s when the Northern Pacific completed its task of linking Lake Superior to the Columbia River. With a strategic position on the rail line, the town grew by the turn of the century to a population of several thousand and was briefly the largest town between Tacoma and Portland. In addition to its mills and the clay-pipe factory to which the clay was hauled on a narrow-gauge railway that passed in front of Cantwell's grandfather's house, the town sported an opera house, several "deluxe" hotels, five saloons, two banks, and a grand Queen Anne–style Victorian mansion housing the local lumber baron.[2]

Cantwell's grandfather owned the store, the gasworks, and the waterworks. But when both the sawmill and the clay factory burned down, a bust cycle began, and his grandfather lost the store. Upon his death in 1912, the town's name was changed to Vader, after a local rival pioneer of German descent who acknowledged the honor of the renaming by departing to Florida, never to return.

Robert's father, Charles James Cantwell, Jr., was one of six children. At seventeen he began teaching at one of the country schools in the neighborhood. Eventually he became the school principal, but did not stay long in that career. In 1905, he married Nina Adelia Hanson from Michigan. Soon after, Charles started work as a carpenter, gradually working his way up to become a construction superintendent. When his father died, Charles Jr.

moved his growing family in search of work to what became Onalaska, a new mill town being built deep in the wilderness.

Charles got a break in 1914 when timber baron William A. Carlisle of the Carlisle-Pennell Lumber Company took a liking to him, taking him on as a personal advisor and putting him in charge of constructing one of the largest sawmills in the United States. Old man Carlisle had something approaching aesthetic standards, and wanted to avoid the worst excesses of clear-cut timber extraction. Ordinarily in building a mill town the area near the mill site was logged first, so that most such towns began their lives as the center of a devastated landscape. But Carlisle and Cantwell wanted something different, a model town. So instead they left a buffer of huge trees, large even by Northwest standards, around the town. The forest was continuous, extending for miles from the town church to the Cascade Mountains. Coming upon the town from the dirt road that connected it to the larger towns to the west, the road opened magically upon a neat, compact little island of enterprise amid a forest as deep as any in the region. In all other respects, the town, dubbed Onalaska, was a typical lumber "company town," consisting of identically designed houses—four-room, five-room, or six-room—all painted shiny gray and trimmed in white, with a company store, company movie house, company barber shop, company meat market, and company pool hall and recreation center, and running on company scrip rather than cash.[3] The larger houses had the rare features of running water and indoor plumbing. The mill was completed in May 1916, and soon the town had 900 inhabitants. The elementary school Robert attended had four teachers and one hundred and sixty students.[4] In later years, Robert remembered this time as one of great joy, full of the mysterious pleasures of play at the forest's edge.

Carlisle was proud of his town, conducted competitions with cash prizes for the best flower garden, and hired local kids each summer during World War I to pick up nails, railroad spikes, bolts, nuts, and other bits of industrial debris scattered in and around the town to both clean it up as well as to donate the materials to aid the war effort. After William Carlisle's death, William, Jr. reassigned Charles Cantwell, and the family moved once again, this time to the other major town owned by Carlisle-Pennell. This much-less-attractive, older mill town was located on the Washington coast north of Gray's Harbor. The primeval cedar forest surrounding this town had been so thoroughly leveled that there was scarcely any green growth in sight. The enormous remaining stumps, "cut high above the swampy ground, were bleached white and stretched away in endless rows like so many tombstones." The natural drainage had been obstructed by the clear-cut such that stagnant pools formed; the rivers were so polluted, the color of tannic acid, that a cut finger exposed to them became inflamed with what locals called "cedar poisoning." This mess of a town was ironically named Carlisle, after the lumber baron whose last project had been to build a mill town that was its antithesis. So corrupting was the degraded condition of this burg that locals would sometimes shoot salmon from the highway bridge outside town then watch them float belly-up downstream.[5]

The Cantwell family did not last long in this dreary place, and moved again so that Robert began his secondary education in the more southerly town of Chehalis. The family moved there not long after the infamous massacre of members of the revolutionary unionist Industrial Workers of the World (IWW) in nearby Centralia had shaken the area deeply, an event that shaped Robert and the fiction he would later write.

While Cantwell's father's status continued to move up and down with the economic cycles, the family never achieved economic security for long. In 1922, the elder Cantwell found work with Gray's Harbor Iron and Metal Works, a shop in Aberdeen that repaired and designed engines for the cargo ships that carried Washington lumber to ports around the world.[6] In moving to Aberdeen, the family entered another stronghold of the radical labor movement. In 1936, looking back on the scene of his adolescence, Cantwell described Aberdeen as a town filled with ethnic and class tension.

> There are twenty-four big mills around the Harbor, capable of producing about a billion feet of timber a year; there is a large Finnish population there, a big Filipino colony, a considerable number of half-breeds from the Chehalis, Quinalt and Taholah tribes, [and] a large proportion of Southerners who drifted to the Northwest.... The town is built on a narrow shelf of flat land; huge anonymous, logged-off hills lie all around it; ... It is almost entirely a working-class community. The major stores are chain stores, and most of the mill officials are hired representatives of Eastern capitalists; the absorbent layer of shopkeepers, small owners and professional people that in other places acts as a cushion to break the clash of class antagonisms—or prevents their being recognized for what they are—

is numerically and culturally unimportant. Consequently, class lines are firmly drawn, and the classes can hardly be said to be in that "state of flux, with a persistent interchange of elements" which Marx once observed to be a condition of American society in general. The history of the town is a record of violent labor disputes. The Wobblies were strong there during the War; the Ku Klux Klan got control of the city administration in 1925; the trade-union movement, intermittently powerful, had no continuity, so that organizational gains made during strikes were dissipated in the periods of relative inactivity between them.[7]

The town's single secondary school, Weatherwax High, was a microcosm of the community, and divisions along lines of ethnicity and income predominated there as well. The local immigrant Finns, Poles, and other ethnic minorities from the south side of town did not generally fraternize with the "Americans," and their children followed suit. "Injuns" and "half-breeds" were far more isolated. Economic class divisions were written into the very geography of the city. The middle- and upper-middle-class children from houses on "the hill" above the city seldom moved in the same circles as children from the lower-class homes on "the flats." The district where the mill workers lived was comprised of acres of closely packed wooden dwellings crowded between the bluff and the waterfront, and was marked by a high incidence of tuberculosis.[8]

Robert was to spend the next nine years in Aberdeen, finishing high school there and, after a brief stint in college, taking up factory labor in a local mill. The Cantwell family was still struggling, their economic status sinking throughout their stay in Aberdeen. Thus the position of their modest home, on the bluff but right at the edge, also is fittingly symbolic. Their income was working-class but their aspirations were middle-class. The Cantwell children moved mostly within the middle-class circle of their high school, and within that circle Robert formed part of an intellectual clique, one that included Clara Weatherwax, a descendent of Aberdeen's founding father, who later became, like Cantwell, a young radical novelist of note (see chapter 4). Robert appears to have been a model middle-class high schooler—a member of the debate team, drama society, and honor society, and editor of the yearbook and school newspaper.[9]

Both of Robert's parents, having been teachers for a time, no doubt provided him with a good deal of what we would now call "home schooling" to make up for what must have been a difficult series of moves from school to school in his elementary years, so it is not surprising that he did well at Weatherwax High. Uncommonly bright, Robert in fact finished high school early, at the age of sixteen. It was assumed that he would attend college, and upon graduation from Weatherwax in 1924, he made plans to attend the University of Washington. He entered the university the following fall, and while he later described his time there as "one barren and miserable year," this seems largely bitter hindsight on an opportunity cut short. At the university he studied drama and playwriting, and contributed a few satiric short stories to the university literary magazine.[10] But by the end of his first year, Cantwell's father lay seriously ill with tuberculosis, and it became clear that he would no longer be able to afford college educations for any of his children. Bob and his elder brother Jim left college and found work in a local plywood factory.[11] When their father died one year later, their mother took up work as a cook in a bakery-delicatessen on the waterfront, and they were forced to move to a smaller house down on the working-class "flats."[12]

In Cantwell's first, largely autobiographical novel, the narrator describes the death of the father of the two brothers (both working in a mill) who are the novel's protagonists: "The last years of his life were spent in a vain almost an hysterical attempt to make some financial provision for the future of his family, as he had planned more pleasant careers for his children than additional lifetimes of drudgery." When the father, an engineer who moved from town to town aiding in the design and construction of mills, falls victim to the "tubercular winds" that blow across the harbor, his sons are forced into just the kind of drudgery he had hoped to spare them. The narrator describes the fate of the brothers: "[Their father] knew more clearly than they could possibly know that poverty, that squalor, inevitably drain the mind of every desire but the desire to escape them. . . . He knew on his death-bed that no matter how intent they were on the family welfare, or how great their affection, there would be a period of revulsion against it—that in the end [his sons] would sicken with a vision of the endlessness of a labor they had not acquired for themselves."[13]

While clearly burdened by a bitter inheritance, the character Cantwell seems to have modeled most closely upon himself is not initially displeased to be working in a factory. Like Robert, the novel's protagonist began work on the night shift:

> He started to work in a factory, working from four o'clock in the afternoon until mid-night. In this strange place, for he never entirely lost his sense of its strangeness, in the upside-down world that working at night seemed to create for him, he was at first reasonably happy; he found his industry rewarded and his awkwardness corrected, his laziness tolerated with a congenial indifference that seemed to indicate to him a more sophisticated, a more vigorous society than he had known at college. He was ambitious, he worked with his mind intent upon some job just over his own, for at this period it was neither hard nor unpleasant for him to imagine himself someday owning the factory.[14]

If Cantwell had ambitions to become a mill owner, and some of his correspondence suggests that this may have been so,[15] he was also forming the literary ambitions that would eventually lead him away from the Northwest. As adolescents, Cantwell and his friend Calvin Fixx had dreamed of "escaping to New York" to make names for themselves as writers,[16] and shortly after Cantwell began work at the factory, Fixx did manage to "escape" to Greenwich Village. When Charles Cantwell died, Fixx wrote Robert from New York:

> I was shocked to hear of your father's death, Bob. It seems such a damned shame that this particular calamity should fall upon your family, so enigmatically unfair. I remember so clearly how you spoke of your father because one's father seldom means much; to me, my own, nothing....
> In your case the particular regret is not that your college career is ended, since school will not deflect you from eventual fulfillment of your present promise, but your freedom is restricted by the necessity of supporting the family.[17]

Through his correspondence with Fixx and by continuing the writing he had begun in high school and college (following upon still earlier work for some local newspapers), Cantwell kept alive a self-image apart from his role as a veneer-clipper operator at Harbor Plywood. While working in the mill from 1925 to 1929, he managed to complete half a dozen short stories, a play, and portions of a novel.[18]

In New York, Fixx, who believed deeply in his friend's talent, began to act informally as Cantwell's literary agent. He cajoled Cantwell to part with manuscripts and attempted to convince the editors of Scribner's, the Dial, and other magazines to accept those he sent east. Rejection followed rejection for several years, but Fixx continued to send word of flattering comments regarding Cantwell's prose from such Village literati as Keene Wallis and Alfred Kreymborg.[19]

In addition, Fixx gave his friend in the "provinces" a vicarious sense of being a part of the New York literary scene. Cantwell was provided with glimpses of the literary world that made it seem less remote and inaccessible. Fixx mentions seeing E. E. Cummings on the street, meeting Edmund Wilson, and hearing Marianne Moore read, and he shared these experiences vicariously with his friend left behind in the "melancholy mists" of Gray's Harbor. Fixx also helped Cantwell keep abreast of literary trends by sending him copies of the avant-garde magazine *transition*, as well as difficult-to-obtain and newly published books. In later years Cantwell recalled the local library as a haven and source of endless revelations. When in a famous exchange with Louis Adamic about "what the working class reads," Cantwell was drawing on his own experience in recalling the many working men reading beside him in the Gray's Harbor county library. He also recalls discovering Edmund Wilson's *New Republic* piece on Sacco and Vanzetti in a hospital waiting room, then returning quickly to the library to track down all of Wilson's essays for the journal. In the process, he also came across the works of T. S. Matthews, a writer who, like Wilson, would later figure prominently in Cantwell's career.[20]

The tastes of the two young would-be writers clearly ran toward the modernists, with whom they shared an interest in things French. Cantwell read Gertrude Stein and James Joyce, sending Fixx a fairly detailed analysis of the latter's *Ulysses*. The two also shared an interest in "Negro music," with Cantwell going so far as to express his appreciation in a short story titled "Homage to Fletcher Henderson."[21] In sum, Cantwell was able to live a kind of low-rent version of the "jazz age" from a distance.

During his years as a mill worker, Cantwell also maintained contact with another young writer from the Northwest by the name of Louis Colman. Colman sent Cantwell a manuscript that seems to have been part of a novel about the radical labor movement in the Northwest that was eventually published in 1931 under the title *Lumber* (see chapter 4). Colman's influence on Cantwell in the late twenties offered some counter to Fixx's self-proclaimed aestheticism and hedonism. Evidence is clear that Colman shared his knowledge of the IWW with Cantwell. When Colman and Cantwell were about to embark upon a trip together, for example, Jim Cantwell wrote that "Louis will probably ply you with the latest dope on the labor situation in the Northwest, something I . . . do not envy you. Lurid tales of hanging IWWs have always failed to arouse any yearning for vengeance in my dilettante [sic] heart."[22] His brother's dismissive tone suggests some fear that Colman's radical sympathies might make a somewhat more favorable impression on his younger brother. Whether Bob was moved by Colman's stories in 1929 or not, an interest in the IWW is apparent in his later work, and the memory of such "lurid tales" likely shaped the radicalism he embraced during the Depression years.

The IWW (or "Wobblies," as they were popularly known) was a powerful force in the Northwest from their founding in 1905 up until the start of World War I. In early decades of the twentieth century conditions in the lumber trade were appalling. Lumberjacks worked twelve to fourteen hours a day, six days a week, under frequently life-threatening conditions for subsistence wages paid in scrip that could only be used at company-owned stores. The IWW believed in the radical decentralization of authority and democratic control over the economy, was open to all races (decades before mainstream US unions were), and argued for one big union across all classes of workers, skilled and unskilled. It opposed political parties (even socialist or communist ones) on the grounds that they create a class of experts above the people. The IWW's strikes and free-speech campaigns had a profound effect on the political landscape of the region, but it was decimated by widespread repression during the war and its "Red Scare" aftermath, in which thousands of political dissenters were illegally arrested, tried, and imprisoned, often on trumped-up charges.[23] By the time the Red Scare subsided, much of the IWW's radical energy had passed on to the Communist Party in the United States, mainly because of the prestige of the successful communist-led Russian Revolution in 1917. But the Wobblies continued to have some influence after the war, especially in the Northwest, both as legendary symbols of the fight for worker rights and as practical tacticians in the labor movement. Cantwell's lumberjack uncle August (his mother's brother) was a Wobbly for a time, and Robert came into contact with Wobblies or ex-Wobblies during his time as mill worker in the mid-1920s. He also read avidly about the IWW in both conservative and labor publications. Clearly, the IWW made a deep impression on him, one that profoundly influenced his political views and his writing as both evolved steadily leftward in the thirties. This influence is seen most directly in a story Cantwell wrote in 1934 titled "Hills around Centralia" that richly recreates the tense atmosphere surrounding the "Centralia Massacre" of 1919 in which Wobblies and American Legionnaires clashed in a town not far from where Bob was living at the time.[24] The story is told from the point of view of a young teen (Cantwell himself was eleven at the time of the events) who experiences the clash among the antiradical ideology represented by his school principal and local authorities, a Wobbly handbill he finds describing their version of the massacre, and an encounter in the woods with two actual Wobblies who bear no resemblance to their stereotype and who give an eyewitness account on the attack on the IWW hall in Centralia, along with the "lurid" details of subsequent vigilante lynching of young Wobbly organizer, Wesley Everett. The story impressively juxtaposes the hegemonic and counterhegemonic rhetorics of this earlier time in ways that could not help but echo ones very much in play in the mid-1930s.

When after four years at Harbor Plywood, Cantwell grew frustrated by the long, exhausting hours and low wages, he considered taking a job on an Aberdeen newspaper. But Fixx, who then viewed journalism as the deadly enemy of the artist, discouraged this move and suggested instead that Cantwell join him in New York (where, ironically enough, years later both Fixx and Cantwell ended up earning their living as journalists). Such a move was financially impossible for Robert at the time. But when Fixx moved briefly to San Francisco in the summer of 1928, Cantwell's brother James, then trying to break into the world of commercial illustrating, joined him there, and Robert followed suit late in the summer. By then Fixx had decided to return to New York, but he had managed to lure both Cantwell brothers out of the Northwest. The brothers remained in San Francisco, where Robert found work as a warehouseman, and continued to write fiction when he could find the energy. He and his brother also continued to send a good portion of their income back to Aberdeen to help support their mother, sister, and younger brother.[25]

Shortly after they had settled in San Francisco, Cantwell and his brother learned that their younger brother was ill with a severe respiratory ailment that dictated his removal from the damp climate of the Pacific Northwest. Even with salaries of the elder brothers and their mother, the family had great difficulty saving sufficient funds to finance the move to Arizona recommended by the doctors. But by March of 1929, the family had managed to scrape together enough money for Robert to take a preliminary trip to the Southwest to scout out a suitable and inexpensive place for the family to live and work. The plan was for Cantwell and James to accompany the rest of the family on the move and to live with them at least until they were settled. In March of 1929, however, Cantwell had also received word from Fixx that his first story had been purchased for the anthology of new writing called the *American Caravan*. Fixx acknowledged the very difficult financial situation of Cantwell's family, but urged him to come to New York anyway to take advantage of the opportunities created by publication.[26]

In July of 1929 the family settled into an auto court near Phoenix where James had found a job as a commercial artist. Meanwhile, Robert had found work on a pipeline construction crew outside of El Paso, Texas. Their combined incomes were sufficient to support the family, but there was almost no money left to finance the trip to New York that Fixx continued to insist was necessary for Cantwell's career.

Fixx's pleas became more urgent in the fall of 1929 when the editors of the *American Caravan* announced plans to hold a party for the young writers included in their new anthology. Cantwell managed, with assistance from Fixx, to secure funds for bus fare to New York, where he arrived just about the time that the stock market plummeted.[27] Cantwell stayed in New York long enough to complete the first draft of a novel, which he submitted to Farrar and Rinehart in the spring of 1930. The publishers liked it sufficiently to sign Cantwell to a contract, offering him an advance that permitted him to spend the next year thoroughly revising his manuscript.[28]

During this period Cantwell also met his future wife, Betsy Chambers of Baton Rouge, Louisiana, at a cocktail party thrown by her cousin, editor Lyle Saxon. Mary Elizabeth (Betsy) Chambers had relocated to New York City shortly before meeting Cantwell, in flight from a stifling Southern family and a less-than-exciting life as a mathematics teacher, perhaps inspired by such independent female forbears as a gun-toting Louisiana suffragette. Soon she and Bob were living together in New York, bohemian style, eventually marrying on February 2, 1931.[29] Betsy's parents were conservative Episcopalians. The Chambers clan had married into a plantation family, and, while having squandered most of their wealth, maintained a high self-regard and somewhat aristocratic airs. While mildly rebellious at this stage of her life, Betsy would prove to be a moderating force on Cantwell's radicalism when later her conservative roots started to show through.

Cantwell completed his autobiographical first novel in 1931, and it was published in the fall of that year with the title *Laugh and Lie Down*. The novel follows closely the outward circumstances of Cantwell's life in the years just before his move to New York. *Laugh and Lie Down* is in certain respects a "lost generation" novel, but one with a decidedly Northwest inflection. Like the beautiful and damned novels of Fitzgerald and Hemingway, both of whom would become major admirers of Cantwell's work, there is a deep mood of disillusionment in this first novel, a sense of the world being played out, of all options being dead ends. The post–World War I mood that shaped this generation of writers clearly extended to the coast of Washington. But in Cantwell's novel, the mood is shaped just as much by economic circumstance as by postwar malaise.

The action of *Laugh and Lie Down* centers on the younger of two brothers, both of whom are vying for the affections of the same young woman. "Laugh and Lye Down" is the name of a Renaissance card game that quickly became associated with women of easy virtue. Cantwell no doubt came across the phrase during his immersion in Shakespeare. Sexual awakening plays a role in this working-class bildungsroman, but the novel's title is soon revealed to be ironic, as the laughing and the lying down prove both short-lived and unsatisfying.

The mood of the story is dominated by the brooding, melancholic speeches of William McArdle, as the younger brother is called. He feels trapped and stifled by his culturally barren environment, and by the economic burden of supporting his family. And, like many in the lost generation, he is too immersed in ennui to take action against his plight. He tells the female protagonist, who wishes he worked somewhere with "a little more class than a factory," that his family "'had some hard luck and I had to go to work—I was going to school. I don't imagine it will last long. My brother has a chance to get some big money, and if that goes through. . . .' Then he flushed, and added rapidly, 'That's a damn lie. We'll never have a dime. We never have and never will. We've hardly got enough to live on: if I stopped we'd starve to death.'"[30]

William feels trapped by this situation, and confides to his brother Kenneth that he is "sick of working," adding, "I don't mean here—I mean anywhere, doing anything. For myself or anyone. I want to get out of here. . . . But I can't just leave and let the family get along anyway—I'm too damn timid to do it—I know I'd regret it the rest of my life. Or I think I would. Probably I'd get over it."[31]

William's attitude toward his work at the factory is one of detachment, but in this he apparently does not differ much from his fellow workers. The narrator notes that it was "impossible" for William "to think of himself as a workman," but adds, "he was relieved when he discovered that no one considered himself a workman. A group of laborers, they considered themselves poets, musicians, mechanics, motorists, politicians, financiers, dissipates, gamblers—anything but laborers, and they were offended at labor agitators, partly because they class them with each other, and partly because none of the agitators could do any work."[32]

But William believes that his troubles lie deeper than the oppression brought on by his financial worries. Where Kenneth has chosen to numb his despair with alcohol, William has found no palliative. He finds life absurd, brutal, and dull wherever he looks. He claims,

> You can accept [society] and try to hypnotize yourself into liking it. . . .
> Or you can try to change it. But you can't, so it's no use trying. You can't because we think as individuals and our imaginations are crippled. We see events as controlled by individuals, and when we don't it only means we have tried to change what we really feel because we think we should. Can you understand how horrible it is?

William mentions radical solutions to this problem, but only to satirize them: "'Join me,' William suggested wearily, 'in the proletariat revolution. Divide up your debts. A sort of merger. The working class must merge its indebtedness.'"[33]

William is seeking, at times desperately, to throw off his ennui, but his self-consciousness constantly stands in the way. He tells his con-man friend Biddle, "I'd like to believe in something. . . . There must be something to work for. Whether good or bad." Biddle merely lifts his eyebrows, flips the pages of a magazine, and replies, "Don't get strident about it. . . . There's the proletariat revolution. As a sort of emotional enema. I take it that's what you mean?" When William does not reply, Biddle adds,

> "It won't work. Not until you convince people they'll get something out of it. And you can't. The present system holds out a vision of superiority to your neighbors. Possible, and according to legend, easily attained. And that's much more appealing as a vision than equality at any level.'"
>
> In reply, William said, rather bruskly [sic], "I believe that. But how much of my belief—my skepticism—is a result of what I would like to be free of? Indecision—negation—self absorption?"
>
> "You can't wish it out of yourself. You can't argue it away."
>
> "But it can't be driven out without a desire to be rid of it. Without an attempt to argue it away."
>
> Biddle said, with an air of finality, "Everyone is right. When you see that, you give up."[34]

The one bright light in William's world is Berenice. He rhapsodizes on the first time he saw her through a "gray afternoon, the gritty pavement, the nut-like smell of sawdust in the air." When his older, more experienced brother steals her affections, he loses his only anchor in the world.

William does not give up, but his search for a way out grows more and more desperately self-destructive. Out of sheer boredom he acts as an accomplice to an act of petty larceny, robbing two lumberjacks of their recently cashed paychecks. He briefly hopes for a mystical religious conversion that will end his living "death." Eventually he is driven toward suicide, and only a mishap prevents him from killing himself. He decides to take another kind of action by fleeing town, but his life continues to careen out of control. The novel ends as he falls asleep at the wheel of his car, sending him and his passengers, Kenneth and Berenice, hurtling toward serious injury or death (the fact that William takes out a life insurance policy before starting on the trip deepens the suspicion that he still had suicide on his mind). The suicide attempt and possibly deadly crash at the end of the novel may reflect a deep melancholy and fragility in Cantwell's character that would haunt him in later years, but its immediate role is as a deus ex machina to solve the dilemma of being stuck between Jazz Age disillusion and not-yet-embraced forms of social struggle.

The novel gives a clear sense of Cantwell's attitudes toward experiences and ideas he will later radically reinterpret after his conversion to Marxism. It also provides an aesthetic benchmark against which to measure the effect of his later radicalism on the quality of his literary work. The existential despair of the character seeps into the structuring devices of the novel, such that the novel fails to really cohere and seems to end out of an exhaustion of authorial ideas more than a resolution of plot. Or, as the reviewer for the *New York Times Book Review* noted at the end of an otherwise favorable critique of *Laugh and Lie Down*, by the end of the novel Cantwell seems as confused as his characters as to his "intentions and meanings."[35] Cantwell's letters of this period make it clear that when he and his wife settled in New York upon publication of *Laugh and Lie Down* in 1931, he was indeed as at sea about his own ultimate values as the protagonist of his first novel.

3 A STUDENT OF KARL MARX AND HENRY JAMES

Cantwell and the Literary Wars of the Early 1930s

New York City in the early years of the Depression was the center of intense debate concerning the political meanings and uses of literature. Cantwell had chosen to settle there during the most unsettling of times. He had come to pursue a literary vocation just as many of America's foremost writers and critics were calling the traditional life of letters into question. With evidence of severe economic and social dislocation all about him, and amid this atmosphere of great agitation among the literati, Cantwell set about to find a place for himself as a writer and critic. As he frequently confided to his friends, he had learned to write fiction and criticism by studying Henry James, particularly the elegant, critically intricate prefaces to his collected works.[1] But James was no guide to the current crisis, and in 1931, after completing his first novel, Cantwell emerged from literary seclusion to begin examining the Marxist ideas that were in the air all about him. Soon he had "immersed"[2] himself in Marxist theory, and when he emerged he had "accepted the Marxian interpretation of history and literature."[3]

What did that mean in the context of the early 1930s? Edmund Wilson, among the most respected critics in the nation and literary editor of the prestigious (then) liberal journal *New Republic*, voiced the views of many writers when he noted that the economic crisis had made the disinterested pursuit of beauty seem utterly irresponsible. Not long after the stock market crash, Wilson had temporarily abandoned literature and gone out among the people to gain a sense of the national mood. The reports he sent back to the *New Republic* in 1930 and 1931 portrayed a profoundly confused populace and spoke portentously of the shattering of traditional American beliefs. Wilson concluded that "Karl Marx's predictions are in the process of coming true," that capitalism, victimized by its own internal contradictions, had totally collapsed, ushering in an era of intensified class conflict.[4]

Wilson was far from alone in these observations and opinions, reflecting a general drift of the intelligentsia toward the Marxist left. Marxist ideas became common currency among intellectuals in the early thirties, and nowhere was this influence greater than among critics of literature and writers of fiction. While, as I indicated in the previous chapter, complex continuities, both political and aesthetic, link "the thirties" to earlier decades, it is equally clear that a decidedly new tone had emerged.[5] Throughout the twenties, Mike Gold and a small band of radical intellectuals centered around the revolutionary literary magazine the *Liberator* and its successor, the *New Masses,* continued the radical literary tradition of the pre–World War I years, but began to modify it under the influence of the then new Communist Party. Gold had cajoled writers to abandon the decadent culture of the capitalists and to align themselves with the working class. He argued that bourgeois culture was dying and would soon be surpassed by the culture of the proletariat. But amid what F. Scott Fitzgerald called the "gaudiest spree in history," the claims of Gold and his comrades seemed to many to be little more than wishful thinking. Many writers agreed that American culture was crass and decadent, but few believed capitalism to be in danger of collapse.

By 1930, however, the claims of revolutionists could not be easily ignored, as revealed by the response that greeted the publication of an article by Mike Gold in the October issue of the *New Republic*. In "Thornton Wilder: Prophet of the Genteel Christ," Gold attacked Wilder in terms long familiar to readers of the *New Masses*. He charged Wilder with writing works that served as a "sedative" to keep a sick "genteel bourgeois class" blissfully unaware of the degradation and misery their greed brought upon the workers who supported them. His analysis still owes as much to Thorstein Veblen as to Marx, but it ends with a call for writers to abandon the empty, "effeminate" humanism that Wilder represents, in favor of the vigorous culture of the rising proletariat.[6]

Gold is here promoting what was increasingly being called the "proletarian literary movement." Although often cited at the center of the decline into uniform, hack writing, the proletarian movement was in fact quite a variegated phenomenon. The term "proletarian literature," for example, proves on close examination not to be the name for a coordinated, well-defined, prescriptively drafted body of work but rather a never very successful attempt, often after the fact, to characterize a fairly heterogeneous set of texts. While Gold used the term in his criticism as early as 1921, the concept of proletarian literature did not enter the common vocabulary of American critics until the early thirties, and it never achieved a stable definition during the decade. While Gold undoubtedly borrowed the term initially from the Bolshevik revolutionaries and the Proletkult group of Soviet writers (1918–21), the translation of the term into the American language and culture brought significant changes. Gold's initial use of it was rather mystical and Whitmanesque, deriving as much from the rhetoric of the Jacksonian and Populist exalters of the "common man" as from Soviet theory, and this American patina was never erased—even after Gold and others attempted to follow more closely certain rather general guidelines set down by Soviet theorists.[7]

By the midthirties Gold had begun to slough off most of the mystical trappings of his proletarian theory in favor of a conception that, though still vague, was essentially an attempt to use literature as part of a Leninist party apparatus.[8] But neither he nor any other critic in the thirties ever developed a consistent, elaborated position on what such use might entail. In 1928, near the beginning of the "Third Period" of Comintern (Communist International) activity, in which precipitation of worldwide communist revolution became an immediate goal, Gold had editorial control over the *New Masses*, America's most influential revolutionary literary magazine. He quickly transformed the magazine from an independent left-wing journal into one closely allied with the Communist Party USA (CPUSA), and changed the format from one dominated by established literary figures such as John Dos Passos, Sherwood Anderson, and Van Wyck Brooks into one dedicated to publishing the works of previously unknown writers drawn from the working class.[9]

To inaugurate this new policy, Gold put out a call for "letters from hoboes, peddlers, small town atheists," for "revelations by rebel chamber-maids and night club waiters," for "strike stories, prison stories, work stories" of all kinds.[10] It was assumed that the respondents would be among the "vanguard of the American proletariat," but initially no ideological sanctions were placed on the work. To foster and guide the creation of a proletarian literature, Gold and his colleagues on the *New Masses* founded a group of John Reed Clubs in 1929, designed as a gathering place and training ground for revolutionary writers and modeled roughly on the "literary studios" of the (by then, ironically, banned) Soviet Proletkult.[11]

From the beginning, the literature produced by these proletarian writers was quite varied and ideologically heterogeneous, and, as Barbara Foley has argued, neither the audience, the authorship, nor the subject matter of this work was ever definitively set.[12] By 1930, Gold and many John Reed Club members had come to identify themselves as writers who used the "weapon of art" to advance the class struggle as interpreted, in the last instance, by the Comintern. But the relationship between the literature and the political policies was far from directly determinate.[13] The John Reed Clubs themselves, for example, included both Party members and nonmembers, and in practice, particularly given differing regional emphases, represented a range of styles and ideological tendencies. As Douglas Wixson has documented, worker-writers, in the Midwest at least, responded favorably to Gold's early call partly because they were already engaged in the kind of efforts he demanded, and many of these same writers continued in a spirit of more open-ended worker writing long after certain sectarian definitions and uses of proletarian literature emerged.[14]

In November 1930, Gold and six delegates from the Reed Clubs attended the Second World Plenum of the International Bureau of Revolutionary Literature, at Kharkov in the Soviet Union. Immediately following the conference, the John Reed Clubs officially affiliated themselves with the International Union of Revolutionary Writers, the literary branch of the Comintern. As a result, thereafter the Comintern and the Communist Party in the United States exerted much indirect and some direct influence on the literature produced by many proletarian writers.[15] But even with the rise of some prescriptive criticism, debate raged among leftist critics and writers, and much room was left for interpreting these guidelines even within the Party orbit, let alone outside among Trostkyists and other dissenting radicals. Sporadic attempts by Gold, his successor as *New Masses* editor Granville Hicks, and others close to the Party to elaborate a "correct" literary line seem to have been greeted by writers themselves with a mixture of indifference and hostility. On one famous occasion, a group of young radical writers were asked by the magazine to comment on *New Masses*' criticism: some twenty-four slavish "artists in uniform" responded, and every one found ways to declare themselves independent of if not openly hostile to efforts to prescribe literary form or content.[16]

The revolutionary movement had attracted many of the most talented of the new generation of writers, as well as many of America's established women and men of letters, and both of these contingents generally argued for a much broader and richer radical literature. Michael Denning identifies three main components of the literary left: the moderns, the émigrés, and the plebeians. Moderns such as Dos Passos, Wilson, and Malcolm Cowley added stability and perspective. Émigré writers brought their ethnic particularity with them into the fray. Plebeians such as Cantwell brought their exuberant revolutionism into literary form. Some of these writers discovered their writer selves in the context of the proletarian literary movement. Others, such as Edward Dahlberg, James T. Farrell, Erskine Caldwell, Josephine Herbst, Henry Roth, Richard Wright, Mike Gold himself, and Cantwell, while still young compared to the moderns, were possessed by a sense of the literary vocation prior to their involvement with the revolutionary movement.[17] These young writers, as well as the older moderns, were particularly likely to ignore any prescriptions from the more dogmatic critics, and pursued their own visions and versions of working-class radicalism. Paralleling arguments by the new historians of Communism that "rank and file" autonomy was a significant phenomenon, we can speak confidently of a significant degree of autonomy among "rank and file literati."

As Alfred Kazin, a critic who later joined the opposition to literary leftism, expressed it, and as the example of Wixson's Midwest "worker-writers" richly confirms, these young writers wanted "to prove the literary value of [their] experience, to recognize the possibility of art in [their] own lives, to feel that [they] had moved the streets, the stockyards, the hiring halls into literature—to show that [their] radical strength could carry on the experimental impulse in modern literature."[18] For many of these young writers, rendering their experiences of class oppression (and in some cases racial or gender oppression as well) faithfully was sufficiently revolutionary without adding particular partisan political passages.[19] The proletarian movement also drew upon many writers from the middle class whose representations of and attitudes toward both their own class and the working classes varied widely. Knowledge of Marxism and conceptions of revolutionary ideas also varied widely from author to author.

These young "plebeians," as Denning calls them, also generally had a deeper appreciation for the accomplishments of their "bourgeois" predecessors than was supposed earlier (even Gold, a notable comment about Proust as the "master masturbator of the middle class" notwithstanding, was not so much hostile to modernism as to certain reactionary currents within it).[20] This meant also that they tended to be closer to the older, established writers who came to identify themselves with the revolutionary movement in the thirties. "Modernists" such as John Dos Passos, Theodore Dreiser, Upton Sinclair, Sherwood Anderson, and Waldo Frank were connected to the earlier phases of literary radicalism (the "bohemian" radicalism of the 1920s and currents associated with such pre-Communist groups as the Populists, the Socialist Party, and the Industrial Workers of the World, or IWW).[21] These older writers added stability, continuity, and a sense of craft to the proletarian movement, and were extremely important in mediating the transition of young writers such as Cantwell. In Cantwell's case, Dos Passos especially played the role of older confidant. Aligned with the best of the young proletarians, these writers attempted to improve the quality of radical literature by pointing out the shortcomings of colleagues whose revolutionary enthusiasm overleaped the development of the skills necessary to convey that enthusiasm to the reader. While important differences of emphasis exist among revisionists on this matter, it is quite clear from recent work that the relation between literary "modernism" and proletarian or radical literature involves absorption, adaptation, and critical appreciation, not just critique and rejection, as previously claimed.[22]

The parallel course of "Marxist literary criticism" was also deeply influenced by those in and around the Communist Party, but, as with proletarian literature, there is far more variety than Cold War–dominated histories claim. Left literary criticism in the thirties begins in a vague, populist radicalism, and becomes for *some* the political criticism of literature in service to the rather vaguely articulated needs of the Communist Party, but is taken up by a variety of practitioners, many of whom believed the CPUSA critics to have distorted Marxism and its relationship to the study of literature.[23]

Already by the time Cantwell arrived in New York in the early thirties, prescriptive Marxist criticism was meeting with a good deal of resistance despite the prestige of the CPUSA, and throughout the decade opposition grew steadily. Among the most prominent critics to call for a more flexible, generous, and complex Marxist literary criticism were Wilson, Cowley, Farrell, V. F. Calverton, and Newton Arvin (all of these save Calverton befriended Cantwell). Long before a serious Trotskyist criticism developed to challenge the Stalinism of the Communist Party, various strong oppositional critical currents existed on the literary left. An array of Party, non-Party, and anti-Party critics objected to the narrowly political nature of certain *New Masses* reviews, to the sporadic attempts to prescribe content for proletarian literature, and to the tendency to view literature as a mere reflex of economic activity, rather than as a complex imaginative structure in which overt ideology was only one of many elements.[24]

The critics who opposed the prescriptive strain of some *New Masses* criticism frequently pointed out that they were in fact closer in spirit to the actual (largely informal) aesthetic criticism Marx and Engels themselves had produced. Indeed, as Barbara Foley has documented, the prevailing criticism in the Union of Soviet Socialist Republics and of such formidable Marxist critics as Georg Lukács, consistently argued against prescriptive or "tendentious" criticism, or "leftism." Many of these critics agreed that, while Marxism was very useful in illuminating the historical ground of a work and could aid in clarifying the ideology of characters within a work, it provided few, if any, guidelines for judging the aesthetic worth of a given piece of literature. Lacking such guidelines, these critics frequently relied on established, "bourgeois," humanistic aesthetic criteria. In this they were again arguably closer to Marx's own appreciation of literature as shaped by his bourgeois education.[25] In support of their position, one strand of dissenting radical critics also frequently cited Leon Trotsky's *Literature and Revolution*, a nuanced work that argues against the notion of a separate proletarian culture, and suggests that because the "laws" of art and the "laws" of political discourse are quite different, the latter are of limited value in evaluating the former.[26]

Drawing on Trotsky and others, James T. Farrell offered a rich, contentious mid-decade critique of some *New Masses* criticism in his book-length *A Note on Literary Criticism* (1936). Still later in the decade, Wallace Phelps (a.k.a. William Phillips) and Philip Rahv institutionalized one key dissenting literary radical position by turning a former John Reed Club journal, *Partisan Review*, into a new force advocating a rather tense mixture of European aesthetic modernism with leftist politics that anticipates certain strains in the neo-Marxism of later decades. In their rich efforts to articulate their own "Eliotic leftism," as one critic has called it,[27] they exaggerated the flaws of Communist critics, putting forth a caricature that under the more virulent anticommunism that followed unfortunately proved useful in helping bury for decades not only the Communist Party critics but *Partisan Review*'s own early efforts and those of other dissenting Marxist critics as well.

The Communist Party USA, because of its prestige as the representative of the tradition of the Bolshevik Revolution and through the activities of a plethora of a cultural institutions such as the John Reed Clubs, did indeed exert a great deal of influence over Marxist thought in the United States, including among writers. Relatively few writers joined the Communist Party, but a great many became "fellow travelers" who supported the main goals and policies of the Party without formally joining. Denning has made a compelling case that this somewhat disparaged category was in fact the more significant one in that it reflected the larger "Popular Front social movement" that encompassed but went far beyond the CPUSA.[28]

Even these categories, however, can be misleading, since some fellow travelers may have been more orthodox in their writing than others who actually joined the Party, and consciously held ideas do not translate neatly into literary practice. But the opposition to various never very consolidated attempts to create a Communist Party literary policy often carried with it an implicit criticism of the political policy of the Party as well, for what was in fact being objected to was the simplistic analysis of American society embodied in simplistic analyses of American literature. Thus the struggle of many American women and men of letters to transform the sometimes crude literary Marxism of some in the Communist Party into a more supple tool of social analysis was also a struggle to, as Wilson phrased it, "take communism away from the Communists." This became quite explicit in the late thirties when many literary figures joined the Trotskyist opposition to Stalinism, but it is implicit in the efforts of many literary Marxists, including Cantwell, from the beginning of the decade, and it surely belies the image of radical writers as Stalinist robots. Cantwell was from the beginning, a "*critical* fellow traveler," a radical careful to eschew reductive aesthetic criteria and dogmatic politics alike.

By the time of Cantwell's arrival in New York, these "literary class struggles" were well under way. Gold had been delivering his message about the need for a radical workers literature in essentially the same terms for close to a decade, but his words had reached only a small portion of the literary community. As the extent and depth of the Depression was becoming apparent, however, his words carried far more weight, and his "Thornton Wilder:

Prophet of the Genteel Christ" touched off a controversy such as the *New Republic* had scarcely seen before. For weeks the journal's letters columns were filled with polemics and counterpolemics arguing the relative merits of Wilder's humanism and Gold's Marxism. Finally, Wilson put an end to the *New Republic's* coverage, but not to the controversy, by printing an unsigned editorial in which he censured Gold lightly for certain personal innuendoes (homophobic jibes) directed toward Wilder in his article, but then added, "The furious protest raised by Gold's attack suggests that there is more point to the Marxist objection to Wilder than one had previously suspected."[29]

Wilson and several other critics later cited the Gold-Wilder controversy as marking the point at which it became clear that the economic crisis was to be accompanied by a literary crisis.[30] Gold had prompted Wilson and a number of other liberal critics to consider the possibility that their work helped to prop up the capitalist system, and soon many concluded that the Marxist analysis of their role was essentially accurate. Critics were rapidly polarized into "bourgeois reactionary" and "revolutionary" camps. Wilson himself was among the first of the major critics to embrace Marxism as a vision of history and a mode of literary analysis, and soon he was followed by such prominent figures as John Chamberlain of the *New York Times* and Clifton Fadiman of the *New Yorker*. By 1932, the skirmish touched off by Gold had escalated to such an extent that much American literary criticism could be accurately labeled "literary class warfare."[31]

Malcolm Cowley, another major Jazz Age critic converted to Marxism, and the successor to Wilson as the literary editor of the *New Republic* beginning in 1931, recalls that in the early thirties his friend Cantwell was "almost religiously committed to the idea that American society would have to be completely remade."[32] Cowley remembers Cantwell as a "slight, sallow, hungry-looking young man who dressed neatly in dark suits that were always too large . . . and who stuttered with excitement—which he passed on to others—as he explained the dramatic value of a strike or imagined the secret maneuvers that went on in a crisis."[33] Critic Alfred Kazin, then a young literary radical himself, recalls Cantwell as among a small group of "young writers who seemed really to be writers," who wore a "proletarian scowl on their faces as familiar as the cigarette butt pasted in their mouths," and who projected a "proud and conscious sense of personal 'vitality,' a flourish of dangerous experience."[34] Critic and historian Matthew Josephson, who was very close to Cantwell in the early years of the Depression, remembers him as a "charming . . . tense and nervous" young man who spoke of IWW members in his family background, and who, like most of the young writers Josephson encountered, would sometimes "talk as if he expected the Revolution to break forth almost any hour."[35]

All of these comments were made retrospectively and have about them something of an air of condescension, but reading between their lines one can glimpse the nature of Cantwell's emerging persona as a revolutionary writer. Cantwell's mood in the early thirties can be read more directly through a short story he published in January of 1932 in the *New Republic*. Titled "The Wreck of the Gravy Train," the short piece develops an elaborate allegorical relationship between a group of one hundred drivers moving a caravan of automobiles from Phoenix to Los Angeles, and the American work force heading for revolt. A disparate array of individuals, "a few tramps, some college boys . . . a few workmen with tool kits," the drivers are molded into a rebellious unit that ends in a mass pile-up.

> What was important was the way we unconsciously acted together as soon as we understood we were running away. . . . At Indio the law stopped us, for speeding, . . . but there were too many of us. We were still keeping in line.
>
> And the owner, too, when he caught up with us, could only walk back and forth, strangled with his indignation but unable to say anything. . . . We could have told him there wouldn't have been any trouble if we hadn't followed his orders. We had kept in line, and it had taken a lot of wreckage to convince us we would never get anywhere following [bosses] who didn't know where they were going.[36]

The wreck is a rather obvious metaphor for the crash of the economy, and the rebellion is clearly meant as a portent of things to come. While elements of Wobbly ideas, such as the intentional disruption caused by a literal interpretation of orders from the boss (a kind of sabotage practiced by the IWW), are apparent in the story, Cantwell's emphasis on "line" and "order" may also be read as an illustration of the Marxist concept of industrial regimen molding individual workers into a cohesive class (a theme that will resurface later in his novel *The Land of Plenty*, as will the penchant for allegory), while the ending of the story suggests the dawning of a sense among the workers that they must become their own bosses.

General expectations of imminent revolution were never higher than in 1932, and Cantwell's rather apocalyptic mood was not uncommon. Radical enthusiasm among the literati peaked in the fall of that year when over fifty prominent writers, critics, and professionals, Cantwell among them, endorsed the Communist Party's candidates for president and vice president of the United States. Cantwell joined such established figures as Dos Passos, Arvin, Wilson, Cowley, Josephson, Fadiman, Anderson, and Theodore Dreiser, and younger writers such his friends Louis Colman, Grace Lumpkin, and Erskine Caldwell, in affixing his name to the pro-Communist pamphlet "Culture and the Crisis."[37] The pamphlet's authors wrote that "the United States under capitalism" was like "a house rotting away," and ended with this plea:

> As responsible intellectual workers we have aligned ourselves with the frankly revolutionary Communist Party, the party of the workers. In this letter, we speak to you of our own class—to the writers, artists, scientists, teachers, engineers, to all honest professional workers—telling you as best we can why we have made this decision and why we think you too should support the Communist Party in the political campaign now under way.[38]

The League of Professional Groups for Foster and Ford, as the signatories of "Culture and the Crisis" designated themselves, was composed of Marxists of many shades of opinion and soon fell victim to the internecine warfare that afflicted the left between 1932 and 1935. But as the winter of 1932, the worst of the Depression, approached, radical expectations were high. In New York City, Cantwell sensed a mood of calm before the storm: "Today the town looks the way you imagine it should during a great Depression; no smoke from the chimneys, no elevated trains, no cars or trucks, only a few children playing in perfect safety in the middle of the streets."[39]

When journalist and fiction writer Matthew Josephson, an older colleague of Cantwell at the *New Republic*, invited the Robert and his wife Betsy to join him in rural Connecticut that winter, Cantwell refused, saying he preferred to stay close to the scene of anticipated activity, writing that to be in the country would be "like being out of sight of some enormous fire and wondering if your house is burning with the rest."⁴⁰ In pursuit of the "enormous fire," Cantwell also joined Cowley on a trip to Washington, DC, in December to report on the Hunger March.⁴¹ Cantwell later declared the event to have been superb material for a dramatist.⁴²

If Cantwell's interest in the Hunger March was in part literary, he may also have felt qualified to join the protesters, for the "hungry look" that Cowley recalled was no cultivated pose. The Cantwells' early years in New York were lean years indeed. In the winter of 1932, with his wife expecting their first child, Cantwell was without a steady income. On the strength of his highly praised (but financially unsuccessful) first novel, and Josephson's recommendation, he had secured occasional book review assignments from New York newspapers, while Cowley assigned him *New Republic* reviews as frequently as possible.⁴³ He quickly developed a reputation as the "best book reviewer in New York."⁴⁴ But even when he sold the books given him to review (a common practice among impecunious New York writers), Cantwell often had only ten or twelve dollars a week with which to feed his family. Josephson recalls that his friend "lived in daily dread of the gas man's visit, when light and heat might be cut off from his Greenwich Village flat."⁴⁵

But if Cantwell was sometimes given to apocalyptic anticipation of the revolution that would end capitalism (and his own poverty), he was also capable of viewing his plight and the nation's with humor. When the left-liberal journalist Stuart Chase published a series of articles in the *New Republic* charting the dangerous courses that an American Revolution might take, for example, Cantwell responded with this letter to the editor (headlined "The Revolution Is Here!"):

> Sir: As I have been very much impressed by Stuart Chase's articles on the horrors of revolution, I feel that he should be informed of some ominous developments now taking place in the metropolis. Not long after I read his prediction of how those skilled technicians, working at certain key valves, could do so much damage to the technological development of the country, I became aware of a sinister movement, similar to that he describes, *but now* actually going on! Skilled technicians, "shock troops," no doubt, but masquerading as employees of the electric company, entered my apartment, and, working with great speed and efficiency, reached

certain key valves *and turned off the lights!* No sooner had they left when another swift and silent group, bent on sabotage (but equally well trained and disciplined) entered and *turned off the gas supply*! I immediately called an officer, but (no doubt having been bought off by the "shock troops,") ... he *turned his back and walked away.* What was to be done? I rushed to the telephone, thinking to inform the public utilities of the "employees" of Mr. Redbonnet or some of his motley crew, but what did I find? That same well trained and well disciplined corps of skilled technicians had worked their way to certain key valves and *taken away my telephone*! What is to be done? Come, Stuart Chase, the crisis is upon us!⁴⁶

But even this humor is pointed, aimed to mock a certain squeamishness on the part of "bourgeois" radicals. And as a joke it nevertheless underscores the financial insecurity that shaped Cantwell's life and his literary decisions throughout the thirties. Though only eking out a meager salary from his two reviewing jobs, Cantwell often sent money to his elderly mother and sister in Arizona. When the Cantwells' first child, daughter Joan, was born on August, 12, 1932, with a collapsed lung, she was not expected to live. Fortunately, she beat the odds and recovered. But now, with a child to feed, Cantwell's economic woes deepened.

Cantwell's expectations of imminent revolution may well have been encouraged by his friendship with a rather bizarre young man given to real and/or fantastical clandestine activities. Matthew Josephson recalls an encounter with the young man in Cantwell's Greenwich Village apartment on March 6, 1933, the eve of Roosevelt's "bank holiday." Josephson had rented a small room at the Cantwells' for his weekly visits to New York, and remembers vividly a strange occurrence upon his arrival that evening. Although he heard voices in the flat as he approached, at his knock, all fell silent. He knocked a second time, waited, and finally called out to identify himself. Cantwell then said, "Oh it's perfectly all right. It's Matty Josephson. You can come out," as he opened the door.⁴⁷

Cantwell then introduced Josephson to a rather sheepish-looking man who "seemed to have come out of hiding." This was Whittaker Chambers, and upon hearing the name, Josephson recognized it as one Cantwell had mentioned once or twice before—a "down-at-the-heel" writer who claimed he was "a communist secret agent attached to the GPU," who lived an underground life full of real or imaginary dangers, and always carried a revolver. Josephson's disparaging account is no doubt colored by his knowledge that Chambers later became the most famous anticommunist informer of the McCarthy era. At this point Chambers was chiefly notable as the author of a number of "revolutionary" short stories who had briefly been an editor of the *New Masses*.[48]

After Cantwell explained apologetically that Chambers had arrived unexpectedly and was temporarily using Josephson's sleeping quarters, the group sat down to drink a little bootleg whiskey. Conversation soon turned to the bank crisis. While Chambers viewed the bank closure as a sure sign that the Twilight of Capitalism was at hand, Josephson demurred, offering certain reservations. At that point, as Josephson recalls, "Chambers exploded with excitement . . . and fairly screamed at me 'Why man you're crazy! With no money, no work, no food, everything stopped, there's going to be a revolution here right now! This is it . . . There'll be barricades the end of the week in Union Square, I tell you!'" Josephson again disagreed, citing Marx to bolster his argument. Suddenly, "Chambers was seized by an access of hysteria. Red-faced, with eyes almost popping out of his head, he began to abuse me, yelling imprecations at the top of his voice, using epithets such as 'bourgeois stooge,' or 'tool of the capitalists'—even at one moment calling me a spy." At this, Josephson instinctively stood up and doubled his fists, but before blows could be struck, Cantwell and his wife jumped between the two men and asked Chambers to leave.[49]

As things cooled a bit, Josephson remarked that, although only a "half-baked" revolutionary, Chambers appeared to be a "thorough-going paranoiac" (though again, one must caution that this account of these remarks is made retrospectively, after Chambers became famous as the chief accuser of Alger Hiss). Cantwell disagreed, attributing his friend's behavior to the strain of actually being a secret agent. Cantwell added that, in any case, he found Chambers "fascinating." Josephson recalls that Cantwell said this "as if with the clinical interest of a writer bent on observing singular characters . . . I gathered that he thought of using the tormented personality of his friend for that of a fictive communist agent in one of his proletarian novels."[50] Whatever clinical or literary interest Cantwell may have had in Chambers, and as we will see there is an element of prophecy in Josephson's remark, their friendship at this point was sincere, though their relationship would undergo a number of radical plot twists in subsequent years. Cantwell's initial interaction with Chambers, at a cocktail party where the latter was accompanied by Mike Intrator and his wife, proletarian novelist Grace Lumpkin, did not go well at all. Chambers was highly critical of the lack of a Marxist perspective in *Laugh and Lie Down*, and they argued about it throughout the evening. Their second meeting, at a John Reed Club event, proved more engaging, and while nothing about his relationship with Whittaker Chambers was ever less than murky, the two clearly became friends over the next decade.

Josephson proved to be better than Chambers as prophet of the future of capitalism: the nation survived the bank crisis of 1933. Cantwell and his family also survived their financial crises, and soon their fortunes began to improve some. The liberal journal *New Outlook* was reorganized under a new editor, former presidential aspirant Alfred E. Smith, and needed a critic to write a monthly book commentary column. Cantwell was awarded the position, which he kept for two years. At about the same time, Cowley managed to secure his young friend a move from freelance reviewer to membership on the review staff of the *New Republic*, at a small but regular salary.[51] With these two forums open to him, Cantwell began to develop his criticism in earnest and shape a role for himself as a literary leftist.

Cantwell's criticism in these two journals in the early and midthirties can best be described as moderate in tone, but radical in intent. From the prefaces of Henry James, Cantwell absorbed a belief in "organicism" and a set of aesthetic principles and ideals that make many of his critical comments sound less like a committed radical than like the New Critics who followed in the wake of, and in reaction against, thirties Marxist criticism. But this seeming contradiction stems in part from the fact that a full-fledged Marxist aesthetic theory did not yet exist in the United States, or even in the Soviet Union, for that matter. Foley notes that Communism existed for most radical critics as a set of political ideas and commitments that did not carry with it a clear set of aesthetic values or rhetorical strategies. And, again contrary to the stereotype, she asserts that even the *New Masses* critics were generally reluctant to prescribe standards for literary performance. Political values could be substituted for aesthetic ones (as some Communist Party critics did from time to time), but even here the criteria for evaluating two equally politically correct literary works would be lacking, and criteria for correctness themselves were often inconsistent, changing from review to review. Foley argues that this forced would-be Marxist critics into a relatively uncritical reliance on "bourgeois" aesthetics. While there is a good deal of truth in this, it presumes the possibility of an absolute break between bourgeois and revolutionary literary perspectives that is highly contestable.[52] In Cantwell's case, as I will detail, the use of "bourgeois" predecessors such as Henry James and James Joyce took the form of a critical working through, rather than an uncritical lapse into, "bourgeois" aesthetics.

Exhibiting none of the revolutionary rhetoric employed by some *New Masses* critics, Cantwell's reviews and essays express consistent support for the Marxist movement in politics and literature, but in a calmly persuasive style almost always confident in its ability to separate out and show relations between what Cantwell saw as aesthetic questions and political ones. Working no doubt under editorial constraints, aware that his audience was composed primarily of middle-class liberals, and always worried of the financial costs to being seen as too leftist, Cantwell did not dwell obsessively on the work of radicals but rather reviewed a wide variety of literature. But his highest praise was reserved for literature written by Marxists and sympathizers with Marxist causes. In treating the work of radicals, Cantwell appears most often in the role of objective observer, drawn toward revolutionary conclusions by the evidence and logic exhibited by the Marxists. This position is generally similar to a group of independent (non-Party) Marxist critics such as Wilson, Cowley, Arvin, and, among the younger writers, Farrell. Cantwell was friends with all of these figures and bears family resemblance to them on a number of counts. But his relation to the putatively more "orthodox" critics around the *New Masses* is a complicated one that makes it clear that one should not be too quick to set radical critics off into neat schools of criticism. Cantwell, for example, actually wrote criticism for the *New Masses* for a time under the pseudonym "Robert Simmons," in hidden tribute no doubt to his grandfather.

While at times Cantwell's posture was, as a later chapter will suggest, a public persona designed to mask his more radical personal views, in general Cantwell's apparently objective treatment of works under review is a fair reflection of his approach to literature and politics. He saw no necessary contradiction between commitment and objectivity, and he consistently paid close attention to all shades of opinion, including the ideas of such conservative critics at T. S. Eliot.[53]

Cantwell's criticism suggests an implicit belief that "organic" art and clear political thinking are intimately related. He seemed to share a viewpoint succinctly phrased by the great German Marxist critic Walter Benjamin, who argued that "the tendency of a literary work can only be politically correct when it is literarily correct."[54] Cantwell demonstrated a keen appreciation for the work of his great literary predecessors, and sought always to judge the level of radical writing by the standards set by the "finest" writers of the nineteenth and early twentieth century, even as he encouraged younger writers who inevitably fell far short of those standards. Henry James, and to a lesser degree, James Joyce, came to symbolize for Cantwell the subtle intelligence required to understand and portray the details of personal reality, while Marxism suggested the general outlines of the larger, social realm. And for Cantwell, the goal of art in the thirties was to seek out and illustrate dramatically "organic" links between the private and the social. An acknowledged gap between this ideal and the accomplishments of the radical writers of the decade, whose views and hopes Cantwell shared but whose work seldom met his standards, is apparent throughout his criticism in the thirties.

Cantwell's most explicit and sustained attempt to articulate a theory that could serve to unite his literary and political beliefs occurs in an essay titled "No Landmarks." Appearing in January of 1933 in the philosophical quarterly *Symposium*,[55] the essay announces virtually all of the central themes of Cantwell's thirties criticism. Divided into two major sections, the piece begins with a discussion of Henry James's novels, particularly *Julia Bride*, and then shifts to an analysis of Grace Lumpkin's novel of working-class life, *To Make My Bread*.

Cantwell opens the essay with an attempt to rescue James from certain critics who had accused the self-exiled writer of having been an apologist for aristocracy. Cantwell remarks that to argue "that people who enjoy reading James' novels do so because they wish to enter the society pictured in them ... is somewhat like saying that a secret urge to hunt for whales is involved in an appreciation of *Moby Dick*."[56] Against the then prevalent image of James as an irresponsible aesthete with little awareness of the social and political currents of his time, Cantwell posits a James so intensely aware of the social forces operative in his time as to have been driven to extremes of abstraction in order to find "landmarks," permanence, in a rapidly changing environment:

> There were no symbols generally accepted or widely agreed upon in America ... the institutions that had developed were, or seemed to James, so unstable, so involved in controversy as to be useless as points of reference. The way of living, the accepted customs, the economic foundations of a whole social order had been forcibly destroyed in the South, while in the North industrialization was rapidly changing the life of most of its inhabitants.[57]

Given this unstable social situation, Cantwell argues, James was hesitant "about bringing anything so perishable as ... a national custom, or a system of government, or a hierarchy of social values, into anything so precious as his art." Or, put more directly, James's "art was too precious in his scheme of values to permit his regarding it complacently as having a future of simple historical interest."[58]

To protect himself from the perishability of modern American experience, James sought meaning in the landmarks of European civilization. But these proved to be only a distraction, too laden with meanings of their own to lend themselves to his art. In the end, Cantwell contends, James was driven to become "a master of the ambiguous definition, of the broad hospitable abstraction." Thus, in his preface to "The Turn of the Screw," James speaks of making the reader's general vision of evil intense enough that she or he might draw from personal experience in imagining the particulars.[59]

Cantwell then notes that to achieve his imperishable art, James was forced to confine himself largely to the private realms of experience. Concentrating on what sociologists would call "milieu," he excluded all but the vaguest sense of the larger historical process. Cantwell then proceeds to a subtle analysis of the method by which James moves his characters from total self-preoccupation and self-deception to an awareness of their milieu, or "predicament," as James chose to call it. The James portion of the essay ends with Cantwell noting that, even given these severe self-limitations upon the historical groundedness of his art, James offers an implicit, and occasionally explicit, social commentary by contrasting the feverish "scramble for money" in his time to the permanent beauty of aesthetic contemplation.[60] (On this latter point Cantwell exhibits an affinity with Marx himself, who noted, in commenting on Balzac, that conservative criticism of the bourgeoisie often parallels that of radical leftists.[61])

Having established the essential elements of Jamesian aesthetics in their attempt to transcend history, Cantwell proceeds to a discussion of the very different purposes of Grace Lumpkin, a fellow practitioner of the proletarian novel (and an unacknowledged friend). With a hint of embarrassment at the comparison, Cantwell begins, "To turn from *Julia Bride* to Grace Lumpkin's *To Make My Bread* involves a certain strain on the imagination; *Julia Bride* is among the last works of an artist whose long career and experience were behind him, *To Make My Bread* is a first novel." Cantwell then proceeds to use Lumpkin's novel as a touchstone for his most sustained rumination on the "meaning" and "possible development" of a proletarian literature. Calling *To Make My Bread* "a step toward" such a literature, he then defines proletarian literature as "a literature about propertyless workers, embodying their point of view, illustrating their position in contemporary society and advocating a revolutionary correction of it."[62] This definition has considerably more precision than most being offered in debates then rampant among Communist theoreticians of the proletarian novel, and, while Cantwell's language remains cautiously distancing, his sympathies are more than apparent.[63] But Cantwell felt it necessary to speak out against the denigration of artistic craftsmanship by the cruder Marxist writers. He notes that Lumpkin has the "distinction" of being "among the few proletarian writers who do not begin with the assumption that a strong belief in a cause excuses any amount of careless writing about it."[64]

Cantwell immediately establishes that Lumpkin has set out to accomplish precisely what James disdained to attempt. He notes that

> as an example of proletarian literature, [Lumpkin's] book has a special application to this essay, for the points of reference in it are not what is fixed and rigid in society, but what is in the process of change. Social changes are defined as mass movements, and the characters are identified by their relation to them. There are two such movements in the story, the first the transformation of the characters from farmers to mill hands, and the second their intellectual and emotional development into class-conscious workers.

Cantwell then compares these "movements" to the character development in James's novels:

> The moment of realization for [Lumpkin's] characters when they recognize the nature of their role in the society, and the implication of it, has for them a significance analogous to that which James gives his characters when they lose consciousness of self and become conscious of their predicament—although the difference is great, for in James the moment of awareness . . . is an end in itself, while to the characters of *To Make My Bread* it is a more vital experience, a step in the movement in which the book itself, the reader's response to it, is thought of as part of the larger continuous process of social change.[65]

What is implicit in this argument Cantwell soon makes explicit: "*To Make My Bread* revolves around a specific historical event, of importance to the movement of which it is a part, and of affirmative emotional value *only* in terms of this movement."[66] Lumpkin, Cantwell is suggesting, has abandoned the effort to achieve a transhistorical "emotional value" for her work, in favor of grounding that work in perishable social reality. This makes clear that Cantwell understood the proletarian literary movement, and worker-writing more generally, as an "emergent literature." As such, he sought to suggest that it had different, more transient values and goals than did the eternity-seeking fiction of a James. But in making this case Cantwell does not find it necessary to exaggerate the quality of Lumpkin's work in comparison to that of James.

The particular social reality upon which *To Make My Bread* was based was a prolonged series of strikes in Gastonia, North Carolina, that had occurred in the spring and summer of 1929 (an extremely violent series of clashes that inspired a number of fictional treatments).[67] Through a synopsis of Lumpkin's transformation of this historical material, Cantwell elaborates a general proletarian aesthetic:

> By dramatizing the Gastonia struggle and celebrating the heroes of it, the novel increases the importance of the happening by strengthening its tradition: there are, to this point of view, no "historic sites" so charged with . . . meaning as to distract the artist from his task; the function of art rather is to charge these sites and events with meaning, so that they become part of the consciousness of class and a point of reference in it.[68]

Charging "sites and events" of struggle "with meaning, so that they become part of the consciousness of class," that is Cantwell's definition of the role of the proletarian novelist. In evaluating this work, he sees no necessary conflict between that goal and the need to be clear about high "aesthetic" standards, while at the same time recognizing that it is a different, developing aesthetic mode.

Thus, as Cantwell moves toward the conclusion of his essay, he makes it quite clear that *To Make My Bread*, while an improvement over the "careless" work of many proletarian novelists, has weaknesses of its own. Primary among these is a lack of fidelity to the "unique sensations and experiences directly connected" with life in a particular work environment. Cantwell attributes this failure, in part, to the lack of any tradition of literature about industrial life. He laments that industry, "the most conspicuous item on the social landscape" for nearly a century, has received little literary treatment. He writes, "Except for whale fishing, there has been almost no writing about a specific industry, with the particular conditions and dangers of that industry made the central matter of the fiction, and it may be that *Moby Dick*, the mystical digressions rejected, gives additional insight into the sort of literature that may be expected when the proletarian tradition becomes more firmly established."[69] Both the exalted ideal and the potential for banality that characterized some proletarian literary theory are evoked in this comment. In appropriating *Moby Dick* for the proletarian movement, Cantwell is attempting to suggest the dramatic capacity latent in the facts of industrial life, a dramatic power as great as that in Melville's masterpiece. But in so doing, Cantwell comes dangerously close to the view he parodied in his opening remarks, dangerously close to reducing an appreciation of *Moby Dick* to interest in the whaling industry.

Cantwell concludes his study by contrasting the dangers of obfuscation inherent in Jamesian withdrawal, against the vitality liberated by Lumpkinian (alas) commitment. But, again, in so doing he is careful not to exaggerate the accomplishments of Lumpkin, nor to deny the richness of James:

> Surely [James's] sense of the high importance of art was directly connected with his sense of the precarious position of art in an exploitative society, a society in which the landmarks of culture were sacrificed for personal acquisition. Thus he searched, in progressively smaller fields, for traditions which seemed to have dignity enough to entitle them to a place in his art, and could not envision a literature so closely allied with the culture of a class as to be occupied with creating traditions rather than using them.

> *To Make My Bread*, in turn, with its weaknesses, gives a new meaning to the term, "beginning of a tradition," while the works of Henry James so richly and fully illustrate what is meant by the end of one.[70]

The phrase "beginning of a tradition" allows Cantwell a certain room to acknowledge what he sees as the aesthetic underdevelopment of the "emergent" literary movement with which he felt himself aligned. It implies, in the manner of Virginia Woolf's famous remarks about Shakespeare's imaginary sister, that greater works of art emerge only over time as writers build one upon the other. Like Woolf's roomless women writers, Cantwell's proletarians have few material supports and few literary landmarks with which to identify as they stumble into the beginnings of a working-class literature.

Cantwell's sense of the complex literary "predicament" besetting the writer who would seek to understand the social processes operating in the thirties is also illustrated by a review titled "Four Novelists of Tomorrow." A discussion of James T. Farrell's *Gas-House McGinity*, Albert Harper's *Union Square*, Meyer Levin's *The New Bridge*, and Marjorie Kinnan Rawling's *South Moon Under*, the essay begins with qualified praise for the efforts of these writers.

> These four novels are by young writers, and in their various ways they indicate something of the impact the crisis has made on the imaginations of their authors. What a deep difference there is between them and the mooncalf, the beautiful and damned novels of the period after the War! Instead of the elaboration of sexual difficulties, there are acute problems of livelihood; instead of descriptions of drunken literary parties, there are descriptions of killings, riots, and evictions. But description is still the proper word. For the most part these authors simply picture events, rather than looking into their causes.[71]

Cantwell proceeds to discuss the novels by Farrell, Harper, and Levin, all of whom were identified with the proletarian movement, finding each marred artistically and as social criticism. He praises elements of characterization and dramatization in each of the three novels, but finds their plots fragmented. As he writes of Harper's study, "There is no form underlying the confusion: the catastrophes are the results of accidents and coincidences; everything moves in a circle."[72] Cantwell's observations suggest that he felt that a sense of social causation could, in these cases, aid in uniting the disparate elements of plot.

Again demonstrating that a sense of "traditional literary values" was not lost amid his desire to foster progressive political content, Cantwell reserves his highest praise for the one nonproletarian member of his quartet, Marjorie Kinnan Rawlings. *South Moon Under*, a tale set in "the Florida scrub," a "country far removed from the violences of the depression" possesses just the kind of formal coherence and clarity that Cantwell felt to be lacking in the proletarian novels. Rawling's characters "always observe clearly," and the very "bends of the river take on a kind of individuality, since their identifying characteristics are so acutely seen and recognized."[73] Where a more narrowly political Marxist might have found only escapism, Cantwell finds a refreshing pastoral vision executed with skill. In fact, Cantwell, no matter how deeply enmeshed he became in contemporary social struggle, never seems to have lost his love for good adventure yarns and romances, and often recommended such fare to the readers of his new *New Outlook* column.

But if Cantwell sometimes refreshed himself in the "garden" of pastoral, he was drawn ceaselessly back to industrial reality. He concludes his study of the four young novelists by noting that the "nostalgic serenity" of Rawlings's novel, the "more consistent artistry" of *South Moon Under*, is possible to "a great extent because Mrs. Rawlings has chosen an easier task" than that faced by the proletarians who confront Depression reality.[74]

Cantwell's sense of the delicate critical balance required to keep social criticism in literature from conflicting with the imperatives of art sometimes led him to recognize that not all writers with revolutionary values should seek to write in a proletarian mode. In two reviews of fiction by Erskine Caldwell, for example, he recognizes that Caldwell, though a writer of revolutionary sympathies who reported for the *New Masses*, was not at his best when portraying social causation directly.

In the first of the reviews, Cantwell counters a *New Masses* review by Edwin Seaver, which had called for more social analysis by Caldwell in his novels of Southern lowlife, by noting that this amounted to encouraging the least impressive aspects of the Georgia novelist's talent at the expense of his better skills.[75] Caldwell's talent, Cantwell insisted, was for picturing the brutal, degraded life of a "white-trash" subculture profoundly alienated from the flow of modern American society. And in his review of Caldwell's next work, *God's Little Acre,* Cantwell reaffirmed this belief by noting that the very powerful novel was marred by Caldwell's unsuccessful attempt "to bring a specific social criticism into his work."[76]

Cantwell's insistence that the literary standards of leftists must remain high led him also to praise the work of James Joyce. In an article from 1933 titled "The Influence of James Joyce," he expresses regret that "in the rush of critical debate, including discussion of Marxian criticism, the really dominant literary figure of modern times has suffered a curious neglect."[77] Cantwell tries to remedy this situation by briefly tracing the effect of Joyce upon such diverse writers as F. Scott Fitzgerald, William Faulkner, and Edward Dahlberg (a writer sometimes included among the proletarians). He then accounts for this influence by claiming that Joyce developed a language "ever closer to the actuality" of modern experience through the inclusion of greater dissonance, complexity, and detail. Cantwell suggests that writers have imitated Joycean technique because

> they have recognized that under the lens of his methods all the overworked scenes of realistic narrative, like drops of water under a microscope, are suddenly seen to be teeming with unsuspected life; the pauses and silences whose meaning could barely be guessed, the nuances of moods, the emotional responses which are scarcely reflected in speech or gestures or facial expression—all this ... is packed with infinite voiceless dramas.[78]

Having paid homage to Joyce's technique, and having suggested its superiority in capturing the complex rhythms of modern urban life, Cantwell proceeds to a question that he notes is more pertinent to "current debate"—Joyce's treatment of the role of the artist in society. Arguing that Joyce has dramatized his political and aesthetic beliefs "with more wit and audacity and scholarship and with more intense labor than the holders of opposing points of view have so far displayed," Cantwell examines the key scenes in Joyce's novels that address the artist's duty. Of these the most important occurs in *Ulysses,* where, Cantwell notes,

> in that most cunning scene in modern fiction, when Stephen finally arrives at his concept of the artist's social role, he has spoken first with Davin,

the revolutionist with whom he cannot establish a firm relationship—he is alternately attracted by Davin's "quiet inbred courtesy" and repelled "swiftly and suddenly by a grossness of intelligence or by a bluntness of feeling or by a dull stare of terror in the eyes, the terror of the soul of a starving Irish village in which the curfew was still a nightly fear."

It is after turning against the revolutionist in this scene, Cantwell observes, that Stephen Dedalus offers his vision of a static art, an art above desire and loathing, and of the artist as a politically neutral seer above the common fray. Joyce follows this vision of the artist's neutrality with a scene of lyric inspiration in which Cantwell finds the artist's intangible rewards expressed as eloquently as they have ever been presented.[79]

Cantwell respected Joyce for having "thought deeply" about, and "understood fully," what each choice open to the artist entailed, and for having dramatized his choice in luminous prose utterly faithful to experience. Thus, while admitting the validity of Marxist objections to Joyce's claim of neutrality, he finds their response inadequate. "It would be easy for a Marxist to prove that such neutrality is in fact impossible, that it works to the advantage of the dominant class, but this is aside from the point; the Marxian novelists and critics have not dramatized their convictions so compellingly as Joyce dramatized his."[80]

Cantwell clearly believes that before Marxists can glibly dismiss Joyce, as some did on occasion with such epithets as "bourgeois" or "decadent," they must first meet the challenge implicit in the Irish novelist's accomplishments. But he also believed that the record of Joyce's accomplishments since *Ulysses* indicated that his choice of neutrality had led to profound alienation, if not sterility. Noting the "strained and meagre production," the troubling "Work in Progress" [*Finnegans Wake*] that few writers sought to understand, let alone imitate, that had followed his masterpiece, Cantwell asks rhetorically, "How much have we lost because Stephen drew back from the revolution that attracted him, rebuffed by the first bluntness of intelligence he found or by an occasional stare of terror he saw in the eyes of those with whom he would have had to throw his lot."[81]

Cantwell's answer is written by his entire career in the thirties. And in a letter to his friend and fellow critic, Newton Arvin, written a month before the publication of his essay on Joyce, Cantwell echoes Stephen Dedalus but declares himself committed:

> The narrowness and harshness of a good deal of the writing done in the movement creates a genuine problem—it's impossible for people who sympathize not to be disturbed precisely because they so earnestly want the work of the revolutionists to be superior. For myself the only counter-irritant against this sort of thing is to subject myself to a careful study of The Saturday Review and the Herald Tribune Books for a few days. Then I go back, I all throbbingly and yearningly go back, as James would say, steeled against almost any grossness of phrase or bluntness of intelligence that the people on our side can show.[82]

The echoed phrase "bluntness of intelligence" and the qualifier "almost" suggest that this "steeling" of himself was not always easy. The passage also seems riddled with sexual anxiety, with Cantwell "throbbingly" "steeled" against the softness of any feminine yearnings for Jamesian or Joycean aestheticism. Cast as it is in a masculinist mode typical of much male proletarian writing, it suggests that, despite his more complicated aesthetic politics, Cantwell did not fully escape the classic identification of aesthetics with the feminine (as reinforced by such works as Gold's on Wilder).[83]

Cantwell clearly moved at times uneasily between the "bluntness of intelligence" seemingly sometimes demanded by revolutionary politics, and the brilliance of a Henry James or a James Joyce. He shared in the desire of radicals to create a literature "about propertyless workers, embodying their point of view and advocating a revolutionary correction of it," but he was also convinced that to be effective at least some of this radical literature must be, to use the problematic thirties metaphors, a sharp and beautiful "weapon" quite unlike the "blunt instruments" produced by the comrades he criticized.

Barbara Foley's claim that proletarian novelists and even the most dogmatic of the *New Masses* critics were heavily indebted to "bourgeois" aesthetic ideas is certainly borne out by Cantwell's criticism. But this fact can be looked at quite differently than does Foley. She argues, in effect, that the proletarian novel and those critics who supported it should have been more open to developing a "hortatory and didactic" approach in their work, that they were held back from creating a truly "revolutionary" literature by their continued embeddedness in "bourgeois" aesthetic values and perspectives. But Cantwell's argument, it seems to me, offers an interesting counter to this thesis.

Cantwell's criticism suggests that what Foley calls "bourgeois" aesthetic concerns are *crucial* to the effectiveness of proletarian literature. While there are times when Cantwell seems drawn back to certain "purely" aesthetic concerns, most of the time his argument is that certain storytelling or "dramatizing" skills one might label "aesthetic" are needed to ensure the political success of the proletarian project *as* "propaganda" (a term that, as we will see, Cantwell was perfectly willing to use to describe his work, but which Foley, among others, cites out of context of his broader vision). While he never rules out the use of the "hortatory and didactic," he suggests that most often such an approach emerges when the dramatizing dimension has failed. The claim that literary discourse is to some degree different from other kinds of political, didactic, expository discourse seems necessary if we are to speak of literature at all. But as I suggested in my opening chapter, this partly depends on defining the kind of genre one is dealing with. No one suggests that radical street theater should compete with Shakespeare, and it is clear that not all proletarian literature needed to compete with Joyce. Cantwell, however, wished that some of this literature would render the experience of radically aligned working-class life with a degree of subtlety approaching the complexity of lived experience.

Cantwell is implicitly arguing, in his remarks on Joyce, for example, that to move an audience from a "bourgeois" position to a "revolutionary" one, one must start with where those audience "subjects" are structurally located. And even most members of the working class, as Louis Althusser has argued most systematically, are "subjected" as more or less "bourgeois" individuals (Foley admits something like this in her own qualified sense that the bourgeois realist tradition is not only a source of limitation but also enables certain proletarian literary gestures). Cantwell rejected the efforts of Marxists who replaced literary criticism with a purely "extrinsic" political criticism of literature, the position most often attributed, with some justification, to Gold, Granville Hicks, Joseph Freeman, and a few other critics around the *New Masses*.[84] But he objected to such an approach not in the name of maintaining some bourgeois aesthetic idea but rather because he thought good craft a key element of good propaganda. He certainly preferred the kind of openness advocated by his friend John Dos Passos, who had earlier censured Gold and called for a radical literature that "will find what it's not looking for."[85] But if Cantwell was at times tempted by the kind of reductive empiricism that Foley sees alternating wildly with the overt political didacticism in much *New Masses* criticism, he resisted this approach as well.[86] He was advocating instead an interaction between Marxist theory and the details of the social world. Cantwell sought in his criticism to chart such a course for writers that encouraged them to interrogate experience in search of the links between individual and social reality, rather than assuming that such links had already been discovered by Marx or Lenin or the CPUSA and need only be illustrated dramatically by the artist—but he did not think such links would simply spring magically from close attention to the real. The real had to be interrogated theoretically, a position that to a degree anticipates such later Marxist literary theoreticians as Fredric Jameson. Cantwell's critique of naive empiricism is made clear in letters exchanged with fellow novelist and critic James T. Farrell from midyear 1934.

Cantwell tells his friend Farrell that his work as critic and fictionist is marred by a certain reluctance to theorize. He first points out that Farrell's own literary strictures are, in their reductive empiricism, as "exacting and arbitrary" as the Marxist critics Farrell was already (in)famous for attacking. Further, Cantwell adds, "Marxist dogmas are much less limiting and confining than those of Aristotle, for instance." He then goes on to specify where he disagreed with Farrell's philosophy of composition by discussing the construction of Farrell's most famous character, Studs Lonigan:

> You evidently feel that you must write of Lonigan in his own terms. The significance of his actions—of his life—must be considered in terms of his whole complex of experience, his friends, the standards existing in his environment. I agree with you. But I wonder if you mean his *immediate* environment and I have a feeling you do. . . . You submerge yourself in that environment; you write of it as it seems to one submerged in it. You refuse to lug in outside meanings, standards and judgments brought from another world. . . . But my observation is that these units, groups, are not self-contained, that they respond to other pressures, propulsions, besides those of the group itself. Lonigan, for instance, may be relatively uninfluenced by someone he is in daily contact with, and yet respond very sharply and dramatically to the decision of someone he has never seen, some banker, say, whose decision critically affects Lonigan's father, which in turn is of influence in Lonigan's career. The banker's decision in turn

may be the result of a complex of pressures over which he has no or little control. I feel that the isolation of these powerful and invisible connectives is one of the tasks of modern fiction.[87]

In this passage and in similar ones addressed to other Farrell characters and milieux, Cantwell tries to demonstrate the limits of a narrowly conceived realism or literary empiricism, arguing that larger social dimensions of the capitalist system are no less "real" for being "invisible."[88]

The ideas announced in "No Landmarks" are reiterated throughout Cantwell's thirties criticism and personal correspondence, forming the core of his literary politics. Several of those ideas—the need to develop a literature dramatizing the struggles of workers, the belief in a creative vitality summoned up through commitment to the class struggle, the withering of one literary tradition and the emergence of another—were common to virtually all Marxist literary commentators in the thirties, and they were often portrayed retrospectively as ineluctably leading to a crudely reductive literary moment. But Cantwell had no difficulty connecting these commitments to an intricate sense of the complex interrelation of the "aesthetic" and the "propaganda" dimensions of literature. His example suggests that it may well have been the conservatives in the 1930s and later the Cold War critics who were reductive in failing to note such complexities. By turning to analyzing Cantwell's own fiction, especially his own proletarian novel, *The Land of Plenty*, we can assess how well his work "dramatizes" and clarifies his critical convictions.

4 A PORTRAIT OF THE ARTIST AS PROPAGANDIST

Cantwell as Proletarian Novelist

In October, 1933, shortly before his essay on Joyce appeared, Cantwell took the opportunity provided by a *New Republic* review of recent fiction about workers to reiterate his strong support for the proletarian literary movement. Calling the literature dealing with the conditions of workers the "most vital" of "all contemporary literary movements," Cantwell insisted that "no one who is interested in literature rather than in politics could disregard" proletarian fiction.[1] In so phrasing his argument, Cantwell was expressing his continued faith that the literary purposes of artists and the political purposes of the radical movement could be fruitfully joined. But, even acknowledging that this may be a tactical maneuver aimed at his liberal audience, it is clear also that his ability to separate out the literary from the political indicates a bit of continuing tension between the artist and the revolutionist. And for Cantwell this faith and these tensions were not only abstract; it is evident that his critical perspectives on proletarian literature were developing in dialogue with, not to say in "dialectical relation to," his practice as a fiction writer. Cantwell's first years as a critic, 1932–34, were also the years in which he produced his superb "proletarian" novel, *The Land of Plenty*.

Land of Plenty is widely regarded as one of the major achievements of the proletarian movement and has received a fair amount of commentary, although not in the context of Cantwell's overall career.[2] It is important also to say that the novel cannot ultimately be contained by the proletarian genre or its subgenres. It is a magnificent, subtle, elegant literary achievement that stands with the best writing of the era. Confining it to the much-disparaged proletarian movement accounts in large part for the fact that it has not received the position it deserves in the broader canon of US literature.

That said, Cantwell felt himself to be very much a part of the proletarian cultural movement, and for the purposes of this book it is most fitting to read it in that context, to read it as an exemplum of the best work inspired by that cultural project. Two of the most perceptive analysts of the proletarian literary movement, Walter Rideout and Barbara Foley, refer to Cantwell's second novel as a "strike novel" and a "social novel," respectively. Rideout views *Land of Plenty* as "the best from most points of view" of a proletarian novel subgenre (consisting of some sixteen examples) centered in the experience of a labor strike. While what he means by "best" remains implicit, he seems to have in mind "traditional" literary values, including believable plot, consistent characters, aesthetically pleasing language, and so forth. Foley, on the other hand, places Cantwell's novel in a slightly broader category, the proletarian "social novel," defined as works centered around "multiple protagonists" rather than stressing either individual development (as do two of the other categories in her taxonomy of the proletarian novel—the "fictional autobiography" and the "bildungsroman") or largely effacing individuality in a mass/class (as does her fourth and final category, the "collective novel"). Foley notes the partially arbitrary nature of such categories, and, as we will see, Cantwell's novel actually displays aspects of all four subgenres. In analyzing proletarian novels, Foley also departs from Rideout in the criteria for judgment. Arguing that proletarian literature as a form did not fully exploit its potential to be a hortatory and didactic discourse aiding the revolutionary movement, she analyzes the novels as various combinations of and tensions between doctrinal politics and generic limits/possibilities.[3]

I want to combine and reconceive of elements of both Rideout's and Foley's criteria of judgment by examining *Land of Plenty* in light of and as an extension of Cantwell's own conception of the nature, uses, and values of proletarian fiction, an approach I would characterize as "nonhortatory propaganda." Then I will evaluate this strategy in relation to its projected audiences via two rather different kinds of review *Land of Plenty* received—those arising from the New York literary scene, and those coming from workers in the factory that is the scene of the novel.

As an extension of Cantwell's critical attitudes on proletarian fiction, *Land of Plenty* takes as its central problem one endemic to the genre—connecting the micropolitical level of workers' daily lives to the macropolitical level of larger questions of capitalism and class struggle. Some proletarian authors solved this problem through explicitly didactic interventions (though Foley notes that this is less common than generally charged). These could range from the situationally credible and subtle to what one might call the "communist ex machina" approach, or what Cantwell called the use of "communist magicians,"[4] in which a radical organizer/agitator appears suddenly to offer Marxist analysis through a speech or conversation. Cantwell uses this approach to a certain extent through the "mentor figure" of Vin Garl,[5] a Finnish worker and former member of the Industrial Workers of the World (IWW) who serves as the voice of labor history and organizational experience in the novel. But Cantwell's primary way of dealing with this problem of connecting levels is to offer, on one hand, a micropolitical analysis in naturalistic detail of the psychology of class as worked out in a particular work site, and, on the other, to offer an overarching Marxian allegory addressing the macropolitics of capitalism in the 1930s. While some might think this allegory (sometimes subtle, sometimes blatant) a mere "frill" on top of the naturalism, in working the allegorical vein Cantwell was, whether consciously or not, contributing to a long tradition of working-class literature extending back through Jack London and Rebecca Harding Davis to the dime novels of the nineteenth century,[6] in which allegory was a key method of conveying class-conscious political analysis.

Drawing its raw materials from Cantwell's four years of laboring at Harbor Plywood in Hoquiam, Washington, and his years of living in mill towns, *The Land of Plenty* is a detailed account of activity in a veneer wood factory and of the workers and bosses whose lives revolve around it.[7] The novel depicts the conditions and events which precipitate a strike as seen through the eyes of a diverse group of characters representing various personality types, political positions, and class interests. Part 1, "Power and Light," traces the events that lead up to the strike, as viewed by workers and management. Part 2, "The Education of a Worker," continues developing the strike as seen by numerous characters, but concentrates a bit more centrally on one sensitive young working-class adolescent who is forced to come to terms with the class conflict touched off by the walkout.

The novel is constructed via twenty-three chapters, each labeled with the name of a character and (de)centered in the point of view of that character. I say "decentered" because each character is carefully constructed in relation to other characters such that we see them at once as individual and *social* beings; they are sufficiently individualized to seem like "real" human beings, but never to the point where we lose sight of them as social types and members of larger classes. Each chapter consists of a mixture of dialogue and free indirect discourse, thus reinforcing a sense of character as emerging socially. At points the free indirect discourse is sufficiently distanced from character to become something verging on a more objective narrative voice. As in Faulkner's *As I Lay Dying*, the distribution of chapters to characters is uneven, divided between what might normally be characterized as both "major" and more "minor" characters in such a way as to minimize a sense of this distinction and to maximize a sense of social interrelation and totality.

The novel begins with the factory suddenly plunged into darkness by a power failure during the night shift. Details of the blackout are handled in naturalistic fashion, but images of darkness and light also form the overarching symbolic structure of the Marxian allegory.[8] Set in 1929 on and around Independence Day, the blackout allegorizes the "power failure" of capitalism known as the Great Crash. Workers literally struggling to restore power have to do so amid the incompetence of the managerial class. Winters, an American Indian sawyer, proves the most militant of the workers by seizing first a flashlight and later commandeering the boss's car to use its power and lights to help an injured worker. I have called the allegory "Marxian," but, more particularly, it seems closest to the anarcho-syndicalist ideology of the Industrial Workers of the World, who, unlike the Communist Party, stressed the ability of workers to organize independently to create One Big Union to run an economy without bosses.

The blackout forms the center of the novel's early action and is viewed by the various characters in succession. We first see it through the eyes of Carl Belcher (shades of Fielding), a former "efficiency expert" turned inefficient supervisor. Being *in* the factory but not *of* it, Carl stumbles about blindly and rather comically in the dark while attempting to devise a way of blaming the power failure on Hagen, the senior-most "old hand" of the mill whose prestige among his fellow workers Carl and the plant manager, MacMahon, both fear. Carl is accompanied in his stumblings by his sycophantic assistant Morely (feminized as "Molly" by the workers). Discussion between Morley and Belcher focuses on the micropolitics of the plant, the struggle to control the pattern of blame with regard to the economic loss brought about by the outage. Hagen's section, which immediately follows, continues this intricate dance as he seeks to protect himself from the blame he knows Carl will try to inflict by gaining witnesses among his fellow workers and by documenting his whereabouts despite the darkness. But soon Hagen's concerns shift away from self-interest when it is discovered that a "hoist man" has been crushed by a huge log set lose by the blackout.

In contrast to the foreman, Belcher and the plant manager, MacMahon, both of whom eventually fall through a hole in the floor and get lost in the swampish, chemical waste-ridden tide flats beneath the plant, Hagen and the other workers, "knowing the floors around their machines as they know their own homes" (14), move swiftly and efficiently through the dark factory in an attempt to rescue the hoist man. Cantwell makes it clear that the workers are quite capable of running the factory alone, indeed, that they must protect it against the incompetent representatives of management. On the allegorical plane, this instills the sense that they are qualified to seize the means of production, and the prolonged situational irony of the foreman's and manager's inaction set against the quick actions of the workers suggests that the power failure of capitalism can be set aright only by the workers.

At the more naturalistic level, the temporary stoppage serves to underscore the structural conditions that make labor organizing difficult, since only such a break gives the workers time to think and talk among themselves about the layoffs, speedups, and wage cuts with which they have recently been burdened. In the Hagen sections and in those centered on Winters, these central characters have a series of encounters with small groups of their coworkers, gradually and cautiously building solidarity. These discussions are structured as concentric circles, moving out from the main characters to other named "minor" worker characters, and then out further to anonymous workers acting as a kind of chorus: *"Listen,* a voice said, *Just say the word and I'll walk out"* (117). The italics (in the original) underscore a different, abstract dimension, functioning synecdochically as a hint of collective forces and the mass voice found in some "collective novels" in the proletarian genre.

Cantwell builds a sense of complicated class consciousness by contrasting an awareness of alienation (both alienating physical conditions and alienation from the fruits of one's labor) with a counterbalancing pride in work. Winters is the character that most fully embodies these contradictions. He realizes that in this factory, as in others he has worked in before, workers are being driven to inhuman lengths to meet a rush order. Just before the lights went out, he was himself a pure embodiment of industrial alienation: "The Indian's face was set and his eyes were half-closed under the bright hanging light. The effort to keep up with the racing saws drove everything else out of his mind . . . ; there was nothing left for him now but the straight edge against which he lined the panels and the rolls that drew them in. Gradually his features emptied of life, only his swiftly moving hands and his intent eyes revealing the spirit in him" (39).

In addition to driving the workers too hard, the new foreman is robbing them of their pride in their work. Sensitive to minute nuances of sight and sound in the factory (17), the mill hands sense that Carl is ruining *their* factory. Winters's free indirect discourse blends toward a collective consciousness:

> [Carl] was tearing it down, he was wrecking the whole factory, letting the machines go to pieces and demoralizing the crew so that no one could get anything done. It had been bad in the old days, it had always been bad, but there had been moments, at least, when it had run smoothly, when the whole factory hummed like a single intricate machine, smooth and beautiful, perfectly coordinated, perfectly timed. Then for a few moments, even for an hour, they would all be refreshed with pride at the way they worked, each man in his place, each tiny act fitting with the swing and drive of the factory. (279)

Retrospectively in 1936, amid the more reformist mood of the Popular Front era, Cantwell wrote that the major motivation in his fiction was to "give workers a sense of their own dignity."[9] That sense is clearly present in this passage and throughout the novel in its careful depiction of the details of various jobs in the factory. But in the context of *Land of Plenty* such knowledge is not an end in itself but a prerequisite part of a larger consciousness of class and the possibility of radical transformation. It becomes a utopian prefiguration of unalienated labor, emerging when the workers work for themselves as the owners of the means of production.

Class consciousness is always built in relatively small increments rather than through dramatic conversions. Winters, for example, building on his anger at Belcher, makes a discovery more profound than the mere incompetence of one supervisor as, in the darkness, a vision of his entire life, touched off by thoughts of his dying wife, passes before him: "His memory would give him nothing but images of misery and terror until it seemed he had lived all his life on the scene of some vast wreck that had strewn the world with its victims; now he remembered the 'accidents' in the logging camps and the mills where he had worked, the ruined bodies of cripples, the loggers whose intestines were ruptured and torn from weights they pulled and the mad pace of their labors" (174). It becomes clear to Winters that these "accidents" were not accidents at all but the direct result of a profit-driven system that pushed machines and workers alike beyond their capacities.

When Belcher eventually finds an excuse to fire Winters, Hagen protests and is fired along with him. The rest of the crew, sensing the injustice of the firings, force the boss, through mostly silent intimations of violence, to overrule Carl and rehire the workers. Thus part 1 ends with the pride of the workers restored by their resistance to the supervisor and the plant manager: "They were proud; they were excited; some of the kids began yelling as they ran toward the factory. They had their first sure knowledge of their strength" (204). The section subtitle, "Power and Light," now shifts meaning to represent not power and light lost in the blackout but power and light gained through solidarity.

Part 2, "The Education of a Worker," traces the parallel emergence of a strike and the gradual development of class consciousness in young Johnny Hagen, son of the "old hand." This section contains elements of what Foley calls the "proletarian bildungsroman," but this individualizing dimension is kept in tension with the more "social" dimension. On a symbol-laden, July 4, 1929, the day after the power failure, Johnny joins his father, the Indian sawyer Winters, Vin Garl, the ex-Wobbly who gives the workers their only knowledge of strike tactics (there is no union organized in the plant),[10] and a few other workers, who meet informally to discuss tactics in the event that Carl attempts once more to fire some members of the night shift (as he was rumored to be contemplating). When Vin Garl begins to lay out a plan of action, one of the workers asks him,

"You a union man?" . . .
"Me? What union is there for a man working where I work?"
"Wobbly?"

"I used to carry a red card [IWW membership card] during the War. . . . was in that fighting at Everett and after Centralia it got so hot for me I had to beat it to Canada. . . . But there's nothing left of them now."

Johnny looked around at the men gathered in the yard. The harshness of the Finn's voice repelled him and he searched the faces of the men, trying to see some approval or disapproval in their responses to his words.

"They didn't die out," Vin Garl said abruptly. "They were wiped out." He said wiped out with a curious intensity, his mouth closing over the words as though he were biting into them.

Sorenson said cautiously, "We don't want to get everybody thinking we're a bunch of Reds."

Vin Garl started to answer him. Then he nodded. (262–63)

This nuanced silence suggests Vin Garl's savvy sense that Sorenson, who represents the most cautious faction of workers, is not ready for a further lesson in labor history that might redefine what being a "bunch of Reds" means.

Following this exchange, the workers begin to dispute the merits of the American Federation of Labor (AF of L), and Johnny leaves because arguing "got on his nerves." Like Stephen Dedalus, Johnny is at first repelled by the harshness of those with whom he would have had to throw in his lot, and is caught up in the ethnic tension that has historically been a bane of the US labor movement. He thinks of Vin Garl and his friend Waino, both Finns, as "foreigners sticking together and living on the wrong side of the river instead of like ordinary citizens" (263), and he resents their potentially dangerous interference in his (work)life. But then he remembers a ghastly story told to him by an older worker, a story about a kid not much older than Johnny who had had both his legs crushed off in an "accident" brought on by a speedup. Johnny begins a slow, groping process that leads him to realize that violence, in its various forms, was constantly being directed against workers, and that their harshness was a necessary and inadequate defense against it.

As Johnny walks away from the scene of the strategy session, he also begins to understand the gulf that separates him from Walt Conner, representative of a tempting middle-class life. Conner, like Cantwell himself, has been forced by economic circumstance to quit college after a year. Initially, Johnny is attracted to Walt's talk about fraternities and campus life. As he and Walt talk during the blackout, Johnny begins to dream of the "ivy-covered halls, the long slopes of green lawn, the beautiful coeds, each with her own sports roadster, giving herself so gaily and passionately with a true F. Scott Fitzgerald abandon." (109). But he soon realizes that Walt was merely toying with him and using him to gain a chance to take advantage of Marie, a young Polish worker whom Walt assumes by her ethnic and class origins to be a "chippie."

This relationship between the two young men functions structurally (though sometimes awkwardly) in the novel, but it also suggests an element of autobiographical displacement, an allegory of Cantwell's own split consciousness. As we saw in chapter 1 above, in his first novel, *Laugh and Lie Down*, Cantwell revealed considerable ambivalence toward his experience as a factory laborer. The autobiographical protagonist of that work felt the factory in which he labored to be a more vital environment than the college he had been forced to leave, but he also felt shame at having to wear workers' overalls and had ambitions to own the factory one day. But as the radical movement, with its celebration of the heroic working class, grew all around him, Cantwell sloughed off most of this ambivalence and began to recreate himself as the gruff proletarian remembered by some of his colleagues. The satiric reference to gay "F. Scott Fitzgerald abandon" is one of several such allusions that suggest a kind of intertextual commentary on the Fitzgeraldesque dimensions of his first novel and of his earlier self. As such, "Walt" serves as a condensed trope both for the discourse of a "decaying middle class" found in much Communist polemic and for the literary embodiment of that decline in much "this side of paradise" fiction (117).

When Conner eventually betrays Johnny, a more directly relevant kind of "decadence" is revealed and another part of the latter's education begun. Johnny learns not only to generally distrust promises coming from the middle class, but when Walt becomes Carl's new assistant, he begins to understand something about the functioning of class in the factory. When Johnny sees Walt riding in the foreman's car,

> something he had not understood before became clear to him. Somehow he had thought that people worked and rose in the world. In one swift glance at Walt riding important in Carl's car the picture was reversed and now in the depth of his bitterness he saw Walt rising in the world, yes, but rising in the way that a corpse rises when it has lain for a long time under

water, rising and rotting as it was pushed out by the strong cold currents at the bottom. (304)

Johnny has begun to identify himself with the "strong cold currents at the bottom" who have nothing in common with the Walt Conners of the world. Foley argues that this portrayal of Conner instills the message that workers themselves must bring change without the aid of sympathetic members of the middle class.[11] Cantwell certainly portrays the middle class in a highly unfavorable light, but later in the novel Walt has some minor awakenings of his own when he sees the forces of reaction frame his old friend Winters for murder and sees the disgusting nature of those for whom he works (339, 344–46); his responses remain ambivalent but at least hold out the possibility of his identifying with those "below" rather than "above" him.

When the night shift returns to work the evening after the blackout, they learn that Hagen, Winters, and twenty other workers have been fired. Spontaneous shouts of "Come on out!" arise from the night shift crew, and as word spreads inside the factory, the day shift shut off their machines to join their fellow workers; the strike begins. Earlier many of the workers had scornfully eyed the cheap display of the town's Independence Day parade, but now a real independence has been declared and the workers are extremely excited. For Johnny, the memory of the moment when the strike begins becomes a kind of talisman:

> Nothing else ever gave him the same strange feeling of excitement and strength, and all during the next week he treasured the memory calling on it like some powerful charm to help him in the moments of despair. At home he used it most, making himself remember when wrangling in the house got too bitter and when the disorder and the lack of any quiet wore on his nerves, but he used it every day on the picket line when the waiting got tiresome or when someone got caught and hauled off by the cops; he called on it when . . . after the third day a part of the factory began to run with scabs who came from nowhere. (298)

But notice how even here the dramatic "charm" is set against the mundane, the quotidian.

As Johnny watches the police protect the scabs and sees how anxious they are to bust the heads of pickets, as he reads the accounts of the strike in the local paper and compares it to what he *knows*, a sense of the wider significance of all that is happening begins to dawn on him. Some day, he imagines, "it would happen again. Some day all the people would come out of [all] the factories, singing in the streets." (301) "Slowly and painfully he learned that what happened did not depend only on how they acted here on the [picket] line. It was not only this strike, he learned, that determined what the police did, something else was in the air; there was a chance that there would be strikes in some of the other factories on the harbor" (304–05). He realizes that the battle is part of a much larger war, and as the importance of the strike becomes clear to him, he loses his distaste for arguments.

> Sometimes at night he sat in on the meetings . . . , sitting back in a corner of the smoke-filled room and listening to the arguing that went on almost all night. Crowded around the table, their faces strained and sweating in the hot night, the men argued fiercely. . . . The police, the unfinished orders, the price of logs, the way men felt in the other mills, the length of time before an election, the newspapers—everything came into these talks. (305)

During one of these arguments, Winters and Vin Garl, both now effectively without family, take the most militant stand, while Sorenson pushes for reconciliation. As Johnny's father begins to lean toward Sorenson's side, pressed as he is by great financial burdens, Johnny's own militancy is sparked, and the class struggle is symbolically passed on to another generation.

The climax of the strike and of the novel comes during a violent rainstorm. Thinking they have been granted permission to do so by the police, a large group of pickets rush into the factory to seek shelter. The scabs, misunderstanding the intentions of the strikers, panic and rush to seek the protection of the police. The police, "with the habitual and unimaginative roughness they are trained to employ," and "grunting" "like speechless animals," push the scabs back into the crowd of workers because they are unable to distinguish them from the strikers. Suddenly the police, "so far off their native grounds," panic, shooting a scab (321).

In the ensuing melee, the elder Hagen quickly reaches the main switchboard and shuts off the lights to again give the workers the protection of darkness just as more shots are fired. He has transformed the accident of empowering "disempowerment" into an active, conscious process. As the scabs and police retreat from the workers' home ground, the strikers discover that, in effect, they have captured the factory. "Temporarily," writes one critic, "the paradox of the estranged forces of production is resolved, for the workers, who belong in the mill by virtue of their knowledge of it, are now in possession of it and are for the first time emotionally at home in their familiar environment."[12]

But the strikers' triumph is short-lived. The workers occupy the mill overnight, but by dawn they are surrounded by a cordon of police. Behind the police, a large crowd of townspeople, some sympathetic to the strike, others hostile, moves restlessly. After waiting all morning for the owner to arrive to begin negotiations, Johnny's father and another worker venture outside the factory to reconnoiter, and perhaps try to open up negotiations. As they do so, a fight breaks out in the crowd and shots are again fired. In the melee Johnny's girlfriend is viciously smashed by a policeman's club, but Johnny and Vin Garl manage to escape through the floor of the factory into the bushes on the tide flats beneath the mill. The same bushes in which Carl and MacMahon had gotten hopelessly lost earlier in the novel offer the workers a refuge out of sight of the rampaging police (365–66).

As Johnny, Vin Garl, and another worker await nightfall so that they may escape undetected, Johnny learns that his father has been shot. His "education" has been completed, and the novel ends abruptly:

> The rain fell hard, drenching them while they waited, not like rain but like some new and terrible weapon of their enemies. Johnny tried to crowd under the driftwood and Vin Garl put his hand on his shoulder. "Come on, son," he said gently, "don't cry," and they sat there listening . . . , their faces dark with misery and anger, listening and waiting for the darkness to come like a friend and set them free. (369)

Darkness has by now revealed itself at the allegorical level as a metaphor for the failing power of capitalism, and thus the novel ends with the strike defeated but also with unspoken portents of the eventual defeat of capitalism.

While Johnny's *bildung* plays a large role in the second half of the novel, it is clearly far from the whole story. As Foley has noted, the expansive field and the expanded cast of the proletarian "social novel" allows room for various subplots. She notes, using *Land of Plenty* as one example, that there is a general dispersal of class consciousness across a range of worker characters, with nuanced differences among them. She later notes that this expansiveness was often beneficial in somewhat displacing masculinist tendencies in much male (and some female) proletarian fiction, and in making for more complex treatments of race and ethnicity.[13]

With regard to questions of race and ethnicity, the treatment is not terribly complex but it is demonstrably "progressive." I have already given some suggestion of how this works with regard to ethnic differences Johnny has to transcend, and there are also a number of other instances in the novel in which ethnic and racial prejudice is exposed. This primarily takes the form of racist slurs and anti-Semitic remarks by the bosses (see, for example, 160–61) and by representatives of the petty bourgeoisie such as Johnny's real estate salesman brother-in-law, Gerald (245). But ethnic prejudice among workers (in addition to Johnny) is also acknowledged and implicitly critiqued. A progressive message is also underscored by casting an American Indian as a central, highly class-conscious character. His racial characteristics are never foregrounded, unless it is through a kind of stoicism bordering on racist stereotype, and the prime message is that race is ultimately irrelevant to his class consciousness. From the other side, signs that the class-ambivalent Walt Conner is moving toward siding with the bosses include his ethnicism (106, 115) and racism in turning on his friend and mentor, Winters, calling him a "God-damned half-breed" (202).

Treatment of gender in the novel is considerably richer and more complicated. There are dimensions of the novel that inscribe some "classic" gender tropes of the proletarian novel, particularly the juxtaposition of masculine workers and their flabby, feminized overseers (like "Molly"), and the paralleling of Johnny's sexual awakening with his emerging class consciousness is a familiar masculinist trope of the proletarian apprenticeship genre (his first sex is virtually coded as a reward for his heroic participation in the strike—girls say yes to boys who say no to the bosses?). But these sexist clichés are also counterpoised to elements of a female bildungsroman that complicate, without fully displacing, such tropes. Class loyalty and sexual loyalty are imbricated in the figures of Marie and Ellen, two sisters working at the factory who become involved with Walt and Johnny, respectively. The differences in treatment each receives form an important, clearly class-coded subplot. Walt's attempt to rape Marie allegorizes the rape of the working class by capitalists, but is also handled in chilling, nonsensationalistic detail, and Marie successfully defends herself without outside (male) assistance (223–26). Ellen is coded as being more class-conscious than Johnny is, and she provides him, through her disgust at his association with Walt, with one of his initial lessons in class consciousness. She is also coded as more feminist than her sister in swearing that she won't let men treat her as badly as they have treated Marie (219). But Ellen's development is not followed carefully during the strike, where she is portrayed only as one of a segregated crowd of "girls" and "women" on the picket line, as a victim of a policeman's club, and, again, as a vehicle for Johnny's achievement of proletarian manhood.

On the other side of the class line, Rose, MacMahon's daughter, while portrayed as rather superficial and self-centered, is far less so than her middle-class twit of a boyfriend. His insensitivity to her possible pregnancy reveals that middle-class girls and women bear an extra gender burden as well. Rose is portrayed throughout as being more perceptive than her father and the other males she is surrounded by (138), and her need to play coquettishly dumb even embarrasses the insensitive Conner (196). She is, however, partly taken in by Conner's social-climbing attentions. Rose's mother is also briefly depicted as a victim of "self-sacrificing," "patient womanhood" (126).

Gendered class differences are also apparent in the plant. The females in the factory office are "girls" (regardless of age) and are portrayed as middle-class observers of the events (296 313), in contrast to the factory "girls" and "women," who side with the strikers and join in picketing. The sexual harassment both groups of women face is also dealt with in a manner meant to suggest distinct levels of social consciousness. Some of the "girls" giggle when they are groped in the dark by stock boys during the blackout, but others react with stoic distaste: "'Oh, get out of here,' she heard a girl's voice, wearily, not in anger but disgust, 'Keep your hands to yourself'" (69).

Gender struggle within the working class, where presumably the class allegory can be backgrounded, is handled more interestingly. The insensitive reaction to Marie's pregnancy and abortion by her working-class boyfriend, for example, entails sensitive identification with the additional burden of exploitation borne by working-class women (71, 219). And there is also a clear critique of working-class male machismo as the plot reveals Marie's boyfriend's reaction to Walt's attempted rape as more involved in his own ego than concern over the effects she might be experiencing (228, 232).

These gender issues never take center stage in the novel, but they are handled with the same respect as, and are never totally subsumed under, the development of class consciousness. This is made possible in large measure by the fact that class consciousness is handled at a very microanalytical level. As I have suggested, there certainly are dramatic moments of newfound power and awareness, and the overarching allegory has portentous dimensions. But even the darkness and light symbolism is brought down to the everyday level in the one chapter not labeled with a character's name, "The Light Man," in which the very practical problem of paying the electricity bill is ironically set against and within the grand themes of struggle. Cantwell's strategy is clearly to slant his text propagandistically in sympathy with the working class, but that does not mean that he presumes to know precisely what they should do in a given situation. While some might argue that the gap between the revolutionary allegory and the day-to-day struggle is a flaw, one could also read it as leaving room for working-class agency and for the specificity of local struggles. The text bears careful witness to the particularities of local conditions and local levels of organization without ignoring larger structures. The main radical character, Vin Garl, accurately reflects both the history of Finnish radicalism in the Northwest and the important regional legacy of the IWW. No Communist "magician" comes in to save the day, but as the Eastern capitalist plant owner Digby declares that the strike must be the work of Communists, the party is ironically invoked (338). The complex message here seems to be both that Communists get the blame/credit for efforts of countless rank-and-file workers, and that in turn those workers may in fact be building a communist future whether they identify with the Party or not.

Not long after the first reviews of *The Land of Plenty* began appearing in the press, Cantwell availed himself of an opportunity provided by the *New Masses* to discuss the intention behind his novel and to assess his own achievement. He began his autocritique, in the form of a letter to the *New Masses* in response to a questionnaire about Marxist criticism that the editors had circulated to radical writers, by stating flatly, "*The Land of Plenty* is, quite simply, a work of propaganda."[14] What Cantwell means by "propaganda" is not entirely clear even in context, but given the critical context I have provided, we can come closer to an understanding of what the term means to him. Near the end of the letter to Farrell mentioned in the last chapter, for example, he uses the term to contrast his position with his friend's:

> You are striving toward an impartiality, even toward ... characters not congenial. You evidently believe that some sort of scientific detachment is possible. I no longer believe it, though I once did. I now consider myself a propagandist and all my works—including this letter—as works of propaganda. If I can contribute toward weakening the prestige of the group that controls this society I don't want to miss an opportunity to do so. It's only a question of trying to find the most effective method.[15]

Cantwell's committed position is clear, but, as we will see, much of what that might mean hinges on the question of "effective method" raised in his final sentence.

What I think is at stake for Cantwell with regard to method is suggested later in his letter to the *New Masses* when he argues that proletarian literature and Marxist criticism should provide a kind of imaginary battleground to test working-class strategy in the growing class struggle. He writes that a "great part" of the task of novelists and critics should be to "work out, in our own imaginations, some of the problems the working-class must face in actuality; we can fight out on paper some of the real battles that are coming and so be a little better prepared for them. If we can visualize them concretely, in detail, the terrible costs of progress may be a little reduced."[16] This call is clearly a rebuke to formulaic thinking and writing on the left, a call to use novels as tools of exploration, not simply representations of already ordained strategies.

In criticizing his accomplishment in *The Land of Plenty*, Cantwell suggests how this process of "visualizing" works, and reveals the extent to which he attempted to work from concrete conditions while also theorizing and strategizing. Some of the problems raised in *The Land of Plenty*, Cantwell argues, deserved greater attention than they had received, not only from critics but from organizers as well:

> In one section of *Land of Plenty*, for instance, the workers take possession of the factory.... It seemed to me that this seizure of the factory devel-

oped naturally out of the situation that had been built up to that point. But when I came to write the actual details of the seizure I ran into some new problems I had not thought of before—I tried to imagine what would actually happen, in the sort of community I had pictured, when the workers entered the factory, what new factors entered a strike situation, what advantages were gained, what new hazards were encountered. It seemed to me that the problem was important, one that the working-class of this country must some day face. When I came to write this . . . I was stopped; I couldn't imagine clearly what would happen, and the novel suffers as a result. But I wanted at least to state the problem, in the hope that it might be discussed, critically, that the imaginations of others might be directed to envisioning it more clearly.[17]

Cantwell's position seems to be that the great virtue of "imaginative" literature is precisely its ability to concretely "imagine" what theoretical abstraction outlines and generally predicts. Cantwell is, in effect, critiquing the imaginative failure of the Communist literary movement to envision in detail the stages leading up to the revolution they too readily prophesied, and, implicitly, criticizing tendencies among Stalinist critics to see literature as doctrinal application rather than exploration.

What Cantwell was up against in making this plea is suggested by Granville Hicks's review of *The Land of Plenty* in the *New Masses*.[18] Hicks gave the novel high praise, but he was also quite predictably troubled by the ending, and for reasons quite different from Cantwell's: "In the second part of the book, especially at the very end, Cantwell relies too much on obliqueness, and the heroism of the embattled workers is a little obscured. As a result *The Land of Plenty* fails to sweep the reader along . . . to high resolve and a sense of ultimate triumph."[19] While Cantwell may have shared Hicks's desire to see his "propaganda" piece end on a note of triumph, his honest appraisal of the conditions he described and his sense of the logic of his novel led him to write an ending that, at least on the quotidian level, left the course of the workers' struggle in doubt. If *The Land of Plenty* as "propaganda" merely tried to illustrate Party positions, then Hicks would have a point. But Cantwell, while openly embracing the term "propaganda" (a move Hicks claims not to understand and which he claims Cantwell probably does not understand either[20]), is registering a tension between a simplistic revolutionism that called for pure affirmation and a radical realism, which called for a more exploratory and critical approach.

It is clear from his letters and criticism that Cantwell was directing his "propaganda" at both the liberal middle class and the workers themselves. How well he succeeded in this task, and a general sense of the critical climate in which proletarian novelists presented their work, may be gleaned by examining critical reaction to *The Land of Plenty*.

On one point virtually all reviews of Cantwell's novel agreed—it was a superb portrait of factory life. Following a line developed in his critical essays, Cantwell had made the "particular conditions and dangers" of an industry, in this case the lumber industry, the "central matter" of his fiction, and he had successfully captured the "unique sensations and experiences directly connected" with that work place.[21]

John Dos Passos, writing in the *New Republic*, claimed that "*The Land of Plenty* really molds your perceptions and leaves them different from what they were when you began; when you have read it you have understood . . . the noise and sweat and grease of the big plant on the mud flats, the feel of the dirty overalls and the tremor of the panels going under the saws."[22] Jack Conroy, himself an experienced mill worker, wrote in *Partisan Review* that Cantwell's novel had captured the rhythm and feel of mill life better than anything he had ever read[23] (and thirty-five years later Conroy felt this still to be the case).[24] Similarly, Louis Kronenberger commented in the *Nation*, "Mr. Cantwell's real contribution here to our better understanding of industrial problems today, and to our being better qualified for taking sides concerning them, lies in his exact yet capacious picture of a factory."[25]

Only on this point of fidelity to shop-floor life was there much of a consensus among *The Land of Plenty*'s reviewers, however. Several reviewers implied that Cantwell's politics had distorted the telling of his story, and Harold Strauss has evoked Cantwell's letter by making his charges quite explicit. His *New York Times Book Review* claimed, "Two years after its publication, a certain vociferous minority bloc among our critics discovered proletarian tendencies in *Laugh and Lie Down*, and subsequently pushed upon Cantwell, directly and indirectly, the necessity of writing a truly proletarian novel." In Strauss's opinion, "Cantwell's service to the Marxists and their essentially non-literary purpose" was warping his considerable talent, and he ended his review by calling for Cantwell to "strike out for himself."[26]

Cantwell's concern for and relation to his liberal readers is clarified in the letter he wrote to the editors of the *Times Book Review* in response to Strauss. He writes,

> I wrote *The Land of Plenty* because I wanted to express as fully as I could, in as concentrated a form as I could work out, something of the oppression under which the working class of this country lives—an oppression that has become so candid and cruel that no human person can free his mind or his imagination of it. I wanted also to give voice to the utter fatuity and depravity which seem to me the distinguishing characteristics of our ruling class. This was my intention; I cannot pride myself that I expressed either the misery of the majority of the working class or the cruelty and blindness of our ruling class; but that was my purpose.[27]

Eschewing such loaded terms as "propaganda," Cantwell's tone here is more circumscribed than in his letter to the *New Masses,* but the message can hardly be said to be ambiguous, and it makes clear that he did not see *Times* readers as beyond the reach of his words.

Cantwell's angry response to Strauss also declared that he was an independent writer and thinker, who, if he was influenced by any critics while writing his novel, had at least selected the influences to which he exposed himself. Moreover, he wrote, "My personal view is that the people who dominate our society have wrecked it so thoroughly that those who will not see it, novelists, critics, and others, can only maintain their denial by rejecting the most elementary promptings of their observation and intelligence."[28]

Strauss's attack had been directed primarily against Cantwell's handling of characterization in *The Land of Plenty*, and about this several other critics of various political hues also voiced objections. Like Strauss, Geoffrey Stone of *Commonweal* felt that a certain flatness in Cantwell's characters was the result of his attempt to write a "collective" novel in which individuals were effaced.[29] For both Strauss and Stone the failure of characterization in Cantwell's novel was the result of his ideological orientation. But John Dos Passos, from an ideologically sympathetic position, made the same objection, noting that only a certain lack of clarity and lack of development of characters kept *The Land of Plenty* from being a "great novel."[30] Do these complaints confirm Foley's claim that "bourgeois," or, less tendentiously, "humanistic," literary criteria formed a real barrier to the development of the proletarian alternative, even among pro-Communist critics?[31] Or do they merely mean that for Cantwell's propaganda to succeed it needed "effective" characterization? The answer lies in a nuanced space between the need to use existing literary norms and efforts to extend those norms. And that issue implicates form in a complicated, context-specific political dance, since not only proletarian but also many avant-garde and postmodern forms seek to undermine norms of characterization.

Another related type of objection to Cantwell's characterization was put most strongly by Kronenberger. He detected a Manichean division of characters in *The Land of Plenty* that he thought fallacious: "Mr. Cantwell's workers, as a group, have punch, guts, fight in them; his executives and bourgeois . . . are weak and watery and inept. At the very least this defies the law of averages; but more than that, it robs the book of a sense of violent clash. Even a dying capitalism can pay for better soldiers than Carl and MacMahon and Morely; taken as a group they disfigure an otherwise provocative and trustworthy book."[32]

Other critics echoed this complaint about the black-and-white nature of Cantwell's portraiture, and in a letter written to Farrell soon after these reviews appeared, Cantwell addressed the issue:

> Several people have accused me of having credited the ruling classes with too little, but when I pressed them for their own experiences they have invariably been reminded of individuals no more astute than Carl and MacMahon. I don't know whether the picture is true in a broad sense. I only know that my own experience has been that extremely stupid individuals seem to be selected for the task of overseeing labor. Brutalized, insensitive—they are perhaps better descriptions. Others tell me the same has been true of factories in which they have worked. Even you. Even H. S. Canby [conservative editor of *Saturday Review* in the 1930s]. I assume there must be something in it.[33]

What is perhaps most interesting here is that rather than argue the relative intelligence of capitalists and their henchmen vis-á-vis workers in the abstract, or the irrelevance of such a question given the larger dialectic of history, Cantwell reverts back to his own particular experience. This approach is no doubt in part in deference to Farrell's own empiricism, but it also indicates just how difficult it was for Cantwell to maintain his more-than-empirical position in the literary climate of the decade. This play between the particularity of personal experience and the abstractions of a revolutionary theory form much of the drama of Cantwell's literary radicalism, and that of his colleagues.

The overall value of *The Land of Plenty* as propaganda among the middle-class reading public is, of course, very difficult to assess. But an anonymous review in *Time* magazine suggests that it was perhaps as successful as such an effort had hope of being. The *Time* reviewer wrote,

> Many a "proletarian novel" is rightly thrown out of the literary court as mere advertising for the Communist cause; but the literary sergeants-at-arms will think twice before they begin hustling Robert Cantwell's *Land of Plenty*. Though die-hard right wingers will call it propaganda, most readers will find it troubling, critics of all stripes will pronounce it a first rate novel. As social criticism, *The Land of Plenty* will arouse plenty of disagreement, but as a tragically true story of human beings it will hit home to most men of good will.[34]

The reviewer has hit upon all of the most salient points regarding the professional reception of Cantwell's novel. Critics of all stripes did indeed praise *The Land of Plenty*. Even the hostile Strauss admitted that Cantwell had "done and done well what he set out to do."[35] The more politically sympathetic Clifton Fadiman of the *New Yorker* called it "the finest novel of the year" and suggested that it be nominated for the Pulitzer Prize.[36] And Granville Hicks, despite the reservations mentioned above, called Cantwell's novel "the finest piece of imaginative writing the revolutionary movement in America has produced."[37]

By submerging his propaganda in the symbolic layer of his story, and by making it an "organic" part of the work as literature, Cantwell had succeeded with middle-class critics in a way that his more didactic proletarian comrades generally did not.[38] But the *Time* reviewer also inadvertently suggests the limitations imposed by Cantwell's subject. Not only could readers, like Kronenberger, dismiss the bourgeois characters as straw men, but they could simply peel off the allegorical layer of social criticism and view *The Land of Plenty* as a "tragically true" story but one that was not representative of thirties America generally, or one that was a necessary part of human (that is, capitalist) progress. Acknowledging Cantwell's success in his portrait of factory life meant a certain validation of the proletarian literary project by non-Communist critics, but isolating that empirical dimension of the text was also used as a strategy for containing the more radical messages.

What this suggests is that radical writers were in a double bind vis-á-vis more conservative critics: if they made their political messages overt, they were dismissed as dogmatic; if they made them subtle, they were ignored or purposefully misappropriated. As part of his letter complaining about Farrell's limited empiricism, Cantwell writes that he used a symbolic dimension in *Land of Plenty* because "if you don't provide such a frame [of clear meaning] the reader will. Or the critics." And rather than leave his meaning up to some "New York intellectual" who might get it wrong, he preferred to "make my own meaning unmistakable."[39] Too clear for the *New York Times*, not quite clear enough for the *New Masses*, critical reaction to Cantwell's proletarian novel clearly suggests that *both* sides of the "literary class war" sought in their own way to formulate the possibilities and limits of writers. And Cantwell's critical reaction to both Hicks and Strauss indicates that neither side wholly succeeded. But the fact that work such as Cantwell's received considerable praise from such diverse critics also suggests that it was strategically poised at a critical juncture. By definition, social contradictions made it impossible for radical writing to succeed with more conservative critics, but the fact that Cantwell's well-crafted work made them uncomfortable and desirous of converting him also suggests that they recognized that his nonhortatory propaganda was potentially an unusually effective "weapon." This is further confirmed by the fact that both the *New Masses* critics and the editors of the then new *Partisan Review* identified Cantwell's novel as among the top handful in the movement.[40]

Working-class reaction to *The Land of Plenty* confirms this image from a different angle of vision. Cantwell's most interesting, and in many ways his most astute, critic was a worker at Harbor Plywood by the name of Dietz. Dietz wrote a letter to Cantwell's friend Calvin Fixx in which he offered a critique of *The Land of Plenty* that he hoped Fixx would pass on to Cantwell. This unique document seems worth quoting at length. Fixx transcribes the Dietz letter as follows:

I am working for the Harbor Plywood Corp. Inasmuch as this plant is the setting for Bob's novel, and has been read quite extensively by my fellow-workers, I find it damned interesting. Also, I am on the night shift under a boss named Carl Lebold; whether or not this is the Carl of Bob's book is irrelevant since his temperament is identical. Two weeks before I picked up Bob's book, the lights went out—is there any wonder that I find his work engrossing? . . . I believe that if I reported to him the reactions of these very characters he has written about, upon seeing themselves in his book, it would be helping him to do a better work when he again takes up the "education of a worker." . . . My chief criticism of the book is not about it, but only that I regret the fact that it was a slice of the Coolidge era. How much richer in significance it would have been were he to write of the Harbor Plywood of this time. Mind now, that I mean this in a sense of revolutionary significance, and not of either a Marxian interpretation, of which the scene is well illumed, or from a standpoint of proletarian literature, of which its significance on the American scene is unquestionable; I mean this only in the narrow sense: as propaganda. How many of his readers, on the job, have told me they felt depressed, discouraged, etc. at the outcome of the strike. You must admit that in leaving his chief character on the bank of the river in a "badly beaten" frame of mind, the effect on a proletarian would be what I have said it was. And somehow, because the book so truly reflects the conditions on the job, he has won their confidence. Only a short time before this we won a 5-cent raise through sheer solidarity, a hundred and fifty men from one department in all shifts acting as one. His book is appreciated by the men on the job, and if this were a Soviet America, and the men that have read it at the plant could have the say, Bob would get more than the Pulitzer Prize. If for no other reason than that he has made the blustering Carl ridiculous in their eyes; I mean he has somehow confirmed the ultimate ridiculousness of all bosses to them. The dialogue between Carl and MacMahon in the swamp, and their idiocy in falling thru [sic] the conveyor and wandering about under the mill, will always remain, for us that work here, a priceless gem of humor. And best of all, we have the feeling that all the work[ers], now, can see them as we do! Another novel like this, but up-to-date, and Bob will qualify as an American Gorki—if only he will go on. Oh yes, tell Bob that I'm running a clipper. And that all the bosses have got hold of his book. They think he has a remarkable memory of the old plant.[41]

Dietz's rather carefully worded critique suggests that he may well have been aware of and trying to mediate the exchange of views between Cantwell and Hicks in the *New Masses*. His comment on worker reaction to the ending seems to parallel Hicks's response, suggesting that on this point at least the "leftist" position may have had some value. But, unlike Hicks, Dietz realized that the novel's ending is more or less compelled by the labor conditions of the times in which it is set. Cantwell's rationale for setting *The Land of Plenty* in the twenties rather than the thirties was undoubtedly that he had direct experience only of the earlier time, but Dietz's point is well taken. Despite his desire to imagine the future, Cantwell seems to have limited himself to that which he had experienced intimately or what he knew of the past. (A similar reluctance fueled his next major contribution to proletarian literature, the short story "Hills around Centralia".[42]) Cantwell's only direct link to the thirties in *The Land of Plenty* is a paragraph quoted verbatim from the 1931 "Census of Manufactures" that precedes the opening of the novel.[43] The excerpted paragraph notes a 65.2 percent drop in lumber production from 1929, and is presumably meant to suggest that the darkness that will set the workers free is swiftly approaching. But such obliquity also suggests that Cantwell is far from certain as to how or when this liberation will be accomplished. Thus his retreat to the earlier era suggests some conscious or unconscious tension with the apocalyptic tone found in some of his other writing. Where Communist Party USA (CPUSA) critics sometimes projected a static, reified image of revolution that made it difficult to explore the present, Cantwell's strictures on himself actually limited his imagination from another direction through a lapse back into a narrow empiricism he had theoretically challenged in his criticism and correspondence. Each, we might say, was ironically unable to think and write dialectically.

Perhaps the most interesting aspect of Dietz's letter is the reaction of his fellow workers to the comic portrayal of the factory bosses. This reaction stands in direct contradiction to the reaction of most bourgeois reviewers and suggests significant class divisions in Cantwell's audience(s). The generally favorable reaction on the part of Harbor workers indicates that, if skillfully executed, proletarian literature could have propaganda value among a working-class constituency. This fact is further confirmed by the testimony of Jack Conroy, who also had occasion in the thirties to test the reactions of workers who read *The Land of Plenty* (workers without the potentially distorting personal interest of Harbor Plywood employees). Conroy found that Cantwell's novel was received with "appreciative interest" by the factory workers of a "serious bent" who read it upon his suggestion. Conroy attributed this popularity to the fact that, unlike many proletarian novelists, Cantwell imbued his worker characters with a sense of pride and dignity in their work.[44]

Thus *The Land of Plenty* had propaganda value among the only workers whose reactions are recorded, but how widespread was the influence of Cantwell's novel? *The Land of Plenty* was the best selling of all proletarian novels but sold only three thousand copies (not an impressive figure, even given the poor book market in Depression America).[45] But as Cantwell himself pointed out, workers were more likely to borrow books from libraries than to purchase them,[46] and the only individual who examined borrowers of proletarian novels from the nation's libraries suggests that the worker audience for such fiction may have been significantly larger than sales figures indicate.[47]

Whatever the exact size of its readership, and the differences of opinion noted above notwithstanding, *The Land of Plenty* does seem to have been rather effective as literature and/or propaganda among those who did read it. Cantwell had bestowed added meaning and dignity to his own past experience as a worker while simultaneously dramatizing his current political and literary convictions. His novel successfully conveyed a sense of the dignity of the working class and the indignities they must endure. Both his readers among the New York intelligentsia, and his audience of factory laborers, thought he had made an eloquent case for a workers' literature. As such, it remains an enduring contribution to this still underdeveloped field of American literary representation. Beyond this, the ultimate effectiveness of *The Land of Plenty* in disseminating the propaganda message intended by its author must be judged in large part in relation to the fate of the radical movement in America in the years following its publication.

AN ABERDEEN EXCURSUS: A TOWN AND ITS LABOR NOVELS

The Land of Plenty must also be understood in relation to the region and the small town from which it emerged. As regional manifestations of radical literary movements have slowly been brought to light, the Pacific Northwest has remained largely unexplored. The region has a rich, complicated history of radicalism, particularly labor radicalism, and this history is reflected not only in and upon by Cantwell but in Northwest literatures of various types. Because of its relative isolation from such major centers of left and left-literary activity as New York and Chicago, the Northwest developed its own strand of literary radicalism, confined primarily to labor newspapers and radical magazines. Both the Populist Party and Socialist Party had strongholds in the region. A significant bloc of Northwest voters supported the Democratic/Populist ticket in 1896, and voted for Eugene Debs and the Socialist Party in 1912.[48] After World War I, the Communist Party had a very active presence in the state's labor movement. By 1936, the communist movement in the state was such that the US postmaster joked, "There are forty-seven states and the Soviet of Washington."[49] But the most important radical influence, as is clear in the case of Cantwell, was no doubt the Industrial Workers of the World (IWW), who were particularly active regionally in the lumber industry and in migrant agriculture up through World War 1. And they continued to influence the region's culture long after their heyday.[50]

The Wobblies are known for their radical individualism even amid political collectivism, and their own rich culture of song, poetry, and the graphic arts must be seen as an element of the region's left cultural legacy.[51] While perhaps best known for their parodic anticapitalist singing as exemplified in the "Little Red Song" book and the career of the infamous Joe Hill, there was a great deal of other cultural production of all kinds around the IWW, and in other unions as well. Poet, journalist, and activist Anna Louise Strong, for example, wrote poetry about the great general strike in Seattle of 1919, and virtually all of the union and left magazines of the period in the region had literary sections with poetry, short stories, and occasionally even excerpts from novels in progress. John Reed, famous as the author of the most widely read account of the Russian Revolution, *Ten Days That Shook the World*, was born in Portland and brought Northwest-acquired sympathy for the Wobblies with him to the East, where he became involved in IWW-led textile worker strikes in Lawrence, Massachusetts (1912), and Paterson, New Jersey (1913). During the latter, Reed spearheaded one of the most spectacular radical cultural events of the twentieth century, the Paterson Strike Pageant. Held in Madison Square Garden, the event included over 1,000 workers reenacting scenes from their strike. With sets designed by artist John Sloan, and Reed directing, the spectacular "play" is unique in US cultural history.[52]

Strong and Reed became Communist internationalists, and are among the handful of Americans granted a resting place in the Kremlin (though Reed never lost his Wobbly spirit, and in the wake of the Russian Revolution unsuccessfully lobbied Lenin to have the IWW designated the Communist labor front in the United States). Cantwell, though he spent most of his fiction-writing years away from the region, kept his imagination mostly closer to home, and focused the vast majority of his writing on the Northwest. Studying Cantwell closely, it became increasingly clear that his literary leftism never lost its local roots. And though no fully developed left literary coterie of the type led by Jack Conroy in the Midwest developed in the Northwest, one of Cantwell's home towns turns out to have been unusually productive of radical writing. Surprisingly that place was not one of the state's major cities—Seattle or Tacoma or Spokane—but the small coastal lumber town of Aberdeen, Washington.

No fewer than three "proletarian" novelists emerged from this town of 20,000 in the 1930s. In addition to Cantwell, the two other Aberdeen literary left novelists were Louis Colman, author of *Lumber* (1931), and Clara Weatherwax, author of *Marching! Marching!* (1934). While neither novel achieves the richness of Cantwell's work, a brief excursus into *Lumber* (1931) and *Marching! Marching!* (1935) provides a wider canvas for understanding Cantwell and the roots of literary radicalism in the Northwest.

A passage I cited in the previous chapter is worth revisiting in this new context. Writing in 1936, looking back on the scene of his adolescence, with a perspective altered no doubt by his deeper immersion in Marxist thought in New York, Cantwell described Aberdeen in terms that offer as good an explanation for its flourishing literary left as any:

> There are twenty-four big mills around the Harbor, capable of producing about a billion feet of timber a year; there is a large Finnish population there, a big Filipino colony, a considerable number of half-breeds from the Chehalis, Quinalt and Taholah tribes, [and] a large proportion of Southerners who drifted to the Northwest.... It is almost entirely a working-class community. The major stores are chain stores, and most of the mill officials are hired representatives of Eastern capitalists; the absorbent layer of shopkeepers, small owners and professional people that in other places

acts as a cushion to break the clash of class antagonisms—or prevents their being recognized for what they are—is numerically and culturally unimportant. Consequently, class lines are firmly drawn, and the classes can hardly be said to be in that "state of flux, with a persistent interchange of elements" which Marx once observed to be a condition of American society in general.[53]

In the small world of Gray's Harbor, the area around Aberdeen, Cantwell knew both Louis Colman and Clara Weatherwax. Indeed, how could he have not known of Clara, since his high school was named after her grandfather, among the founders of the town. Clara also worked with Robert on their high school newspaper. Of the three, Colman was most clearly situated in the working class, while Weatherwax, like Cantwell, seems to have grown up perilously teetering between the middle class and working class.

LUMBER

Like Cantwell, Louis Colman worked in a plywood mill after high school, in his case as an off-bearer at Wilson Brother's in Aberdeen. Colman's radicalization seems to have preceded Cantwell's. He was active in the local labor movement in the twenties, and it was in fact during a strike at his mill that he wrote his one and only novel, *Lumber* (1931). As reviewers noted, *Lumber* was the first novel to tackle the twentieth-century timber industry. Reviewers praised it for this innovative content (the *New York Times* called it "painstakingly accurate"), but inevitably its ideological directness was also criticized.[54] During Cantwell's years as a mill worker, he maintained contact with Colman, who in 1929 sent him a manuscript that must have been a draft of *Lumber*. Not much else is known about their relationship, but the fact that Colman married one of Cantwell's ex-girlfriends attests to their close connection (and perhaps a falling out?). It is also clear that Colman shared his knowledge of the IWW and labor struggles in the region with Cantwell. When Colman and Cantwell were about to embark upon a trip together, for example, recall that his brother Jim wrote, "Louis will probably ply you with the latest dope on the labor situation in the Northwest, something I . . . do not envy you. Lurid tales of hanging IWWs have always failed to arouse any yearning for vengeance in my dilettante [sic] heart."[55] His brother's tone suggests a dismissiveness partly growing out of a fear that Colman might make a somewhat more favorable impression on Robert, as the latter's subsequent writing would seem to indicate. Little is known of Colman's later career. The next and last time his name appears as a writer is in *Night Riders in Gallup*,[56] a pamphlet published by the International Labor Defense organization, famous for their efforts on the Scottsboro Boys case. Colman's details racist antilabor attacks in New Mexico during a major coal mining strike begun in 1933 that eventuated in murder charges against some strikers and a trial in 1935. But Colman never published another work of fiction, despite the modest success of *Lumber*.

Lumber starts out as what critic Barbara Foley has called the "proletarian bildungsroman"; it tells the story of a young boy, Jimmy Logan, whose father has been killed in a logging accident. At sixteen, Jimmy becomes a vagabond, wandering the Northwest by freight car and eventually settling in Aberdeen, where he marries and, like his father, enters the lumber industry. His travels allow the reader to get a sense of the dangers and injustices facing workers in various aspects of the timber industry, and we see Jimmy gradually radicalized by his experiences, in particular by the tutoring he gets from some old-hand Wobblies. The labor unrest of the era is vividly portrayed, with strikes and boom-and-bust economic cycles a constant feature of the terrain. Class strife depicted in the novel includes Jimmy nearly losing his life when a mob of locals attacks IWWers in an echo of the Centralia massacre. Poverty stresses his marriage to a local girl, and their two sons die of a spinal meningitis outbreak during which the family cannot afford proper medical care. It is hardly a tale of labor triumph (indeed, none of the Aberdeen novels ends in unambiguous triumph), but it does provide a redolent account of the physical dangers and political treachery surrounding the early lumber industry and was surely aimed to instill anger at capitalist exploitation.

MARCHING! MARCHING!

Clara Weatherwax was born in Aberdeen in 1905 to the town's most prominent family. Her father's death when Clara was twelve, however, sent the family on an economic downswing, and she and her four siblings started working at an early age. During her high school years, the precocious Weatherwax formed a literary salon that discussed modernist art, literature, and music. Cantwell, three years her junior, was invited to the salon a few times but largely stayed away, most likely due to shyness and insecurity (he was sixteen when it began). She eventually saved enough money to make it through two years at Stanford University, but ran out of funds before completing. In the Bay Area she met and married Gerald Strang, an avant-garde twelve-tone composer who later became an arranger for Arnold Schoenberg, and later still a professor of music at Long Beach State.

Weatherwax, along with her husband and brother, seems to have reconstituted her salon in the 1930s while living in the hills above Berkeley. There her guests included Frida Kahlo and Diego Rivera, friends of her brother John ("Jack") Weatherwax, a cultural figure close to the Communist Party USA, who wrote pamphlets on African and African American history. Jack Weatherwax was also close to Northwest Communist icon Anna Louise Strong, with whom he cowrote the radical anthem "The Trumpets of Freedom." Salon members also included avant-garde classical composer Henry Cowell, likely the basis, along with Strang, for the modernist composer Steve in *Marching! Marching!* and Carlos Bulosan, the radical Filipino novelist who apparently used Clara Weatherwax as a model for the proletarian novelist Laura Clarendorn in his classic *America Is in the Heart.*[57]

While living in Berkeley, Clara wrote poetry and short stories (never published), while her husband had several of his compositions performed and published. In June of 1934 Weatherwax read of a literary contest for the "best novel on an American proletarian theme" sponsored by the Communist Party's literary magazine, *New Masses*. She spent the next year working on the novel that became *Marching! Marching!*, submitting it to the contest in late summer 1935. To her great surprise, she won the $750 top prize, and the book was published that fall by radical publishing house John Day Company. Soon after publication Weatherwax began to suffer from a severe case of rheumatoid arthritis that made work very difficult, though she continued to work on a second novel, as well as on poetry and some stories. Eventually the disease rendered her unable to walk, and by 1952 she was also legally blind. She died in 1958 in Los Angeles, where she and Strang had moved with the money from the *New Masses* prize, having published no further work.

Weatherwax's biography on the jacket of *Marching! Marching!* is an unintentionally self-parodic example of the CPUSA's line of the time that "Communism Is Twentieth-Century Americanism":

> Clara Weatherwax stems from pre-Mayflower New England stock, which has pioneered across the American continent.... One of her outstanding forebears was Roger Williams. Fourteen of her direct ancestors fought in the first American revolution. Others fought in the War of 1812 and the Civil War, and many of her family were in the World War.
>
> Her grandfather was an early settler and mill owner in Aberdeen, Washington.
>
> Miss Weatherwax was born and schooled in Aberdeen, with the sound of sawmills in her ears. Her earliest days were spent in a papoose basket her mother got from the Indians of the Quinault Indian Reservation....
>
> Since high-school days Miss Weatherwax has had a variety of jobs—both white collar and proletarian, mostly for fifty dollars a month or less, and the kind of work mentioned or described in the book she knows through experience or close contact. She has participated in the labor movement on the Coast, and is now living with her husband in California, where she writes and he composes.[58]

One could speculate that the chance to write this biography may have played a role in the selection of Weatherwax's novel for the *New Masses* prize.[59] A local historian in Aberdeen notes that the Weatherwax family was known to exaggerate its importance and pad its lineage. And by the 1920s, most branches of the family tree, including Clara's, had fallen from the "sawdust aristocracy" into the working class.

In the midthirties the Communist Party literary corps was seeking to maintain a hard line on revolutionism, while also defending itself against charges that its limited socialist realist literary ideals were stifling creativity. So Weatherwax was quite probably equally attractive to the Party because of her biography as well as her attempt in *Marching! Marching!* to unite modernist experimentalism and CPUSA ideology. The novel is full of experimental elements drawn from a host of modernist and avant-garde writers, a style existing in sometimes harmonious, sometimes cacophonous relation to its apparent attempt to reflect then dominant strands of ideology within the Communist Party political and cultural hierarchy.

Marching! Marching! offers a broad, if sometimes superficial, view of the complex labor situation in the Northwest in the 1930s, and also draws upon the 1934–35 general strike in San Francisco that Weatherwax, like Cantwell, witnessed firsthand. The book represents sympathetically the complicating ethnic diversity of the workers—Finns, Poles, Filipinos (from the canning industry), American Indians, Irish, Germans, and more.

The novel also seeks to deal realistically with the ideological diversity in the labor movement. The forces of labor conservatism, especially the American Federation of Labor are represented and summarily dismissed as reactionary. One key element of ideological struggle in the novel reflecting Northwest history lies in the war of rhetoric between an old Wobbly worker and the two Communist Party labor organizers in the novel. Their exchanges over strategy, in which the labor organizers clearly prevail, in some ways accurately represents the triumph of the Communist Party over earlier US radical labor groups in the wake of the Russian Revolution of 1917, and symbolizes the triumph of nationalism over regionalism in the sense that the Western roots of groups such as the IWW are subsumed under ideas largely conceived in the East (New York) and far East (Moscow). But it is not as simple as that in the novel. While the Party agitators get the better of the argument, they ultimately are not at the head of the force of working men and women that confront the capitalist state (in the form of the National Guard) at the close of the novel. Instead, there is a strong sense of the old wobbly spirit that workers organize best when they organize themselves; "party discipline" at the end of the novel is perhaps less prevalent than Communist Party leaders might have liked to see, with more than a hint of spontaneous Western collectivism-in-individualism peeking through. The novel ends on a quasi-apocalyptic note, with strikers facing that battery of armed, bayonet-pointing members of the National Guard; it hardly portends a fair fight, let alone victory for the proletariat, but it is surely emblematic of a working class ready to fight for justice, whatever the cost.

While subsequently often vilified as a "typical" example of the failed nature of the proletarian novel, in its era *Marching! Marching!* received some very positive reviews, even from mainstream sources such as the *Saturday Review of Literature,* whose editor, Henry Seidel Canby, praised the novel as "not a tract" but a "humanitarian" representation of "a workers' world seething about a revolutionary idea." Many left critics, including Cantwell, wished it had been more successful in form and less blatant in ideology. But few were as virulent as a reviewer associated with a rival Trotskyist branch of thirties Marxism who wrote that *Marching! Marching!*

> is a travesty on literature and a libel against the working class. Its style is the dregs of the Joyce tradition, drained off through the worst of Wolfe

and Faulkner, combined with school-essay "straightforward" writing. Its characters are wooden monstrosities, conceived with a kind of horrible masochistic delight in repulsive details and an infantile pleasure in trivial nobilities. The book is liberally interlarded with long speeches on war, strikes, trade unions, Fascism, apparently lifted from back copies of the *Daily Worker*.[60]

While not a wholly inaccurate description, this review is more ideologically reductive than the text it criticizes, and hardly does justice to the complexity of the novel, which, despite serious flaws, can be read as far more than a CPUSA tract.[61]

Clearly, as with most proletarian novels published in the political maelstrom of the decade's literary class warfare, the reviews of *Marching! Marching!* were quite mixed. But any careful reading of the novel makes clear that it cannot easily be pigeonholed as nothing but CPUSA tract. While deeply flawed in traditional literary terms, the novel is a complex document riddled with the literary and cultural contradictions of its era.

As noted, critic Barbara Foley, in her exhaustive study of the proletarian novel, identifies three main subgenres of the radical novel—the social novel, the proletarian bildungsroman, and the collective novel—and each is represented by one of the Aberdeen novels. Foley categorizes *Land of Plenty* as a "social novel," *Lumber* as "a proletarian *bildungsroman*," and *Marching! Marching!* as a "collective novel."[62]

Two additional minor Aberdeen labor novels appeared in the 1940s. *Disillusion*, by Ben Cochrane and William Dean Coldiron,[63] takes place, like *Land of Plenty*, during a strike at a Gray's Harbor plywood factory. While socialist in sympathy, it is written from the point of view of a strikebreaker. And *Viewless Winds*, by Murray Morgan,[64] tells the story of the murder of a labor leader's wife, and is based on the death in 1940 of Laura Law. Neither novel offers much in the way of literary or even historical interest, nor were they widely read (Malcolm Cowley said of *Viewless Winds*, "That book wasn't published, it was printed"), but they stand as further evidence that the literature of labor did not end with the thirties. Taken in concert, the Aberdeen labor novels make clear that this corner of western Washington contributed significantly to the wide swath made by the literary laboring of American culture in the mid-twentieth century.

5 THE REVOLUTIONIST MEETS THE CAPITALIST

Cantwell as Biographer and Nonfiction Novelist

Cantwell remarked in a letter to Ernest Hemingway that he had finished *The Land of Plenty* at "forced draft" in order that he might begin work on a new, very different project: the biography of millionaire department store magnate Edward A. Filene.[1] The proposed biography, commissioned by Filene himself and supervised by muckraking journalist Lincoln Steffens, occupied Cantwell from late 1933 until early 1935. The work was never published, but extant fragments of Cantwell's manuscript describe a fascinating encounter between the aging progressive capitalist and his extremely hostile biographer, an encounter that the latter transformed into a symbolic struggle between reformism and revolution.[2]

Late in 1933, Filene, who had made his fortune by expanding the idea of the "bargain basement" into a multimillion-dollar merchandising operation in the city of Boston, felt that it was time to have the story of his long and checkered career recorded for posterity. As the apostle of enlightened self-interest among American capitalists, he had championed a number of unpopular progressive causes aimed at bettering the lot of the masses, upon whose purchasing power he felt the continued success of capitalism depended. His story was thus not one only of successes but of failures as well, and, putatively detesting the familiar testimonials of other millionaires, he hired an old friend but stern critic, Lincoln Steffens, to oversee the writing of his biography.[3]

Steffens, in his late sixties and in poor health, set about in November of 1933 to find a younger writer to bear the major burden in composing the projected work. He first sought the services of Whittaker Chambers, whose short stories in the *New Masses* he had admired for being both "proletarian and literary."[4] But Chambers declined his offer, and Steffens turned next to Cantwell, apparently on Chambers's recommendation. Cantwell struggled with the decision. Some of his literary colleagues, including John Dos Passos and Meyer Schapiro, advised him to do it. Others, especially Cowley, were set against it; in fact, Cowley later came to believe that it ruined Cantwell as a writer by distracting him from fiction in his prime. Pressed by his ever-practical wife Betsy, lured by the offer of a substantially higher salary, and with the assurance that Filene would not interfere in the writing of his biography, Cantwell accepted, quit his job at the *New Republic*, and made plans to move his family into an apartment next door to Filene's Boston mansion.[5]

Steffens's reasons for selecting Cantwell are not known, but given that Chambers had been his first choice, it is clear that the old muckraker's choice of a radical to write the millionaire's life story was an intentionally provocative one likely to lead to something less than harmonious cooperation. In their initial discussion, Steffens had told Cantwell that Filene's career could illustrate an important point: "... in itself [it] proved that American business, that capitalism, could not be reformed or reform itself."[6] Such was surely not the lesson intended by Filene, who remained a dedicated Progressive, and thus from its inception the proposed biography was a battleground of conflicting interests and conceptions.

When offered the role of biographer, Cantwell's only knowledge of Filene was an exclamation by Lenin he remembered from a biography of the Bolshevik hero: "So, Mr. Filene!" Lenin had remarked, "You believe that all the workers of all the world are fools!"[7] Why should a man who could elicit such an outburst from Lenin, Cantwell mused, wish to hire Steffens and himself, neither of whom, the latter noted with understatement, were "known for a particularly uncritical attitude toward the methods and practices of capitalists," to write the story of his life? Cantwell made discreet inquiries among friends and acquaintances of the elderly merchant and could elicit little but negative responses to questions about Filene's character—"pretentious bore," "self-centered," and "untrustworthy" being typical. But each description seemed to add complexity and contradiction, and the "more Balzacian and cryptic Filene seemed," the more intrigued the novelist in Cantwell became.[8]

The manuscript of Cantwell's projected biography of Filene is actually two separate and quite different works. One is a rather straightforward work originally cast as a biography but later transformed into a ghostwritten autobiography through the substitution of "I" for "he" at appropriate points throughout. But by far the more interesting work is a two-hundred-and-fifty-page manuscript in which Cantwell interweaves the details of Filene's life with a description of the initial encounters between the capitalist and his "very Desperate Ambrose of a biographer."[9] (Cantwell refers to himself throughout in the third person as "the biographer" or "the author".) Early in the manuscript "the biographer" notes that his aim, like that of Steffens, is to use Filene's life to reveal the impossibility of reforming capitalism. But to this he adds a second reason more suited to his skills as a political novelist: to discover how a millionaire's mind worked, and particularly "how [capitalists] justified to themselves the exploitation on which their wealth was based."[10]

Like James Agee, with whom he later worked, Cantwell detested patronizing studies of the poor and dispossessed, "those smug and dehumanized inquiries into the social customs of delinquent women, or slum dwellers, or foreign language groups, or Kentucky miners." Noting that at the time of "this writing" a monthly magazine was publishing a series of articles by a Smith College graduate who had gone to live among the miners of Pennsylvania, Cantwell suggested that he would prefer that "a striking miner . . . go to live among the girls of Smith College, and report on their practices and beliefs." In lieu of that study, he hoped that his report on the practices of a millionaire might offer a similar antidote to such "presumptuous social studies."[11]

But Cantwell's study of the habits and beliefs of a capitalist almost ended before it had begun. In December of 1933, he met Filene for the first time (at the latter's home on Otis Place, a mansion formerly owned by Filene's lawyer and friend Louis Brandeis).[12] The first words the millionaire spoke to his would-be biographer informed him that Lincoln Steffens had recently suffered a stroke and that the project would probably be canceled. Upon hearing this, Cantwell grew secretly enraged that no one had bothered to inform him of this turn of events sooner. Had he been notified promptly, he would "not have quit his job, or gone into debt, or moved his family to Boston."[13]

When Filene began asking a series of naive and seemingly unrelated questions, Cantwell's outrage turned to suspicion and defensiveness. "His [the author's] distrust of capitalists in general, and of Filene in particular, was so great that he was convinced" that the millionaire's inquiries were some kind of "test."[14] As the conversation progressed, Cantwell came to view it as a subtle game, a kind of chess match in which the future of American capitalism seemed somehow at stake: "Again and again the author thought he saw Filene drift into a line of thought, a logical associative sequence of ideas, which if steadily followed would have led to the approach of some invisible contradiction, draw back, or change the subject."[15]

Cantwell felt as though he had descended into Wonderland as he listened to Filene ramble on almost incoherently "like a Joycean interior monologue," "his sentences such a jumble of short-hand rhetoric, so full of non-sequiturs" that at times "his biographer thought him mad."[16] Filene's first "false move" was to confirm, amid one of these rambling discourses, Cantwell's suspicion that the National Recovery Administration, the Massachusetts branch of which Filene headed, had been established "in part to head off and dissipate a nationwide wave of strikes and in order to make possible suspension of anti-trust laws without provoking labor and farmer and progressive hostility."[17]

Cantwell noticed almost immediately that the old merchant seemed to be at pains to create an air of "busy-ness" about himself, and it soon dawned on the biographer that "the myth of the American business man, the great executive and hard practical organizer . . . had so burrowed into [Filene's] consciousness" that he felt a need to prove his own worth through manic activity. He wore the businessman's image, Cantwell writes, "in much the same spirit that some minor poet might wear a black cloak or a Byronic melancholy." Cantwell thus concluded that "The proper training for success in business is not economics or accounting, but a course in dramatic arts; and the successful executive puts on the appearance of doing something in a haggard endeavor to conceal from himself as well as from others the social uselessness of his life."[18]

Cantwell appreciated the "acting" of the millionaire because he had already come to view Filene less as a living human being than as a character in a novel, his novel. After a second day with the old merchant, Cantwell was in a state of "imaginative excitement": "The author kept repeating to himself, with a kind of secret enthusiasm and delight, 'What a character!,' conscious of the fact that he had tried to imagine, for a work of fiction, a progressive capitalist and enlightened employer, [but] could not, could never, have thought of anyone who so completely fitted the part." Cantwell adds that "he would have preferred to study a bigger and more important millionaire than

Filene; ideally he would have chosen Dupont or Mellon or Rockefeller, for their conspiracies would have thrown more light on the system as a whole. But with Filene he felt he could clearly detect other significant values—particularly the psychological punishment suffered by a millionaire who permitted himself to remain conscious—from the point of view of human welfare—of the weaknesses of the capitalist system."[19]

During his third visit to the millionaire's mansion, on New Year's Day 1934, Cantwell plunged into the thirty bound volumes of Filene's public speeches that occupied a prominent place on the bookshelves in the study. Most of the speeches, Cantwell quickly discovered, "were dull, and all of them were familiar; and many were hollow and hypocritical with that strained baccalaureate optimism that can only be attained, in times of crisis, by the amputation of great areas of experience."[20] But as Steffens had remarked, "the man is a bore, but not his life."[21] Cantwell found in Filene's speeches a "startling" picture of counterrevolutionary activity on the part of Progressive Era capitalists. He was surprised and delighted "to find a capitalist theoretician in Boston in 1904 urging two young capitalists to inaugurate reforms for the purpose of aiding socialists 'and the masses they influence' to see the folly of their ways; and it was startling to find two budding millionaires [Filene and his brother] so conscious of their counter-revolutionary aims." "No revolutionist," Cantwell remarks, "could have asked for a clearer statement of capitalist principle."[22]

After reading one volume of Filene's speeches, Cantwell felt "that he had caught a glimpse of the broad horizons of Filene's thought, and before that terrible desert, marked with the decayed ruins of empty platitudes and thickets of vicious conspiracies he drew back in horror.... Averting his eyes he hurried on hoping to find, somewhere in the thirty volumes, greener vistas and less coldly-cunning counter-revolutionary planning."[23] He analyzed his "character's" thought and found it "hopelessly involved in that social democratic dilemma ... that inevitable perplexity of all reform.... How to discuss profit sharing with workers without 'leading to the idea' that all profits belong to the workers? How to strengthen the labor unions and yet be confident in maintaining control?" Cantwell discovered a "vast uneasiness, a sleepless preoccupation, a deep sense of the power of the masses" apparent, "however dimly," in Filene's speeches.[24]

On his fourth day in Boston, Cantwell paid a visit to Filene's store with its vast company archive. After poring over massive cross-referenced files, boxes and boxes of correspondence, clippings, memoranda, and other company-related documents, he felt confident that with a year of research he could complete his task. And not only would he become well informed on the psychology of capitalists, but by the time he was through he expected to have "seventy-five years of American history pretty clearly in mind."[25]

But upon returning to Filene's home that evening, Cantwell's plans were quickly and totally demolished:

> His character fired him, quietly, mysteriously, politely and finally and without explanation; and the writer, whose characters had never acted this way before, felt himself grow pale. Some of his characters had, in the past, acted queerly—in one novel . . . a leading character had a way of dropping out of the story entirely—but never before had one attempted to dispense with his service as an author.[26]

At first Cantwell was dazed and disbelieving. He had just read a speech in which Filene had spoken of the painful and difficult process of firing employees, and he thought the ease with which the old merchant had revoked his commission must indicate that it was all a dream. But when Filene's secretary confirmed that Cantwell had indeed been given three weeks' notice, his astonishment turned to rage and defiance:

> The writer could not just quit writing the life of E. A. Filene, no matter how much the old devil desired it. He had quit his job; he had gone up to his ears in debt; he had moved his household to Boston on Filene's insistence . . . ; and now he could neither get his job back, borrow any more money, get out of Boston or do anything except write the life of E. A. Filene. Besides both his wife and baby were ill, and he had no money.
>
> Slowly at first, but with gathering momentum and intensity, he began to develop a rich and luxurious hatred of this character whose moods were so unstable. . . . He began to tramp the streets of Boston, going mad . . . ; as he had no money, he did not have anything to eat for three days. . . . He attempted to draw on his salary, or borrow in advance on it and was humiliated. At this point all desire to write anything about capitalists left him. . . . He merely wanted—was determined to have—his revenge.

Day and night he plotted Filene's downfall, mad as a hatter, letting his fancy roam unhinged from all realities.... [But] even in his madness ... he could not escape a feeling that his understanding had somehow been confirmed by the fact that he was going hungry while living next door to a millionaire.[27]

When Filene returned from a business trip, on the fourth day of Cantwell's "going hungry," he invited his former biographer to a sumptuous venison dinner. As the old millionaire talked on glibly about his conversation with President Roosevelt, Cantwell's desire for vengeance peaked and he became determined to write the biography whether he was to be paid for it or not.

During the remaining three weeks of his contract, Cantwell labored "madly" and intently, managing to complete drafts of three chapters covering the first twenty-six years of Filene's life. Throughout he must have harbored the hope that the chapters, presented as a fait accompli, would convince Filene to change his mind. And in his "madness" he never lost sight of the larger goal, which lay behind his vengeance, for during this period he wrote to his friend Newton Arvin,

> I'm ghost-writing a biography of Filene for Steffens, who hasn't enough energy left to do the book himself. It's as far as possible from a millionaire's testimonial; it's a biography of a failure, of a progressive capitalist who tried to reform business practices, tried to turn his store over to his employees, and an analysis, a social analysis, of the reasons for his failure. It is fascinating material, no less, and after my first week of examining the documents I feel that I've learned more about the way our society is controlled than I could have learned in any other way.[28]

The first chapters were good enough to convince Filene to retain Cantwell, but relations between the two, at least according to Cantwell, were far from cordial: "At the end of three weeks, the biographer and his character were still engaged in their conflict; they looked upon each other with distrust and suspicion, the character doubting that the novelist-biographer could do justice to his career, the biographer still nursing plans for revenge and a growing conviction that his character had never done anything that amounted to anything anyway."[29]

In the meantime, the unfortunate Steffens, who had hoped to use the Filene project to recoup some recent financial losses, was gradually recovering from his stroke. When well again, he proved to be a master diplomat, somehow succeeding in keeping both Cantwell and his old friend Filene happy. As Justin Kaplan expressed it in his biography of Steffens: "Caught between Cantwell's savagery and Filene's mercurial interventions, Steffens derived what humor he could from the situation."[30] "The situation," after all, was partly his fault for bringing the two unlikely individuals together, and he understood Cantwell's financial plight even if Filene could not. Moreover, he believed in Cantwell as a writer, particularly after *The Land of Plenty* was published, and he believed in the novel biography. When the young radical biographer wrote complaining that the Filene life was keeping him from his fiction, Steffens replied, "Terrible! What do you think you are doing now? I think you are writing a novel now. You ought to think not only the same but that you are engaged upon the only work you ever have or ever are going to do."[31] By offering similar reassurance to Filene, Steffens kept the rather dubious project alive.

As Cantwell probed into Filene's life he discovered that the old merchant had led him to look for "certain characteristics that had no reality except in Filene's imagination." The novelist-biographer discovered, for example, that "all through the [childhood] years that Filene described as poverty-stricken and miserable, the Filenes lived and traveled in a manner that seemed luxurious to a single son of the proletariat."[32] And as the months of research wore on, Cantwell met a good many more capitalists possessed of a similar need to mythicize their pasts. He also found that, like Filene, these wealthy men all strained to create an air of busy-ness to camouflage "the social uselessness of their lives."[33]

Alerted by Filene's distortions, Cantwell began to scrutinize every word and deed of the capitalists he met or read about. Again he was startled by what he found:

> With his growing interest in the extent of willful exaggerations, the high-powered ballyhoo, that seemed so prevalent in this, as in other capitalist circles, the biographer found himself constantly occupied with small comparisons of words and deeds, claims and performances, and his findings were so shocking that [soon] . . . he distrusted nothing so much as capital-

ist fact.... Extending [this skepticism] ... to such other capitalist claims as came his way—to statements made in newspapers, for instance—he now found himself in a world in which statements of "fact" had significance only in so far as they threw light on the plots and aspirations of different groups and individuals.

He found himself then as a writer, and as one whose standard was relatively high, in world dominated by a fearful abuse of words, by a criminal debauchery of their significance; and for the first time he felt that he understood what Lenin meant when he wrote of the "shameful gap between bourgeois words and deeds."[34]

Cantwell himself may well be exaggerating here, exaggerating the extent of the naïveté with which he approached his subject. But he seems sincerely to have found his study of capitalists even more appalling than he had anticipated.

As he examined each of Filene's many schemes for humanizing the labor system, Cantwell also confirmed his belief that reform of capitalism was impossible. He was especially intrigued by Filene's advocacy of workers' credit unions that "the biographer" viewed as an even more ingenious scheme for co-opting workers than profit-sharing because it did not involve workers directly in the unstable stock market. But the credit union too was doomed, and in the history of its failure Cantwell discovered one of his favorite themes: "The record of credit unions effectively dramatized the differences between the workers' ability to manage and the hopeless incompetence and vicious deceptions of their employers."[35]

The single common thread Cantwell discovered running through Filene's life was failure, and as he became more and more aware of this his hatred turned to pity:

As the biographer watched his character move from one intrigue to another, frustrated in each; as he saw him suffer from a harrowing sense of futility about his "work" in the store, and as he found, among Filene's former associates with whom he talked, a veiled or candid dislike, or an intense hatred, a lack of respect or complete contempt....—as he observed all this a kind of desperately denied pathos loomed in his character's career, loomed so sharply that the biographer's own vindictive observations began to appear to him as cruel and base. The pathos was denied and the cruelest thing that one could say of Filene was that his life was sad, miserable, lonely, and touching.

For Cantwell the pathos emerged, or should have emerged, from the Quixotic nature of Filene's efforts. He had tried to give his store to his workers, only to have it stolen from him by his own brother; he had helped to found the national and international Chambers of Commerce as citadels of enlightened capitalism, only to watch them become thoroughly reactionary; he had even lost control of his own philanthropic endowment fund: "One after another the great efforts of [Filene's] life had slipped from his control. The store, the Chambers of Commerce, the Boston City Club, and credit unions—even the Twentieth Century Fund, the research endowment he had founded—and now his biography as well."[36] Filene had indeed lost control of his biography, and just before his manuscript breaks off, Cantwell completes, or at least makes explicit, the transformation of his "character's" life into a revolutionist's symbol:

> The biographer began to see [Filene], after a time, not merely as a capitalist, a millionaire, but as a kind of personification of American capitalism, not merely as a representative of his class, but an embodiment of it. Well-meaning, tasteless, awkward, shrewd, limited—he seemed to sum up a thousand capitalists whose personalities emerged dimly from behind the concealments of popular journalism. But most of all, he was old, and he concealed his age; he was weak and like capitalism itself he denied and concealed his weakness. The heart had gone out of him; and there was nothing left but the front.[37]

Clearly, working on the Filene biography confirmed, and probably intensified, Cantwell's conviction that American capitalism was doomed. But while fueling Cantwell's radicalism, his association with Filene also made it more difficult for him to function openly as a literary radical. Soon after Steffens hired him, Cantwell wrote to Newton Arvin about the problems that being in the employ of E. A. Filene were already causing him:

> I cannot work on the N[ew] M[asses] as a regular contributor without imperiling most of my income, the public announcement of my purpose

would only make it more difficult for me to make a living. Yet I can contribute from time to time under my own name, and am submitting a short story under my own name for one of the first issues if the editors want it. I can do this under the limitations imposed on me by the people for whom I work. At the same time I am actively cooperating as a staff member under another name [Robert Simmons].... If from time to time it seems like good tactics to publish something under my own, I'll do it, gauging my freedom on this point by my observations of the general atmosphere around me. This is troublesome, frequently unpleasant and involved a good deal of tacit deception and occasional outright lying, yet the alternative would only mean that the difficulties of making a living would be increased ... and I would have less time to spend writing the things I want to write—not to mention the emotional consequences, the disruption of my family and other problems.[38]

Cantwell seems in this letter to have absorbed some of the passion for "secret" maneuvers he correctly attributed to his friend Whittaker Chambers. And his duplicitous dealings with Filene encourage the speculation that Cantwell may have restrained public profession of the extent of his radicalism on other occasions for the same reason—to protect his job security. It may, for example, have led to a toning down of his reviews in the rather conservative *New Outlook*.

There is a new urgency and stridency in Cantwell's public and private writings throughout 1934. This may in part be a result of his intimate glimpse into the world of capitalist machinations, but the larger reason has undoubtedly to do with the course of political events during this year. Nineteen thirty-four saw the peak of the decade's radical activity, and the scene on the literary left was never more animated. Violent strikes led by radicals rocked New York City, Milwaukee, Philadelphia, San Francisco, and other cities. At the same time, the popularity of economic panaceas championed by such figures as Father Coughlin, Dr. Townsend, Huey Long, and Upton Sinclair seemed to place Roosevelt's piecemeal reformism in jeopardy.[39]

During this same period the Marxian literary movement was expanding and showed signs of maturing. The *New Masses* was reorganized in January of 1934, shifting from a monthly to a weekly format, under a new literary editor, Granville Hicks; and two months later the *Partisan Review* began publication as a literary journal designed as a forum for a more subtle, sophisticated approach to Marxian aesthetics and dedicated to combating the kind of narrowly partisan and formulaic literary criticism deplored by Cantwell.[40]

Thus the early months of 1934 were exciting ones for a literary radical, and Cantwell expressed understandable regret at being marooned in Boston away from the scene of the action.[41] But he remained active despite his distance from New York, and despite whatever "limitations" were "imposed" upon him by Filene and Steffens. As the following letter to Newton Arvin makes clear, for example, Cantwell felt an urgent need to bring unity to the literary left and initiated an effort to do so:

> I have been corresponding with [Granville] Hicks, and the thought has kept coming up that a chance to discuss things might clarify critical and other problems a lot. Would you be interested in a quiet little conference sometime in the spring? We might be able to get [Malcolm] Cowley, [John] Chamberlain, perhaps [Edmund] Wilson, if it seemed advisable—or others who are thinking along common lines? I am thinking of a day or so of discussion of the actual cultural scene, of the people whose work is or promises to be important, of potential allies and how they can be won, of present and future enemies and how they can be disarmed. My own plans are not clear—I am merely sending up a trial balloon. This seriously...— no one of us can doubt that the next few years are going to bring terrible and violent changes, that the threats to everything we live for have never been so fearful. How are we going to act? It may be that these people I have named are not the ones we want at all, that they have already shown themselves intimidated and only want to take refuge from the future. But if so, there must be others, and finding them ought to be one of our concerns.[42]

The "threat" perceived here is incipient American fascism, and Cantwell's desire to unite these major figures of the literary left is clearly a deadly earnest response to a sense of deepening national crisis.

Cantwell's published work throughout 1934, both in his *New Outlook* column and in the reviews he still occasionally contributed to the *New Republic*, reflect the same sense of deepening crisis expressed in his private correspondence. In the *New Outlook* he frequently chastised established writers for ignoring the contemporary scene and praised young writers for their attempts to understand the Depression: "Facing a world in which the process of change has been enormously accelerated, and one in which social conflicts have grown more and more intense and violent, the major writers [he mentions Joyce, Eliot, and a few others] have turned to tending their own gardens, while their followers are making the first tentative efforts to resolve the confusion they find all about them."[43] Among the younger writers Cantwell praises André Malraux, Edward Dahlberg, James T. Farrell, Erskine Caldwell, and the then little read Nathaniel West—all writers associated with the revolutionary movement. But even as his sense of crisis deepened, Cantwell felt no impulse to judge works solely on the basis of their political content, for he also praised the Gothic tales of Isaak Dineson, as well as Ferdinand Celine's surreal, anti-Semitic, misanthropic, perhaps protofascist, novels.[44]

Cantwell's political beliefs are also reflected in the works of nonfiction he recommended to his *New Outlook* readers. He was consistently hostile, for example, to books by reformers such as Stuart Chase, while giving his highest praise to works by such Marxists as John Strachey, Lewis Corey (Louis Fraina), and his friend Matthew Josephson. He praised Josephson's *The Robber Barons* for the evenness of its tone, which allowed the "facts that set your teeth grinding in rage" to speak for themselves. He expressed similar admiration for the dispassionate tone of Strachey's *The Coming Struggle for Power* and Corey's *The Decline of American Capitalism*. Strachey was something of the British equivalent of Lincoln Steffens, a progressive, Labor party member of Parliament who was driven by the Depression to embrace Communism. Both his work and Corey's carefully chart the reasons why reform of capitalism is impossible, why only revolution can solve the economic crisis. Cantwell says of Corey's book: "American capitalism more or less declines before your eyes, its claims shrivel and all but disappear, its prophets and apologists are confounded, and the pretensions of the New Deal seem more and more hollow and base. Mr. Corey strains and struggles and repeats himself while he lugs towards his proof, but the proof is convincing, and the book, for all its load of facts and figures, is dramatic in the best sense of the word."[45]

These works by Josephson, Strachey, and Corey were praised by most left-leaning critics, but for Cantwell they had a special relevance, for each of them confirmed the impetus behind the project upon which he was working when he reviewed them. Throughout the winter and spring of 1934 Cantwell continued his research on Filene's life and times, sending progress reports to Steffens (then recuperating at his home in Carmel, California). In April, Steffens remarked in reply to one of these missives, "The impression grows upon me that you are writing this biography out of as much pains, agony and doubt as I put into an autobiography."[46] The comparison is perhaps more apt than Steffen knew in that *The Autobiography of Lincoln Steffens* (1931) is the kind of chronicle of failed reformism which the decline and fall of E. A. Filene was becoming. Unfortunately, Filene did not feel himself to be declining or falling, and some of the "agony" and "pains" recorded by Cantwell stemmed, no doubt, from this complicating factor.

When the biographer's doubts grew severe, Steffens wrote to remind his young colleague that "the Thing you are writing is the great, modern American novel."[47] And when he had read the publisher's proofs of *The Land of Plenty* in late April, Steffens sent similar word to Filene, calling Cantwell's novel "an event in literature" and assuring his old friend that his biographer "is, in his line, what you are in yours: a leader."[48] Thus the project staggered on.

Throughout the spring Steffens urged Cantwell to join him at his home in Carmel, and in the summer Cantwell accepted the invitation. The trip might in another time have been a vacation, for Steffens's home was situated in a lovely seaside resort setting, but because of both the difficult biography and turbulent events in nearby San Francisco and in Carmel itself, the trip proved to be far from a respite from the politics of the East Coast. Soon after he had settled into Steffens's household, Cantwell wrote to James T. Farrell of his feelings about the Filene project: "The job I'm doing gets more and more complicated. Interesting but difficult; I'm on thin ice most of the time. I'm getting a chance to see a lot of people—business men and politicians generally—that I wouldn't get to see if I were doing literary journalism in New York. And I have a piece of writing to do that is so hazardous and difficult that I think it must be good for me. Otherwise the rewards for the trouble I go to are a little thin."[49]

The difficulties must indeed have been great, but, as Cantwell tells Farrell later in the letter, his new contacts confirmed him in his view of the incompetence of business leaders and made him more determined than ever to combat capitalists by whatever tactics he could devise. The word "propaganda" that, as we have seen, occurs frequently in Cantwell's writing of this period, is partly deployed in reaction to his increased inside knowledge of the propaganda practices of capitalists and the capitalist media. But this insider's view also confirmed Cantwell's belief that the propaganda mechanisms against which he railed were sophisticated, and he continued to hold up to others and set for himself a similarly sophisticated example of what counterpropaganda, or as we might now say, counterhegemonic rhetoric, should be. In an article surveying current "little magazines," for example, he notes that, while proletarian literature had now found a permanent place in American writing, it was still necessary to combat "leftism," which, consistent with his political aesthetic, he defined as "the attempt to force the reader's responses through a barrage of sloganized and inorganic writing." Cantwell said that "nine-tenths of the revolutionary stories" he read were "mechanically written" and "monotonous," but he still embraced the promise implicit in such works: "If they give rise to strong hopes for the writing of the future, it is for this reason: they show that the barriers that have separated writers from the great masses of the people are breaking down, and that the beginners, the majority of them, are trying to develop a literature that will be based on the details of workers' tasks and on the casual, Elizabethan poetry of workers' speech."[50] Such literature would serve to give readers a sense of the dignity of the working class, while works like the proposed biography of Filene attacked the shallowness, hypocrisy, and incompetency of the rich.

In July, Cantwell was unexpectedly granted the opportunity to unite both of these propaganda impulses when violence erupted in San Francisco and he was given the assignment of covering the events for the *New Republic*. A strike among Pacific Coast stevedores met employer resistance in San Francisco, leading to a bloody clash on July 5, 1934, in which five persons were killed. In the wake of this battle, militant unionist and head of the International Longshoreman's Association, Harry Bridges, played a key role in persuading locals throughout the city to call a general strike against shipments of food and fuel that effectively shut down the city. The ILA had already shut down the entire West Coast maritime industry, from San Diego to Seattle, and the four-day general strike in San Francisco involved more than 180 unions. The events became one of the great labor battles of the era.[51]

Cantwell's report of these events in the *New Republic*, "San Francisco: Act One," begins portentously:

> It is to change everything in San Francisco, and to be of historic significance, but you don't know that, when the parade starts; you only see the workers moving slowly and silently away from the International Longshoremen's Association hall and turn up Market Street, bearing the bodies of Howard Sperry and Nicholas Boredeis. Sperry and Boredeis were killed; they were shot in the back, while they were trying to escape from police who on July 5 were carrying on a massed offensive against all workers who came within range of their guns and clubs. When I say that their funeral changed things in San Francisco I mean that before it started the business people of the city and the arbitrators appointed by the President and the newspapers had been acting on the assumption that everybody was against the longshoremen's strike except a group of radicals, and after the parade had started no one with eyes could doubt that the masses of the people were for the strike and would defend it.
>
> When the funeral march got under way the life of the town stopped in wonder and surprise. Nobody expected so many. It had not seemed there were so many in San Francisco. They were only plain working people, thousands of them, sober and resolute, marching in ranks to bury their dead. It was a week before the business men of San Francisco got back their nerve and convinced themselves that they had had a nightmare, that there had not really been so many after all. But it was clear that the capitalists of San Francisco faced something they had not had to deal with before. They faced a general strike.[52]

Through the remainder of the article and another one a week later, Cantwell carefully details the collaboration between the federal government (in the form of general Hugh Johnson, head of Franklin D. Roosevelt's National Recovery Administration), San Francisco business interests, armed police and guardsmen, and the press in breaking the strike. He portrays their strategy as one of brutal assaults followed by announcements that a settlement was near.[53]

The second of Cantwell's articles on the strike, this one, titled "War on the West Coast," begins with the same sense of drama as the first:

> There is a reign of terror in San Francisco. . . . For the past two and a half months a reign of terror has meant just one thing: it has meant that the

employers, the city officials, the government arbitrators or the reactionary group within the American Federation of Labor—or all together—were going to announce a "settlement" of the strike. If the terror was relatively light, if only a few workers were arrested and beaten—the terms are synonymous—it meant that the settlement was to be only one of the often-rejected compromises.... But when there were wholesale arrests, the smashing of workers' meeting places, the shooting of bystanders and "Communists," it meant that some wonderful new scheme ... was to be made public. So it was that whenever faint murmurs of an approaching settlement reached the people, they knew that a new reign of terror would soon begin to pave the way for it.... And when, on a single day, both Johnson and Roosevelt announced that they believed the strike would soon be over, all those who could fled in terror to the mountains.

After detailing the violence that accompanied each new period of arbitration, and making it clear that it took all of the combined forces of business, government, and the media to defeat the strike, Cantwell ends with this message to workers:

Out of all these facts a general development is apparent. First of all, [General] Johnson has recaptured some of his dwindling prestige by his decisive action in a situation in which so many of his subordinates had acted with a strange indecision. But more importantly, the administration has revealed again, and more strongly and dramatically than ever, that in a conflict between organized labor and a group of open-shop capitalists, its support goes to the latter, the most reactionary group within the American social structure....

With the annihilation of civil rights in San Francisco, with Johnson's provocative attacks and with the blood of a great many working people, Section 7A has been clarified for all time.[54]

Cantwell was clearly more than a disinterested observer of these events. On one of the major battle days of the general strike, he showed up at his brother Jim's place on O'Farrell Street with "a rough looking friend," wanting to hide him from the police. Jim Cantwell was furious and wanted nothing to do with radicals.

The strike continued to grow more confrontational each day, until two protesters were killed and hundreds were wounded on what came to be knows as "Bloody Thursday." Soon the National Guard was called in, 1,500 troops having been told that a communist revolution was taking place in San Francisco. On Monday, July 9, at least 20,000 striking workers and sympathizers marched quietly in a funeral procession for the two martyred workers, Howard Sperry and Nicholas Bordoisie.

The *New Republic* articles Cantwell wrote on the strike stem from his deepest, most complex encounters with labor struggles in the age of the CIO. The Carmel and Bay Area sojourn left profound, contradictory impressions on him. Aptly, his reading matter while there included *The Eighteenth Brumaire of Napoleon Bonaparte*, one of Marx's most novelistic writings and a subtle analysis of the complex interactions of classes and class fractions during a political crisis. He met with all of the major figures in the strike, including Harry Bridges, head of the International Longshoremen's Association, and Sam Darcy, head of the Communist-led Marine Workers' Union. Some of the important information Cantwell drew upon for his *New Republic* articles had come from a clandestine meeting with Darcy arranged by Steffens's Communist Party activist wife, Ella Winter. The meeting was held in secret because Darcy was in hiding after Communist Party and union offices in the city had been hit by a series of vicious raids by vigilantes (paid by the Shipowners' Association) and the San Francisco police.

Fear that a revolution was afoot in California was widespread, and the spirit of anti-Red vigilantism was also rampant in the normally sleepy burg of Carmel. A meeting of the local John Reed Club at which Cantwell spoke was surrounded by a mob of American Legionnaires threatening to maim or kill the Reds inside. Death threats to Steffens, Winter, and their guests became an almost everyday occurrence. Winter had been charged by the Party to recruit writers, artists, Hollywood luminaries, and other left-leaning celebrities in California. The role included helping to found the John Reed Club of Carmel, a group whose literary lights included Langston Hughes. Hughes, as a gay black man, was a particularly vulnerable target, and he wisely left town soon after the first vigilante attack.

For Cantwell, the Legion attack must have brought up terrifying memories of the Wobblies who had been beaten, castrated, and hanged by Legion members in the nineteen teens. Cantwell was never a physically imposing or particularly brave man, and his experiences in Carmel left him even more fearful of radical association than he had been. His fears of exposure as a Red had largely been fear of loss of income, but to this was now added a fear for his own and his family's safety. Betsy had been accosted by police outside a Longshoremen's meeting place, and while she bluffed her way through with "Southern belle charm," she was deeply traumatized by the event and by other encounters with the rough-and-tumble world of labor struggle. When things got particularly heated in Carmel and the local police began deputizing some of the vigilantes, Cantwell and Betsy fled to Oakland.

In the autumn, Cantwell drove straight across the country and arrived back in New York "like a soldier returned from the battlefield." Having driven East at "breakneck speed" in order presumably to leave behind the ghosts of vigilantes and other Red-hunters, he, Betsy, and their daughter Joan stopped along the way in Baltimore. There Cantwell had long talks with Chambers about all that he had seen. In light of the West Coast events, Cantwell was more frightened than before by Chamber's apparently now more serious underground work. He had wanted to borrow money from Chambers, but when Betsy threatened to go to the FBI and tell them of Chambers's treasonous activities, he demurred.

When back in New York, Cantwell wrote a follow-up piece, "The Press as Strikebreaker," a satiric exposé of the complicity of key publishers and journalists who formed the ad hoc Publishers' Council, a conspiratorial effort to blunt the strike.[55] Cantwell was particularly incensed that members of his profession had played a signal role in the suppression of the strike. Publishers had actively suppressed even neutral stories about labor grievances in favor of slanted reporting and Red-baiting headlines such as this one from the *San Francisco Examiner*: "Communist Chiefs Declare Open War in California; Its Object Will Be Overthrow of The State Government to Be Followed by a Soviet Form of Government."[56] Lorena Hickok, in California as a roving observer for Harry Hopkins's Federal Emergency Relief Administration, sent a message back to Washington on August 15, 1934, reporting that "all over the state in the last few weeks newspaper publishers have been getting together in secret sessions and laying plans publicly to put on a campaign to rid the state of Communists, but privately to fight Roosevelt" by painting the New Deal with a Red brush.[57]

Cantwell's *New Republic* articles make clear that his sympathies remained solidly on the side of workers and against liberal union bosses, government complicity in strike breaking, and a corporate-manipulated media. But his up-close and personal encounter with the general strike complicated his view of the Communist Party. He was, for example, appalled when a Party functionary callously mentioned that the death of the two strikers was a good thing because the movement needed martyrs. More seriously, Cantwell was disillusioned by the duplicity of one of his mentors, Ella Winter. One of Winter's celebrity recruits was Hollywood actor James Cagney. Cagney became a major "angel" helping to fund, among other things, work Winter was doing in support of California agricultural workers. But, for obvious career reasons, he did so in secrecy. Cantwell was shocked to discover that the Party had threatened to expose Cagney in an effort to extort more money from the actor. By the end of his time on the West Coast, Cantwell had become more leery of the Communist Party, and felt bitter that Winter had pushed him into a more radical public posture than he was comfortable with. In response, in subsequent years he was even more careful than before to hide his fellow traveler views.

If Cantwell was disillusioned by some of the things he had seen and heard in California, events there had clearly also moved and inspired him. The events in San Francisco had in addition stirred Cantwell's literary imagination. Before the year was out he had begun to plan a new novel based on the story of the general strike. He noted that he had written far more about the strike than appeared in the *New Republic* and planned to turn those thoughts in a fictional direction. The strike seemed to provide the perfect canvas for an epic that would move beyond the story of workers to encompass all levels of the social structure. A letter Cantwell wrote to his friend T. S. Matthews hinted at some of the themes that his new novel would assay:

> The general strike in San Francisco was great and heartbreaking. They came so close to winning and were betrayed so shamelessly. The longshoremen and seamen could defeat the efforts of the employers to break the strike, the efforts of the government arbitrators, the city officials and police; they could, counting on to help other unions, have beaten the National Guard. But they hadn't clearly realized that they have got to beat the A.F. of L. officials just as much as the employers; there isn't any real

distinction between them, but it wasn't so clear before. Meanwhile the patriots are busy driving the god damned reds into their holes. They're frightening away all mild liberals and taking down the license numbers of the cars seen at alleged radical meeting places; it's sickening, but serious. They have built up an organization that will be ready next time.[58]

In a letter to Dos Passos about that summer he wrote that the planned new novel would imagine future struggles and help the masses see a clear path to change.[59] Armed with his now intimate knowledge of the capitalist mind, he imagined a panoramic work that would be a microcosm of America in class struggle. But events in America were moving faster than any young novelist could hope to absorb, and both his new strike novel and the biography of Filene were soon jeopardized by changing conditions in this country and abroad.

6   *TIME*, DOUBT, AND THE POPULAR FRONT

Cantwell and the Ideological Storms of the Late 1930s

As Michael Denning has brilliantly argued, events such as the San Francisco general strike in the summer of 1934 were part of a large-scale "Popular Front social movement" in the latter half of the 1930s and beyond, which included a broad-scale left-liberal cultural front. Denning's work counters the claim that the Popular Front was nothing more than a front for Communist Party machinations. He shows that, while the term "Popular Front" may have derived from the Party, it names a far wider set of forces. Unfortunately, the era of vicious anticommunism that came with the Cold War obscured this larger movement in favor of the false claim that the Communist Party USA (CPUSA) was nothing more than a spy ring for the Soviet Union.[1]

Cantwell's relation to the CPUSA was a very complex one. His close friend from Aberdeen, Calvin Fixx, was a member, and Chambers made him privy to much Party activity (though Cantwell, like everyone else, frequently had trouble separating fact from fiction in Chambers's accounts). The FBI later believed Cantwell to have been a member, but their evidence is circumstantial. Given his generally cautious, nervous, and at times near paranoid behavior, and given his often-stated concern that greater public radicalism could imperil his always shaky financial situation, it seems likely that Cantwell never formally joined but rather worked at a distance and quite clandestinely in critical support. In late April 1934, he was asked by Chambers's friend John Sherman to write a book about the DuPont Corporation in the hope that through his contacts via E. A. Filene he could help the Soviets to infiltrate the company records of this major arms manufacturer. Although tempted by the offer of $25,000 for the job,

Cantwell declined the opportunity to engage in Soviet espionage.[2]

In any event, Cantwell, however sympathetic in general with CPUSA goals, frequent held views on both literature and political policy that were out of sync with Party views. From 1935 to 1939 the public policy statements of the Communist parties in the United States and abroad became increasingly conservative, while behind the scenes a "secret" commitment to revolution was maintained. During these years duplicity, at least at higher levels of the Party, became a way of life, and thus it becomes extremely difficult to gain an accurate sense of the true beliefs and feelings of party members or sympathizers. Communists and fellow travelers were asked to sublimate their revolutionary rhetoric and work with all progressive forces—socialists, New Dealers, and moderates—in a united front, until the greatest immediate threat, fascism, could be eliminated.

In Party terms, this strategy was in certain respects a great success. Between 1935 and 1938 CPUSA membership swelled from 30,000 to 75,000 members, while the development of the bold new CIO-led labor movement, in which Communists played a significant role, seemed to give greater substance to the claim that American workers were becoming class conscious.[3] But beneath the surface, doubt and confusion as to the ultimate direction and moral values of the Communist Party leaders, compounded by dissension on the left resulting from the trumped-up Moscow Trials of left deviationists such as Trotsky and his associates, as well as deep internal rifts in the left provoked by Stalin's treachery in Spanish Civil War began quickly to erode the unity of the front.

A policy repudiating the revolutionism of the "Third Period" of Comintern activity began to germinate in the Kremlin in 1933 when it became clear that the split between Communists and Social Democrats in Germany had been a factor aiding the Nazis in their rise to power. And as the bellicose Hitler looked eastward, he sent a chill across the Soviet Union. In response, Stalin and the Comintern tacticians evolved a new international Communist strategy designed to downplay the ideological differences separating the Soviets from potential allies in the Western democracies over the course of 1934 and 1935. Given the name "United" or "Popular" or "People's Front" in America, the new approach was experimented with in France in 1934, and became official Comintern policy in August of 1935.[4]

The new strategy was to alter completely the face of American Communism, leading eventually to a policy of Communist support for the New Deal that made the Party seem to be in the mainstream of American liberalism. But the movement toward this new position was gradual and was welcomed initially by most American leftists as an approach much more appropriate to conditions in this country. In the literary field, for example, the movement toward a less harshly revolutionary image began in 1934 with the elimination of the John Reed Clubs, and was welcomed as a move consistent with the growing attack on ultraleft literary criticism. To the Party, the move was a part of a long-term strategy to attract well-known liberal writers who could give added respectability to a literary front against fascism, a strategy that would eventually lead to a virtual abandonment of the very idea of proletarian literature and even of the idea of class conflict that it encouraged. But most writers saw the move only as a mild "purge" of the most rabid left-oriented writers, and as a victory for the style of analysis that Cantwell and others like him had championed.

Thus there was great excitement on the left in January of 1935 when a manifesto was published in the *New Masses* calling for a congress of revolutionary writers to convene in the near future to form a new, broader-based organization of writers committed to the fight against fascism. The manifesto was directed toward "writers who have achieved some standing in their respective fields," and thus suggests the new effort to enlist prominent authors at the expense of the relatively unknown writers of the proletarian movement. But in addressing itself to writers "who have clearly indicated their sympathy to the revolutionary cause" and who "do not need to be convinced of the decay of capitalism," the new manifesto showed no signs of a shift toward reformism. Drafted by Granville Hicks, the document was signed by thirty-nine prominent American leftists, including Kenneth Burke, Theodore Dreiser, Langston Hughes, Nelson Algren, Nathaniel West, Erskine Caldwell, John Dos Passos, James T. Farrell, and Robert Cantwell.[5]

The call for a congress of radical writers was answered in April of 1935 when 216 writers from twenty-six states and 150 representatives from foreign delegations assembled in New York City for three days of discussion and debate. Delegates read papers on the state of revolutionary criticism, poetry, and fiction; discussed the role of the writer in the revolutionary movement as a whole; and pledged themselves anew to the struggle against fascism. The assembled writers formed the League of American Writers and voted to affiliate their organization with the International Union of Revolutionary Writers (the literary arm of the Comintern) to help in forming a worldwide front of writers against "fascism, against imperialist wars, and for the defense of the Soviet Union, the fatherland of the toilers of the world."[6]

How wide this front was to be, and the extent to which it was to undermine much of the vocabulary, if not the substance, of the US Marxist movement in fiction and criticism, was not apparent for more than two years after the congress. In 1935, the new tone seemed to correspond with Cantwell's own feelings about the drift of American society, about the real danger to civil liberties, and thus he soon became one of the first American writers to absorb and publicize the new mood and policy.

Less than a month after the Writer's Congress, Cantwell published an article on the developments in California since the general strike of the previous summer. Titled "Better News from California," the essay begins by announcing that, while ten months earlier "the state of California seemed the most violently reactionary in the country, a new mood of resistance was now discernable among liberals and radicals of the state who were pushing back the right-wing forces." He notes that a "move to repeal the [California] criminal syndicalist law brought Democratic assemblymen, representatives of [Upton Sinclair's] EPIC, liberals, members of the Townsend groups, and of the Utopian society into united-front activity with communists and trade unionists." Cantwell is careful to add that these "signs do not mean that the struggle for civil liberties is over," but he concludes that they "do mean that further repressive measures must be forced past an aroused and suspicious electorate."[7]

Cantwell had never been enamored of the Party line on politics and literature, and in its early days at least he must have welcomed the emerging Popular Front ideology as a vindication of the tone and style he had long advocated. As the papers read at the Writers' Congress make clear,[8] the ultraleft criticism against which Cantwell had spoken out was being repudiated by the new policy. And the new, more moderate tone apparent in the pages of the *New Masses* throughout 1935 and 1936 was much closer to his own. In a letter to Cowley, Cantwell made clear that his support of the new policies would come largely by not using their terms, which he feared were easily co-opted. Cantwell expressed support for the term "United Front" and for various forms of more open-minded "Marxist criticism," but urged critics to avoid both terms as much as possible. Rather, he argued, they should more generally assure young writers that their revolutionary efforts would be supported, and that older writers (he mentions Carl Sandburg, Upton Sinclair, and Charles Beard) were good models.[9]

But the Popular Front era policies also presented Cantwell with numerous difficulties, the first major one being the doubts they cast on the fate of the Filene biography. The attack on Filene that he had begun at the height of his revolutionary enthusiasm was precisely the kind of effort being discouraged under the new Communist strategy. To verbally assault a leading progressive capitalist, one of the few prominent business persons to support Roosevelt's New Deal, was to run directly against the new spirit on the left, and might weaken the type of fragile coalition Cantwell saw growing in California. It is small wonder, therefore, that the novel-biography was abandoned before reaching completion. As for the ghostwritten "autobiography" version, Cantwell rushed to finish that manuscript in March of 1935 so that he might begin a new, more lucrative job with *Time* magazine, but the results did not apparently meet with Filene's approval, for it was also never published.[10]

The new job Cantwell was offered was that of coeditor of the literary section of Henry Luce's news magazine. He was recruited for the position by T. S. Matthews, then *Time*'s literary editor, who although he had never met Cantwell, greatly admired his fiction and considered him the best book reviewer then writing in New York.[11] In many ways the new position seemed ideal to Cantwell. Not only was the salary two or three times more than he had ever earned before, but in addition Matthews had arranged for each of them to work only six months a year, leaving the other six free for their own work.[12]

But despite these inducements, Cantwell hesitated to accept Matthews's offer, perhaps because many New York writers thought *Time* less than respectable, perhaps because editor Luce was known to press his conservative opinions on his staff. For whatever reason, he was unsure and called upon his friend Whittaker Chambers for advice. Chambers recalled later that he had urged Cantwell to accept the job, in part because he thought the salary and experience would be good for his friend, and in part because in the back of his mind he imagined that having a contact at *Time* "might be useful to the underground."[13]

Probably knowing nothing of Chambers's ulterior motives, Cantwell accepted his new position. And from May of 1935 until mid-1939, he worked as a reviewer for *Time*, except for brief sojourns with two other Luce journals, *Fortune* and *Life*. But Cantwell's book reviews for *Time*, when it is even possible to be certain of the authorship of the unsigned critiques, usually have no strong, consistent political cast to them.[14] He seems to have confined expressions of his political beliefs to the essays that he continued to write for the *New Republic*, and it is these essays which best suggest how his role as a radically socially conscious writer evolved over the course of the Popular Front years.

Cantwell's political-literary opinions do not shift greatly during the early years of the Popular Front. His central concern—to encourage a high-quality proletarian literature—remains a focal point in his criticism. His critical essays extend and elaborate on earlier ideas, rather than depart greatly from them. If there was a change, it was that he placed greater emphasis on the need for a more complex radical fiction capable of illuminating the relationships between members of *all* classes in American society.

Late in 1934, for example, Cantwell returned to Henry James in an essay aimed at encouraging a more ambitiously complex type of radical fiction. He cites a long passage from one of James's famous "prefaces" in which the Master argues that only the most sensitive and intelligent of the characters in a given author's work can be counted on "not to betray, to cheapen, or, as we say, give away, the beauty and value of the thing." Of this passage Cantwell writes,

> If that text had sunk more deeply into our literary traditions, we might have been spared some of our epics of bewilderment, some of our prose celebrations of spinelessness and fatigue. Our proletarian novelists, for instance, might be induced to part company with that story of the defeated strike as seen through the eyes of one of its more backward victims, and take up the more dramatic issues of leadership, of organization and strategy, as visualized by the most highly developed individuals involved.[15]

Here Cantwell is clearly elaborating on the idea of fictionalizing possible situations in which the American proletariat might find themselves that he had expressed a few months earlier in the *New Masses*. But by speaking of moving beyond "that story of the defeated strike," he is implicitly criticizing his own novel as well as those of other proletarian novelists.

In the conclusion to this article, Cantwell makes still more explicit his belief that revolutionary novelists could gain much by appropriating certain techniques developed by James, and in so doing he suggests the direction in which he then intended to take his own fiction:

> Although James seems to provide a whole arsenal of argument and illustration for the critics who advocate the conscious isolation of the artist from political and social conflicts, his deepest meaning is reserved for those who hold more revolutionary philosophies. They can understand his [dubious] attitude toward his own class, and perhaps add the indignation that he never expressed; his "hierarchizing" of characters according to their individual awareness is close to their own concepts of class and political consciousness. The question of technique is another matter, but it can be said of him, as it cannot be said of Proust and Joyce, that the technique is equally good for both sides.[16]

As elucidation of Jamesian aesthetics, this is confusing nonsense, but it reveals the ingenious manner in which Cantwell brought his cultural heritage to bear upon the effort to create a favorable climate for the flourishing of Marxist fiction.

Soon after this article on James was published, Cantwell received a letter from his friend and fellow radical-novelist John Dos Passos. The letter suggests that Dos Passos felt the overly clever appropriation of James to be a sign that his friend was drifting into a dangerous mind-set. Dos Passos expressed doubt that the proletarian movement in which Cantwell continued to place great faith was the wave of the future. "It seems to me," Dos Passos writes, "that . . . the time for a man to be a communist [was during the Russian Revolution] . . . and that all this literary Gorkyism we have now is an ex post facto performance, more of an afterglow than a daybreak. . . . I'm unloading this social fascism or what not on you because I thought I detected in your article on Henry James in the NR a slight touch of communist holier than thouishness—. . . something I've been guilty of myself."[17] Elsewhere in the letter Dos Passos makes it clear that it is not merely the James article that had set him worrying about Cantwell. Cantwell had apparently informed him that his proposed novel on the San Francisco general strike was to be an attack on fascism, and in response to this Dos Passos warned that "it would be dangerous for anyone who is trying for objective reality . . . to start with any such rubber stamp as 'Fascism' even in the fringe of his mind." To this he adds a more general caution against "sectarian opinions" such as those of "Comrade Hicks" because such views lead a writer to accept "the formulas of past events as useful for the measurement of future events and they never are, if you have high standards of accuracy." Dos Passos continued, "I thought you pulled off what you intended pretty thoroughly in *The Land of Plenty*—I agree with you that it might have been even more useful if it had been possible to indicate more ramifications into the mass population of the continent—but it was certainly better to leave the strings untied than to gum them together with obsolete labels out of Daily Worker editorials." Lest Cantwell still fail to get his message, near the end of the letter Dos Passos becomes even more explicit in his cautioning: "The writer works out of what he's picked up in the past life—his present attitudes can light it but once they begin to change it, the work is no good."[18]

Dos Passos was not telling Cantwell anything he had not already heard before elsewhere, and near the end the older writer declared himself "more or less out of order" and apologized for his pedantic tone. Coming from a writer of Dos Passos's stature, however, these caveats no doubt hurt. But if Cantwell's spirits were dimmed at all by Dos Passos's remarks, they were soon brightened again by the mood of rededication that arose on the left in the wake of the First Writers' Congress. As an article Cantwell published in the *New Republic* a few months after the congress makes clear, his belief in proletarian literature was undiminished. This piece, titled "What the Working Class Reads," was a rebuttal to an essay by Louis Adamic that had appeared in a recent issue of the *Saturday Review*.[19] Adamic had charged that the working-class audience for proletarian fiction was so small as to be virtually insignificant, and that, furthermore, workers showed almost no interest in serious literature of any kind, preferring instead the pap proffered in the commercial pulps. For these reasons, he concluded that politically motivated writers should direct their messages solely to the middle classes and cease talking of a workers' literature.

Cantwell begins his rebuttal of these charges by challenging one of Adamic's basic premises:

> It may be observed in parenthesis that Mr. Adamic began his inquiry with a basic misunderstanding of what constitutes proletarian literature, and that his major premise—that its "strongest justification" is "that it is addressed to the working class"—would be disputed by most proletarian novelists and their critics. Proletarian or any other literature can only be "justified"—culturally, artistically—by the extent to which it advances the heritage of human culture; even, its defenders would insist, by the extent to which it promises to advance human culture, the extent to which it incorporates and hands on and revitalizes and makes significant to the present the great achievements of the human imagination. It is a cultural product and its value cannot be determined in any important way by the size of its immediate audience.[20]

These are noble sentiments which Cantwell no doubt believed on some level, but the emphasis on continuity of cultural tradition sounds conservative enough to please humanist critic Paul Elmer More or Cantwell's favorite, Henry James. How is such a view compatible with the idea of a proletarian literature with revolutionary aims? As Cantwell spins out his defense of a workers' cultural matrix, he seems to become caught in his own web of convolutions to such an extent that he directly contradicts his first definition of the "justification" of literature. He argues that if an individual "believes as Mr. Adamic believes, that . . . the broad masses of the working people accept a kind of cheap commercial fiction" and are incapable of responding to more serious work, then "creative literature becomes of such dubious value, its possibilities seem so limited in comparison with the strain and patience it demands, that the inspiration of the individual writer is constantly threatened by a sense of the social meaninglessness of his labor."[21]

While his first "justification" of literature would seem to countenance even the most elitist work so long as "it advances the heritage of human culture," "no matter what the size of its audience," Cantwell now, as if sensing a drift toward heresy, has made the support of the "broad masses" necessary not only for "inspiration" but to ensure that the writer's labor remain socially meaningful. Cantwell's confusion here is not simply personal but rather reflects a growing confusion on the literary left generally during the transition period between its revolutionary phase and its Popular Front reformist phase. Different, but in some respects parallel, attempts to unite traditionalism and radicalism in the cultural sphere can be seen at this time in a number of places, most notably in the work of *Partisan Review* editors Philip Rahv and William Phillips, whose tense fusion of modernism and independent radical politics must have appeared attractive to Cantwell.[22]

As the rest of his article makes clear, Cantwell was not fully cognizant of any conflict between the long-term demand to "advance the heritage of human culture" and the immediate demands of radical politics because he was still mesmerized by the image of the aroused masses rising to demand their rightful place in, and to advance the course of, American culture. To refute Adamic's thesis that American workers simply did not read serious literature, Cantwell drew upon the one source the other writer had overlooked, the public library system. From a statistical survey of public library readership, he carefully constructed a portrait of workers thirsting after the works of Mark Twain, Thomas Hardy, George Bernard Shaw, and even the Greek classics. Cantwell was forced to admit that the "fact that most library readers of these 'serious' books are members of the working class does not mean that they constitute an audience receptive to revolutionary or radical fiction." He acknowledges, in fact, that a "taste for the higher achievements of bourgeois culture may, on the contrary, encourage rather backward political and cultural convictions . . . , may tend to make him less class-conscious or lead to a feeling of superiority over other workers whose cultural interests are not so highly developed as his own."[23]

While acknowledging these complications, Cantwell was not dismayed by them. The statistical survey of libraries from which he drew his information contained sample letters from worker-patrons, and from these Cantwell drew tortuously hopeful, if cautious, conclusions. These letters, he argues, "suggest, though dimly, that while serious cultural interests on the part of a member of the working class do not necessarily heighten his class-consciousness, they nevertheless tend to raise political issues, and lead, somewhere along their way, to his questioning the structure of the capitalist system." Based on this premise that all good literature is slightly subversive, Cantwell asks rhetorically if the lack of available good, cheap books is not "altogether a technical problem" but "also a social problem, deeply involved with the whole question of the bourgeois domination of American cultural life?"[24] It is not entirely clear if this indicates that Cantwell's suspicions of conspiratorial capitalist intrigue had not waned, or if he is indicating a more diffuse "hegemonic" process of influence.

The image which Cantwell creates in contrast to Adamic's is of a working-class cultural constituency that is not only intelligent but "a growing and groping and eager audience, acquainted with the higher achievements of bourgeois culture and actually straining the resources of the library system in its search for intellectually adequate reading."[25] Cantwell's reassertion of the existence of a mass audience for proletarian literature was of very great personal importance, because in a paper read before the First Writers' Congress three months earlier, Henry Hart revealed that *The Land of Plenty*, having sold barely 3,000 copies, was the best-selling book the proletarian movement had yet produced. "What the Working Class Reads" was, therefore, an extremely timely effort to boost morale on the literary left by promising that the proletarian cultural flowering to which writers had dedicated their work was indeed going on.

A few months later, in October of 1935, Cantwell reaffirmed his faith in the proletarian movement and suggested that it was in fact beginning to achieve maturity. The occasion was the publication of Grace Lumpkin's second novel, *A Sign for Cain*, and in reviewing the new work he took the opportunity to sketch briefly the course of the Marxian literary movement, including what he believed to be its future course:

> Grace Lumpkin's first novel was published in 1932, at a time of intense, embittered and generally confused controversy on proletarian literature. Her second appears at a moment when that argument, in its original form [i.e., what determines that a novel is *truly* proletarian] at any rate, has been more or less abandoned.... The issues raised have not been settled, but discussion of them has grown wearisome and arid, primarily because the Marxists and their opponents have argued persistently at cross purposes. "To Make My Bread," Miss Lumpkin's first novel, was one of the first creative contributions to these discussions, and as such it foreshadowed, in both its strength and weakness, the type of proletarian fiction published in the next few years—a novel about a defeated strike, ending with the realization on the part of the workers of the monumental difficulties they were up against. The pattern has been repeated so frequently that it has been in danger of becoming a formula.... Miss Lumpkin's second novel is a venture into other fields, an attempt to apply a Marxian analysis to a typically demoralized Southern family of the landowning class, and to picture an experienced Communist organizer in action. It suggests, in a vivid way,

the kind of writing that is likely to be produced when the proletarian novelists leave the circumscribed fields of unsuccessful strikes and industrial disputes and enter the complex realms where the class struggle is hidden in politeness and guile.

Later Cantwell adds, "Miss Lumpkin seems to me to possess a clearer political understanding than any other American novelist. She understands politics, that is, not in the sense of interpreting partisan intrigues and maneuvers, but in the deeper sense of knowing how society—in this case rural and small-town Southern society—is organized and controlled; she understands that such simple entertainments as dinner parties can be analyzed as political gatherings, consolidating or strengthening class and group allegiances."[26]

Cantwell's analysis of how Lumpkin executes her portrait of Southern class relationships is rather vague, and it is clear that once more the promise of her work is greater than the accomplishment. He writes that, while *A Sign for Cain* is, "as a political document, an enlightening book," it leaves the reader dissatisfied aesthetically. Even though Lumpkin was a friend (met via Chambers and Lumpkin's husband, Mike Intrator), Cantwell refuses to ignore the failures of the novel. Cantwell feels that its "weaknesses as a novel are obvious, and arise principally from the fact that the characters are seen too narrowly in their social roles, that they are too consistently true to type, without the elements of waywardness and unpredictability that are as truly possessions as eyes or class background." Nevertheless, he concludes,

> *A Sign for Cain* is a pioneering work and its stereotyped characterizations do not invalidate Miss Lumpkin's contribution. She has shown that an analysis based on an understanding of the class struggle can throw its light on the commonplace activities of upper and middle-class life as well as on the explosions of violence during a strike. In the present status of the literary school with which she identifies herself, that demonstration is almost the most valuable that could be made.[27]

Cantwell titled his review of *A Sign for Cain* "A Sign for the Future," and while it may not reveal much about the direction in which proletarian fiction was headed in 1936, it does suggest a good deal about the direction in which he hoped to take his own work. As his letter to Dos Passos indicated, and as similar remarks addressed to James T. Farrell confirm,[28] Cantwell was dissatisfied with the narrow focus he had employed in *The Land of Plenty*. And as his remarks about the defeated strike formula indicate, he now saw this route as a dead end. But more than this, as an article published early in 1936 makes clear, he felt his own novel and its genre to have been not merely limited but also inaccurate about even that which was within their limited range.

In a *New Republic* article titled "A Town and Its Novels," Cantwell examines *The Land of Plenty* along with two other proletarian novels based on conditions in Aberdeen, Clara Weatherwax's *Marching! Marching!* and Louis Colman's *Lumber* (see chapter four). He finds that all three had failed to portray the labor situation in the early thirties adequately. All three of these novels, Cantwell writes, "have pictured strikes which were strikes of desperation and despair, and in which workers who were very militant but not very sensible took an awful beating at the hands of their exploiters." Cantwell then concentrates his analysis on one of the novels, *Marching! Marching!* the work that won the *New Masses* award as the best proletarian novel of 1935. He describes Weatherwax's book as "melodramatic, full of revolutionary forebodings and violent death.... The characters, for the most part, seem to be communist magicians ... they appear, get involved in the most intricate and terrifying complications, and then, when their troubles have reached a climax, they vanish from the novel, uttering revolutionary sentiments. The book ends when a strike is called and the masses of workers are shown parading towards the ranks of troopers, who are drawn up ready to shoot them down." Cantwell concludes,

> It happens that the labor novels based roughly on the life of Aberdeen have all pictured strikes that had such unhappy conclusions. In actuality, however, the general lumber strike that took place there last year was won hands down—the Sawmill and Timber Workers' Union was recognized, a measure of job control was established, the town as a whole was unionized, the Labor Party elected a few people to office. The lumber strike itself, although it received little publicity, was one of the biggest in American labor history, and the conflict in Aberdeen was decisive in determining the immediate future of the organized labor movement of a whole area and a major industry. But you could never have anticipated that from the general picture of the working class described by the novelists of that center of

Western culture. If you based your judgment on Miss Weatherwax's picture of the workers, or on the pictures of her revolutionary confederates, you might have expected the workers to make a desperate lunge for better conditions; you could not have imagined them going through the sensible drudgery of organization, changing their tactics or winning their strike. They knew that the masses were on the move, but they did not know where they were going; and in their hearts they feared that the militant working class, its ranks solid and its morale high, was marching! marching! smack against a stone wall.[29]

Coming from one of Weatherwax's "revolutionary confederates" (and "homies"), this analysis represents considerable honesty, if not courage.[30] But it raises important issues without suggesting how they might be resolved. And what did it portend regarding Cantwell's own future in the radical movement, particularly his future as a proletarian novelist?

Cantwell answers these questions by implication in a *New Republic* review of a book by Samuel Yellen titled *American Labor Struggles*, a review that appeared only a month after "A Town and Its Novels." Cantwell calls Yellen's book "a broad panorama of ten great labor struggles" that is "the best introductory volume to the history of American labor that has yet appeared." The review suggests that Cantwell had been reading deeply and widely in labor history, and may explain the source of his reevaluation of labor fiction. But he is far from believing that previous mistakes have rendered the whole idea of proletarian fiction suspect. On the contrary, his only major criticism of *American Labor Struggles* is that "Mr. Yellen sticks . . . too close [to the individual strikes surveyed] to give voice to the more daring and poetic insights that you feel must have bubbled up out of so much concentrated thinking on the story of the working class." The book therefore, Cantwell concludes, fails to capture the "'sweep and grandeur' of the American labor movement . . . , qualities which, as Engels once pointed out, could be appreciated more fully by observers in Europe than by those at the scene of conflict."[31]

Clearly Cantwell is still moved by the drama of the American labor movement. And more than this, his assessment of Yellen suggests that far from having lost his desire to write another strike novel, Cantwell now desired to write the greatest strike novel of all, one that would also illuminate complex class relationships reaching even across national boundaries. He notes that Yellen's book ends, "logically," with "the San Francisco general strike, the most complex and widespread struggle in American labor history."[32] Cantwell argues that the general strike reached out to involve every stratum of San Francisco society, and had ramifications for international trade as well. Given the knowledge that Cantwell was then at work on a novel treating this strike and its aftermath, his discussion here may be taken as an indication of the ambitious plans he had for *The Enchanted City*, as he had titled his new manuscript. His faith in the need for and in the potential of fiction based on the struggles of the American working class was apparently undiminished.

In a letter to his editor, John Farrar, in July 1934, Cantwell offered an outline for *The Enchanted City*; the cast of the novel was to include Whittaker Chambers, Sam Darcy (California Communist Party leader during the general strike), Harry Bridges, Ella Winter, Lincoln Steffens, Langston Hughes, Tillie Lerner, and others. It is not entirely clear the extent to which some of these "characters" were to be fictionalized, or how much Cantwell's work on Filene had him thinking in terms of what would later be called the nonfiction novel.

Nor was Cantwell's faith in Marxist criticism shaken, despite the fact that it too had not yet lived up to its promise. He had long felt that the young proletarian novelists were not receiving the kind of critical guidance they needed, and blamed many of their shortcomings on this fact. On several occasions he had urged his friend James Farrell to publish an extensive and tough appraisal of the work of the most promising young radical writers, because, he wrote "there is literally no good criticism of fiction being written" in America.[33] Farrell agreed, and held Granville Hicks of the *New Masses* primarily to blame, at least with respect to criticism by leftists. In January of 1936 Farrell sent Cantwell a satirical manifesto signed by "Johnathan Titelescu Fogarty" and "Abraham Lefkowitz O'Halloran," two "noisy and irresponsible Irishmen," which declared a strike against "the Granville Hicks School of Proletarian Writing and World Literature." Farrell, as a student who had received a "B plus" from Hicks, feigned contempt for these upstart pupils and asked Cantwell to join him in forming "The Literary Sympathizers of Granville Hicks."[34]

Continuing in a more serious vein, Farrell mentioned that he had been discussing with Edmund Wilson, then just returned from a visit to the

Soviet Union, the "depressing state of mediocrity" into which contemporary criticism had declined. Farrell added that he was at work on a book-length attack on vulgar critical practices by writers of the Hicks ilk, and he invited Cantwell to join him for lunch to discuss this and other matters pertaining to the scene on the literary left.[35]

Cantwell accepted the invitation, and soon after their discussion, he wrote to Farrell as follows:

> A note to tell you how much I enjoyed our talk the other day—it cleared my mind of a number of creeping confusions and some worm eaten doubts left there, along with other debris during the period of intense literary political activity. I have only one observation to make that I thought about afterwards and which seems more important than it seemed at the moment. It is this: I have personally hesitated about attacking the hair-splitters of the left because I did not want to be playing Henry Siedel Canby's game for him. As bad as the boys of the *New Masses* are, I think they are still better than the boys at Saturday Review, The Herald Trib, and other papers. This is not a tribute to the N.M. It only means that the Marxian point of view, even if imperfectly grasped and crudely applied, supplies a superior method of criticism than any that our reactionary colleagues can possibly achieve. Bad as Granny [Granville Hicks] is now, he would be a thousand times worse if he did not have the rudimentary understanding of Marx he has picked up. And this isn't said in his defense. All I mean is that the attacks . . . shouldn't be construed as an attack on the method they have adopted and the philosophy they profess.

Cantwell then added that, while he "simply cannot read Hicks, Mike Gold, or Joshua Kunitz," three leading *New Masses* critics, rather than attacking them, he hoped someday to go after the "big shot" conservative critics because "the things we object to in the critics on the left have their source—at least to some extent—in the intellectual depravity of the right."[36]

But if Cantwell was dubious about Farrell's plan to attack the *New Masses*, he was more favorably disposed, at least initially, to another approach to the problem of mediocre leftist literary criticism that his friend had discussed with him. Farrell had suggested that the Marxist literary journal *Partisan Review* showed signs of developing into the kind of sophisticated forum for Marxian criticism that the *New Masses* had failed to become. Thus, with Farrell's encouragement, Cantwell sent a letter to the *Partisan* in February of 1936, congratulating the magazine on its recent merger with the proletarian short-story journal *Anvil*, and expressing his hope that the magazine might take the lead in revitalizing Marxist fiction and criticism. Cantwell also took the opportunity to lash out at the conservative critics, whom he blamed for much of the mediocrity he felt typified American letters in the midthirties:

> Reading a good many unpublished manuscripts and talking with a number of talented writers whose work has not yet received recognition has convinced me that there is a wealth of material awaiting publication, and a large number of writers whose talent would mature if they received the guidance and criticism publication inevitably brings. . . . We have passed the stage of undiscriminating support of writing on the basis of its political and theoretical position. There is a need—a healthy, old-fashioned, crying need—for critical leadership. There is scarcely an established—that is to say, a bourgeois—critic in this country who commands, or deserves even the elementary respect of the younger generation of writers. Their concept of criticism has been reduced to simple logrolling, and they are inexpert and obtuse even in that. Their knowledge of politics, and their understanding of theory, amounts to an inability to deal with either. . . . The combined *Partisan Review and Anvil* has an opportunity to take over intellectual leadership in the field of creative literature such as no other publication in the history of this country has possessed; it can become the dominant influence in the intellectual lives of the serious and sincere writers of this period. The difficulties are enormous, but the potential value to American culture is sufficiently great to justify any and every effort to overcome them.[37]

Cantwell's high hopes for the future of *Partisan Review* were shared by many of the most talented writers and critics on the left, and to some degree they were justified, for throughout 1936 the magazine did sustain a higher level of Marxist critical discourse than had previously been typical of the American left. But *Partisan Review* also fostered just the kind of leftist backbiting which Cantwell had long disdained. And, rather than bringing unity to the intellectual life of the nation, its penetrating analyses of the relationship between literature and politics raised issues that were soon to tear the literary left asunder.

If the *Partisan Review* did not fulfill all of Cantwell's hopes for the future of revolutionary fiction and criticism, developments centered on the *New Masses* were quickly dashing those hopes altogether. As 1936 wore on, it became increasingly clear that the Popular Front policies were leading the *New Masses* wing of the communist movement beyond mere coalition with liberals toward what amounted to capitulation. The Party's liquidation of the John Reed clubs and the spate of left-wing little magazines they had spawned was coming to be seen by many leftists as part of a general plan to eliminate virtually all revolutionary literature because it threatened to alienate important liberals needed to make the Popular Front a success. As early as June of 1936, Joseph Freeman could write glibly in the *New Masses* "of those radical writers who in the 'sectarian' days were engaged in what used to be called proletarian literature."[38] Communist Party financial and moral support for the proletarian movement, always an important aid in the early days, was now completely withdrawn. Critical support from the *New Masses* was similarly withdrawn, gradually, while the new policy of pursuing the support of name writers, regardless of their politics so long as they opposed fascism, left the young radical writers of the proletarian movement behind. In 1936 the number of proletarian novels published dropped by 60 percent from the previous year, and the following year the number declined still further.[39] It must have seemed that Dos Passos had been right and Cantwell wrong; the proletarian literary movement was collapsing.

But the arc of this decline is no doubt much clearer in retrospect than it was to most participants, for if Cantwell sensed that the revolutionary fiction movement was waning, neither his public attitudes nor his private correspondence reflect it. Moreover, the spectacular rise of the CIO during these years, suggesting that at last the workers were rising, clearly reanimated Cantwell's imagination. The publication late in 1937 of Upton Sinclair's *The Flivver King*, for example, brought forth a suggestion from Cantwell for a new genre of workers' literature that seems more in keeping with ideas of the Third Period. Sinclair's biography of Henry Ford had been distributed to 200,000 members of the newly formed United Auto Workers for only twenty-five cents a copy. In a review of *Flivver King* for the *New Republic*, Cantwell praised the biography as an example of "what unions can do in the way of making good relevant writing available for their members, and it suggests subjects for other books that could be of general interest and yet have practical value in union organizing campaigns." He adds that "as a rule, workers know very little about the histories of the companies they work for, or the personalities of the men who dominate them, but they are usually interested in finding out, and a series of books modeled on *The Flivver King* could be a contribution to working-class literature as well as a social survey of importance."[40]

As for Sinclair's book itself, Cantwell finds it basically sound, but, like the Yellen book he had reviewed a year and a half earlier, he thought that the biography failed to capture the excitement of working-class history. It failed to give a sense of the "tremendous drama of Detroit—the Auto Workers rising in the greatest drive in trade-union [sic] history, the tragic factional fights in its leadership, the national issues at stake in its current battle with Ford—when you think of the book in relation to the personal rivalries, you see that it does not throw light where illumination is urgently needed. . . . We need to know more: the subtler influences that paralyze organizations of workers from within; the sources of the conflicts that enfeeble them or prevent them from realizing their aims."[41]

A few months earlier, in a *New Republic* essay assessing the achievements of Sinclair in his long career as a writer and activist, Cantwell had indicated even more clearly that his faith in the radical literary movement was undiminished. At the close of the article he wrote,

> [Sinclair] is the first important American novelist to see in the struggle between capital and labor the driving force of modern industry; he has hammered away for a lifetime at the cruelties and injustices of exploitation as well as at the grossness and insensitivity of life among the exploiters, and his books, with all their unevenness and vacillations, have a simple literal honesty about them that makes the work of most of his contemporaries seem evasive and affected. . . . In his concern with the moral aspects of exploitation, his strong religious feeling, his indifference to Marxian theory, his reformism and his hope for a peaceful solution of the class struggle, he has been the outstanding literary representative of the Second International, in the way that a writer of the type of André Malraux—intense, defiant, scornful—promises to become the voice in fiction of the hard-pressed and violent life of the Third.[42]

Cantwell's mood in this passage probably reflects the exhilaration that passed through the American left during the early stages of the Spanish Civil War. But events in Spain and in the workers' fatherland itself soon sent sentiments of a very different kind sweeping across the American left.

Beginning in 1936 periodic reports reached America of startling and confusing events taking place in the Soviet Union. Each new report of the trials of former Soviet officials accused of treason by Stalin raised new doubts about the Soviet leader's charges. A number of Cantwell's closest and most respected colleagues, including Dos Passos, Farrell, and Edmund Wilson, were convinced by 1937 that the trials were not trials at all but frame-ups disguising a brutal play for power.[43] All three of these writers, further, took part in an investigation, headed by John Dewey, into the specific charges brought against Leon Trotsky. The investigators found Trotsky innocent, and as a result his prestige as the leader of the most vociferous communist opposition to the reformist policies of the Communist Party grew enormously. Trotsky's claim that Stalin had betrayed and distorted the heritage of the Russian Revolution appeared more and more plausible to many American Marxists. Cantwell's friend Farrell was only one of many literary leftists who joined, or at least flirted with, the Trotskyists in the period from 1936 to 1938. More important, in 1937, *Partisan Review*, after briefly suspending publication, reemerged as a virulent anti-Stalinist quarterly still dedicated to communism but increasingly skeptical of attempts to unite politics and literature.

At the same time, such old friends of Cantwell's as Newton Arvin and Malcolm Cowley remained ardent supporters of the Party, the latter going so far as to write an intricate defense of the Moscow Trials for the *New Republic*. At the same time, commitment to the struggle against fascism in Spain gave new impetus to the broader Popular Front social movement. Soon, however, the complexities of the Spanish civil war would add further fuel to the growing anti-Stalinist movement on the left. Reports in the *Partisan Review* and elsewhere charged the Soviet Union with subverting the cause in Spain by encouraging the Loyalists to attack Spanish anarchists and Trotskyists. These reports seemed incredible, but when John Dos Passos returned from Spain, he gave eyewitness substantiation to the charges. Indeed, the war between the various radical factions in Spain so disgusted him that he began a rapid retreat to the far right.[44]

Throughout this period of charges and countercharges, conversions and counterconversions, Cantwell continued to plot his novel *The Enchanted City*, but apparently not actually to write it. Reports that it was near completion appeared in the *New Republic*. Once the magazine reported in its biographical information on contributors that Cantwell's new novel would be "published late in the spring [1937] by Farrar and Rinehart."[45] Either Farrar or Cantwell may have encouraged this announcement to spur the writing. But the novel did not appear, and in 1938 Cantwell's friend John Chamberlain suggested the difficulties Cantwell was experiencing in trying to complete his new strike novel. Without mentioning Cantwell by name, Chamberlain uses him to illustrate the difficulty many radical writers were experiencing in the late thirties:

> The dilemma of the socially conscious writer is illustrated by a young novelist of my acquaintance who has been trying for several years to finish a book about the San Francisco Waterfront strike of 1934. He cannot finish the book because he is all at sea concerning the motivating philosophy behind it. From month to month and year to year his attitude towards the personal value of his protagonist keeps fluctuating with the movement of radical values, of radical morality, in a world of Moscow trials, undeclared wars, "Trojan horse" tactics, and political "timing" that frequently works out into two-timing.[46]

The doubts and disequilibria engendered by the course of world events bearing down upon Cantwell were increased by life at *Time*. As his friend and coworker there, T. S. Matthews, recalls, by 1937 their plan to share the post of book editor in six-month cycles had collapsed as both of them "got caught up in the machinery," eventually finding themselves working full-time in the *Time* office. And working full-time for the demanding Henry Luce often meant six or seven days a week and several thousand words of copy each issue.[47] Moreover, the *Time* office itself in the late thirties was a microcosm of the ideological conflicts then raging in America—the staff included New Dealers, Communist Party stalwarts, Trotskyists, and middle-of-the-roaders, in addition to those who shared the conservative views of editor Luce. And as World War II approached, tension on the staff intensified.[48]

Cantwell's correspondence during the late thirties makes it clear that both his work as a journalist and his ideological uncertainties were factors in his inability to complete *The Enchanted City*. To a cousin back in the state of Washington he wrote, "Working at *Time* is making it difficult for me to finish my third [novel], which deals with San Francisco."[49] And to poet Weldon Keys he wrote that his manuscript of the new novel was too full of the "changing moods and changing styles and changing opinions" of the period of its composition.[50]

Cantwell's opinions were still in flux as late as January of 1939, but they were moving steadily in a conservative direction. I will speculate in the next chapter about the variety of forces behind that transformation, but it is clear that the change would prove the undoing of Cantwell as a novelist. In February of 1938, Cantwell was still capable of defending the Communists charged by Benjamin Stolberg of having "infiltrated" the CIO in massive numbers.[51] The essay reflects Cantwell's continuing belief in the need to rework American literature to represent seriously the dramatic story of the laboring classes, to capture the laboring of American culture going on all over the country. The piece ends with a renewed call for "a working class literature—candid and realistic accounts of every strike, the set-up of every industrial town, matters of policy and strategy and disputes within and without—that by its very existence would make [distorted writing] like Stolberg's impossible."[52]

But by this time Cantwell was already urging his friend Chambers to leave the Party, and when he did so Cantwell found him a job at *Time* as a book reviewer. Cantwell gave *Time* associate editor T. S. Matthews one of Chambers's *New Masses* stories, urging him to see in it qualities reminiscent of André Malraux. In one of his memoirs, Matthews recalls that the story had led him to expect a somewhat dashing and heroic character. But when Matthews met the unprepossessing and unkempt Chambers, his main impression was that "there was such a suppressed air of melodrama about him that I should not have been greatly surprised if one day a Communist gunman shot him down in the office corridors."[53] As we will see, Cantwell's increasing entanglement in Chambers's melodramatic life would shape *his* life for many years to come.

By the time of the signing of the Nazi-Soviet Non-Aggression Pact in August of 1939, Cantwell was convinced that Hitler and Stalin were equally dangerous representatives of totalitarian political regimes. And two months after the pact was signed, he could pass the following harsh judgment on his former comrades: "The Communists modeled their press on the worst performances of those they presented as their enemy, and in their hysteria, vindictiveness and fatalism, belonged with Hearst rather than with the working class which, like Hearst, they claimed to represent."[54]

In a sense Cantwell had anticipated the outcome of his odyssey through the literary left of the thirties in an article written in 1937 while he was still an ardent fellow traveler. A propos of Henry James's deep personal disappointment at not having foreseen the approach of World War I, Cantwell wrote at the time that, "to [some] extent every writer must set himself up as a prophet. It is not part of his task to conceive the exact sequence of coming events, but his general picture must square with the literal living history of his time and his dramas—the motives he ascribes to people, the potentialities he sees in them—must line up with the actual conduct of masses as it becomes known in crisis." Thus, when the Great War arrived, catching him by "surprise," Cantwell observes, James felt that he had "somehow missed the real drama of his time." "The implication was obvious [to James]," Cantwell continues, "history had become the most savage critic of his work. A true representation of a society or of a class is a revelation of its future, and if his pictures of the society he knew best had been true, no such development [as the War] could have taken him so completely by surprise . . . or left him at such a loss in facing it and trying to understand it."[55]

By 1939, history, as he then interpreted it, had become a most savage critic of Cantwell's own work, and the hubristic words about the prophetic power of literature with which he closes this essay seem to stand in judgment of his own efforts:

> The miniature world of [the novel] is not only a representation of the social environment [the author] observes around him. It is also his implicit judgment of what the future holds in store for the social equivalents of the types he creates, and an infallible revelation of his outlook on the future of the class to which he is tied. It is his task to isolate and lift into consciousness the invisible connectives between the little things of daily living within the normal life of that class . . . and the great upheavals of the past and the volcanic upheavals of the future; to dramatize and make concrete

the secret ties between the common life and the sweep of historical movements. This is the primary function of fiction and criticism. Only when it has been realized can we become steadily conscious of the potential significance of our lives, and be made to see that the minute coral atoms of our acts are inevitably building the structure of history. When it is evaded the end is as it was with James—the catastrophes and surprises of life so "belie" the imagination's products as to force them out of the mind and prevent their being written at all.[56]

The "implication was obvious" to Cantwell in the late thirties. Swept up by dramatic images of historical change, he had failed to see that the "secret ties" between socialism and the common life of most Americans were not being made strongly enough. Worse still, lost in the drama of a sweeping historical movement, Cantwell had failed to observe the many signs that the Soviets were betraying his vision. The piece also reflected his growing concern that a new world war was approaching. Thus, at the decade's close, the "catastrophes and surprises" of life had so belied "his imagination's products as to force them out of his mind and prevent their being written at all." That savagely capricious critic, History, left Cantwell at such a loss in "facing" or "trying to understand" his past as to send him reeling in disillusionment toward almost total repudiation of a decade of effort. But another, subtler rereading of his remarks on James might have led him to other conclusions. For the further lesson here is that Jamesian withdrawal or aesthetic neutrality is no better guarantee of prophetic insight into the vicissitudes of social change than is Marxist commitment. The rapid ideological shifts of the late thirties were certainly cause for soul-searching, for exploring the contingent nature of historical and literary judgment. But it is far from clear that the errors of the decade should issue in a blanket indictment of politically committed literature and criticism. Such a reaction was and is in its own way as misguided as the most dogmatic reactions of the putative "literary commissars."

7 BREAKING DOWN, MOVING ON, LOOKING BACK

Cantwell in the Wake of the 1930s

"Robert Cantwell, literary leftist" ceases to exist with the end of the nineteen thirties. But to understand that earlier Robert Cantwell more fully, it is necessary to know something of his life in the wake of the thirties, to understand the ways in which the decade did not leave him, even as he, in many ways, left it behind. Before turning to my final assessment of his work in the context of the thirties and the larger question of the "reworking of American literature," I need to explore briefly the twists of Cantwell's fascinating post-thirties life and career, and to critically examine Cantwell's late rethinking and reimagining of the decade.

As suggested at the end of the last chapter, Cantwell began a slow drift toward the right in the latter part of the thirties, and "drift," at least initially, appears to be the correct term. There does not appear to have been a dramatic, revelatory break such as that experienced by his colleague Whittaker Chambers and other famous converters from Communism. Cantwell's rightward movement was subtle and had a number of complex components, including financial and familial pressures, a deepening involvement in mainstream journalism and the Luce milieu, and mental instability that may at once have been cause and effect, as well as the broader shifting historical currents, especially the Nazi-Soviet Pact and the coming of World War II.

Despite Cantwell's bravura in predicting the imminent demise of capitalism, some of his letters during the thirties reveal a deeply insecure man. That personal insecurity was partly driven, and was certainly compounded, by constant financial insecurity. By decade's end he had two children to feed, clothe, and care for (daughters Joan and Elizabeth Ann were born in 1932 and 1937, respectively; the third daughter, Mary Elizabeth, was born in 1943). In addition to his immediate family, Cantwell often had to send money both to his family members in Arizona and the state of Washington, and to his wife's family in Baton Rouge, all of whom had been hard-hit by the Depression and frequently looked to him for financial assistance. Like his father before him, Cantwell struggled to stay above water. At the same time, his wife, a not very political person from a traditional Southern family with strong religious convictions, no doubt pulled him away from radicalism for both temperamental and practical reasons. But given his public cautiousness, it is reasonable to conclude that Cantwell's views and associations throughout the decade were more left than is apparent. As noted, his involvement with Chambers entailed at least one request to engage in clandestine activity. In late April 1934, Cantwell was asked by Chambers's friend John Sherman to write a book about the DuPont Corporation in the hope that through his contacts via Filene he could help the Russians infiltrate the company records of this major arms manufacturer. Although tempted by the offer of $25,000 for the job, Cantwell declined this opportunity to engage in Soviet espionage. Whether there were other such unrecorded episodes we do not know, but his association with Chambers certainly increased Cantwell's long-standing tendency to be overly cautious, not to say mildly paranoid, in protecting his privacy in regard to his political views and activities.[1] Critic John Chamberlain, who, like Cantwell, was among those moving to the right at the end of the thirties, recalls that "[Cantwell's] wife Betsy distrusted the Communists, but Bob, caught up in a growing movement, became implicated with them in ways that made him uncomfortable even though he considered it his duty to be a revolutionist."[2]

Cantwell's job at *Time* was the first more-or-less full-time regular job he had held since arriving in New York in 1931. Originally, he struck a deal with T. S. Matthews to share the book-reviewing responsibilities in six-month shifts, with the plan being to have the other six months free to write fiction. But both the difficulties of the fiction he undertook, and financial need, made the job full-time, and eventually it came to overwhelm all else. Some sense of Cantwell's mood can be gleaned already in this letter to Matthews composed in February of 1936, and the pressures and troubles mentioned only grew from then on: "I have got to get settled down to some kind of concrete program for my [writing] and for my life itself—I am getting so God damned rattled and so crowded with so many obligations in so many directions that it is becoming literally impossible for me to concentrate on any one. I am in that deplorable state of mind that comes when the saturation point of fruitless trouble and unresolved—in terms of writing—worries—is reached. I am fed up with 'Time,' book reviewing, the steel workers, politics; I am fed up with trying to get Wilson to write anything."[3]

Surely overwhelming also was the influence of Henry Luce and his infamous empire. Life at *Time* and *Fortune*, deadline pressures notwithstanding, initially offered a taste of and thirst for more security. This included not only a degree of financial security but also the security of being close to someone like Luce with the kind of undeniable social power that led him to meet routinely with the highest-ranking officers of government and heads of state from around the world. This must have seemed like the "real world" compared to the rather more low-level power plays of left literary circles. Where proximity to E. A. Filene had bred only contempt and a little pity in Cantwell, proximity to the mighty Mr. Luce bred some quite different things—initially an awe that slowly evolved toward respect and friendship. That respect appears to have been mutual, since Luce moved Cantwell quickly from the relative backwater job of book reviewer to more and more central roles in *Time*. In 1939 Cantwell produced a series of articles called "Background of War" that he later claimed represented the best writing he ever did. The series won him a post in the increasingly central "Foreign Affairs" section at the magazine. Researching and writing the articles convinced Cantwell deeply of the need for US involvement in what became World War II, and drew him closer to the interventionist Luce.

Cantwell's deepening interventionist views meant that the Nazi-Soviet or Hitler-Stalin pact of 1939, a move that proved a hard blow to many literary and political leftists, hit him particularly strongly. Still, his diary of the time reveals that even after the pact he attempted for a time to justify the Communist position. His move from pro-interventionist to anti-Communist evolved over many months. But by late 1939 he could note in his diary, "Talked with [Calvin] Fixx—Politics, the end of the left."[4] Such conversations with his old friend Fixx, whom he had helped find work at *Time* as he had Chambers, apparently became common. By the early forties Cantwell, Fixx, and Chambers were identified, along with Cantwell's old friend Chamberlain, as forming a "violently anti-communist" clique at the journal. Chamberlain mockingly refers to this group as "an anti-Communist cell" within Luceland.[5] Chambers, still years away from becoming America's most infamous FBI informer, apparently regaled the circle with endless tales of Communist treachery, and offered them tactical advice on how to anticipate and outmaneuver the Party members at *Time*.[6] An FBI report summarizing one of their many interviews with Chambers reports the latter's recollections of Cantwell in the late thirties as follows:

> Chambers indicated that when he broke with the Communist Party in 1938, he trusted ROBERT CANTWELL to the point where he was willing to provide him with his address. In turn, CANTWELL gave him odd jobs, helped him and loaned him money. During the period, however, ROBERT CANTWELL remained close to the Communist Party in spite of CHAMBERS severance from it. CHAMBERS stated further that ROBERT CANTWELL maintained his Communist Party affiliations until the time of the Russian-German Pact. At just about that time, CANTWELL was writing a series of articles for "Time" entitled, "Background of War." When the above-mentioned pact was signed, according to CHAMBERS, CANTWELL wrote a "humdinger" concerning what had happened to Marxist's ideas. As a result of this article, the Communists employed at "Time" Magazine berated ROBERT CANTWELL extensively.[7]

The "humdinger" of an article in question was titled "The Future of American Journalism," and it no doubt added fuel to the incendiary atmosphere among *Time* personnel.

According to his friend T. S. Matthews, Cantwell was as "out of place" in this heated *Time* milieu as a "canary in a coal mine." From Matthews's point of view the situation led to his friend's undoing: "He never published another novel and his career at *Time* ended in a breakdown."[8] Both Malcolm Cowley and Granville Hicks also felt that Cantwell's political move to the right was his undoing as a fiction writer.[9] The picture is more complicated than that, but there is a kernel of truth in it. Leftist critic F. W. Dupee, running into Cantwell in the later forties, thought he seemed "a stranger, an amnesiac." Dupee discussed the matter with Edmund Wilson, who "thought Cantwell a tragic victim of Stalinism, the anti-Stalinism of Chambers, the Luce publications ambiance, and his marriage to the fiercely possessive little Betsy."[10]

Mary McCarthy did not share her ex-husband Wilson's view of figures who moved from left to right as tragic.[11] She rather saw them more as comic and bathetic figures that moved too easily across political and intellectual positions. McCarthy, who worked under Cowley at *New Republic* in the late thirties, also occasionally was "on loan" to assist Cantwell. McCarthy's short story "Portrait of the Intellectual as a Yale Man," composed mostly in Cantwell's New York apartment, which she sublet in 1941, draws apparently upon figures such as Chamberlain, Cowley, and Dwight Macdonald in her unflattering composite portrait of a man for whom ideas and real-life consequences somehow disconnect. Her memories of Cantwell are more positive—as she put it in her memoirs, "Cantwell was nice, Cowley was not"—and he may have been the source of some of the more positive dimensions of her portrait. But if McCarthy had a corrosive view of literary communism, she had an even more corrosive view of literary Lucism. McCarthy's knowledge of the Luce world was intimate, and her views of it are suggestive. She argues throughout the story and in her memoirs that Luceland subtly corrupted fiction writers such as Cantwell through many interconnected forces, including an assembly-line production process that ultimately distanced the writer from responsibility for their words, the safety and refuge provided by relying almost exclusively on the gathering of "facts" as the basis of one's views, and the seductive self-importance that came from being close to real power.

Matthew Josephson, writing in 1977, recalls that Cantwell "turned ambitious at the *Time* mill; then one day Luce promoted four men ahead of him, and he cracked up. . . . Small, frail, timid, Cantwell broke down, went to a mental institution. Luce, guilty, paid for his treatment for years." Josephson adds, gratuitously, "I remember that his Louisiana cracker wife Betsy used to beat him up just for fun."[12] This portrait is no doubt colored by Josephson's disappointment at Cantwell's rightward turn, and his suspicion that his former friend had "named names" during the McCarthy era. And, as we will see, the story does not jibe with Cantwell's account of the same incident.

Clearly many folks have speculated about the matter, but what did Cantwell himself think about his own transformation and breakdown? In a letter to Ernest Hemingway in 1950, Cantwell offered a self-assessment that seems to me to correctly identify many, though not all, of the forces that undid him as a novelist. In the letter to which Cantwell is responding, Hemingway had asked about why Cantwell had ceased to write, or at least publish, fiction. Cantwell's reply begins superficially and moves haltingly back and forth in time, but eventually offers a rather full revelation of the forces at play:

> As for why I haven't done any more novels—I haven't had time enough. The first two were pretty hasty. I usually spent two years on the first third of them and three weeks on the last two-thirds. The problem was usually trying to raise a couple of hundred dollars rent to keep from being evicted. After The Land of Plenty was published I got a job with *Time* and worked there from 1935 to 1942 without a break—usually a couple thousand words of copy a week, the money being ample compensation for not having to write any more novels, or at least not under [such] conditions.

Cantwell then describes the Filene fiasco, which not only wasted his literary energies but left him broke and ready to leap at the chance to work for *Time*. He goes on:

> I got about a third of another novel done in my first two years [at *Time*]. Before the war, things got pretty tense in the office. Most of the staff was isolationist and a lot of them were New Dealers and quite a few were party members. By the time of the Nazi-Soviet pact I was practically the only member of the staff who was not. Since Luce was not, I did a hell of a lot of writing directly under him, by-passing the staff and in some cases the editors. This did not make for very cordial relations except with him.

Not very cordial indeed. Clearly the already tense political atmosphere was made far worse by perceived favoritism toward Cantwell. This pushed him further into Luce's political and personal orbit. The various stresses began to affect Cantwell's mental stability, and even when he describes it more than a decade later, his thoughts seem confused:

> However, things kept happening, and finally it got so bad that whenever I wrote anything good somebody would call me up and tell me some other catastrophe had taken place, or one of the children had been taken to the hospital, and I gave up trying to combine literature and journalism. Or, rather, I thought for a while, I could blur it until we got in a better position. Also, I found that there was a definite physical effect after a while, and

certain subjects connected with this period, whenever I began to write on them in any way that had any impact, made me extremely uncomfortable.

Cantwell goes on to tell Hemingway that, unlike in Josephson's version, about the time of Pearl Harbor, Luce offered him the assistant managing editorship of the magazine, but that he turned it down, "largely because I knew how vulnerable we—meaning the people who were not isolationists or New Dealers or party members—were."

> All three of us: Chambers, myself, and a friend of mine who has since died [Fixx]. Shortly thereafter I found it difficult to concentrate. I sent the family South [to my wife's parents'] and tried to settle down to work, but couldn't make it, and after a few days yelled for help and asked the friend . . . to put me in a sanitarium. My knowledge of them was extremely limited, but I thought I'd be able to sleep. They damn near killed me in the first one. My wife returned in time to get me out of that one. In the second—by this time I couldn't talk above a whisper, or say anything coherent if I did—they really gave me the works, but in a nicer way, and after the electric therapy [sic] and the insulin therapy I was sufficiently pleased to be still alive not to worry about not writing novels.

Cantwell concludes, "That is the fullest explanation I can give you. I have recovered to the point where I can get around with a car and a companion and not too exacting a routine of work."[13]

The "nervous breakdown" was clearly severe if after almost a decade he is still in such a state. In fact, he spent seven months (March to October 1942) in the New York State Hospital in White Plains. When released, as is clear from the passage above, he was not in any condition to return to work. In addition to ideological pressures and stress at *Time*, Cantwell became involved in an extramarital affair with a staffer, and the discovery of the infidelity no doubt also contributed to his collapse (his letters from the hospital include several tortured apologies to his wife). Electroshock and insulin therapies were the standard treatments of the day, and Cantwell underwent a full battery of both. He emerged from the hospital in many ways a shadow of his former self, and in certain respects he never fully recovered, at least in terms of accessing the full range of his personality.

Upon Cantwell's release, Luce, one of his few visitors in the hospital, gave him an unprecedented severance package from *Time* that allowed him to purchase a small farm near Sherman, Connecticut. Some *Time* writers saw this as a gesture of guilt, others as an act of sincere friendship. In any event, in the peace and quiet of the countryside, Cantwell spent the next several years working on a biography of Nathaniel Hawthorne. As he explained to Hemingway, "I wrote the Hawthorne [book] when I got out of the hospital in order to get used to writing again. I couldn't write anything very close to me without beginning to shake. Hawthorne seemed the ideal subject . . . sufficiently academic so I wouldn't be getting into the kind of skullduggery that made foreign news and national affairs pretty hazardous toward the end."[14] The Hawthorne book proved a financial disaster upon publication in 1948, and Cantwell, apparently having exhausted his pension from Luce, freelanced some, while his family continued to rely as well on his wife's earnings as a nursery school teacher.

Any peace and quiet his life in Connecticut may have provided was soon shattered, however, by the rise of McCarthyism and Cantwell's entanglement in the spy case that was second only to the Rosenberg case as a cause célèbre in the era of anti-Communist witch hunts. When Chambers made his decision in the late 1940s to answer inquiries from the FBI with the claim that he had helped state department employee Alger Hiss pass secrets to the Soviets, it was inevitable that Cantwell would be drawn into the profoundly murky affair. In large part because of his apparent closeness to Chambers, several of Cantwell's former acquaintances assumed that he had become an informer, and they were correct, although it is not clear that he "named names."[15] Cantwell became an informer for the FBI (Confidential Informant T-11, interviewed October 12, 1950)[16] in the emerging context of the Hiss-Chambers spy controversy, the climactic event of his long and troubled association with Chambers. But, as we will see, Cantwell's attitude toward Chambers was far from wholly positive, and his association with America's most famous ex-Communist "witness" continued to haunt Cantwell until his death.

The files don't suggest that Cantwell had much to add to the Hiss-Chambers case. He was probably only asked to confirm some claims made by Chambers, and it is unlikely that he could have done so with much conviction, since at the end of his life he himself was still unsure as to whether his late (and at that point not lamented) colleague Chambers had really been a spy. The FBI files on Cantwell reveal that the situation was just as confusing to the most famous investigators in America. They could not fully distinguish Cantwell from Chambers, mostly because the latter had once used the alias Lloyd Cantwell, but also because the question of Chambers's sanity was much in question from the Hiss camp. Cantwell's institutionalization was one source of a mistaken rumor pursued by Hiss's lawyers that Chambers had been in a mental hospital.

The FBI was also initially reluctant to approach Cantwell. Knowing of his mental instability, they began their investigation via acquaintances and with discreet inquires in the neighborhood of his Sherman, Connecticut, home. The result of those inquiries was typically contradictory. One unnamed informant, probably a colleague from *Time*, remembered Cantwell as a member of the Communist Party before the time he knew him, but said Cantwell had "renounced Communism in 1938–41 and now appeared violently anti-Communist." Testimony from Chambers himself from 1949 is more ambiguous on the membership question. Chambers said that during the period after he left the Party, Cantwell was one of the very few folks he could trust. As quoted above, he claimed that Cantwell "remained close to the party" after Chambers's own break, but that this changed at the time of the Russian-German Pact. Chambers told the FBI that around that time Cantwell wrote a "humdinger" concerning what had happened to Marxist ideas, for which the Communists at *Time* "berated Cantwell extensively." The humdinger was as noted "The Future of American Journalism," in which Cantwell denounced the Communist press as being no better than Hearst, and asserted that both the right and the left had equally betrayed the American worker.[17]

Cantwell had steered clear of Chambers for the most part after his breakdown, but was drawn back into his orbit first by the Hiss trial and then by Chambers's best-selling memoir, *Witness*. When that book was about to be published in 1951, letters exchanged between Chambers and his good friend *Newsweek* writer Ralph de Toledano recount an intrigue that potentially places Cantwell's radicalism in a new light. Here is Chambers's account.

> This has to be brief and to the point. Last night I got a curious call from Bob Cantwell . . . I have been on the point of mentioning him and certain relevant matters to you, but refrained on the theory that talking about

unfortunate things only gives them a false life. He still seems to have some very odd ideas which do not conform to reality....

Long ago he communicated with me and made it clear that he did not want me to say anything [in *Witness* or in his Hiss testimony] that could hurt his job. From what you have read of the book, you will recognize, I think, that I've actually stretched a point to let him off the hook.[18]

What does Chambers mean here by "stretching a point" to get Cantwell "off the hook"? Since there is only one substantive mention of Cantwell's politics in *Witness*, Chambers is no doubt referring to this passage:

[My friend Robert] Cantwell had asked me whether he should take the job *Time* had offered him. I had urged him to, in part because I thought the experience and the salary would do him good, in part because, at the back of my mind, was the thought that my having a friend at *Time* might some time be useful to the underground. The Communist mind works in that thrifty way. Cantwell, of course, was not a Communist and knew nothing about what was on my mind. He was one of the people who urged me to break away from the Communist Party.[19]

In his letter to Toledano, Chambers expresses fear that Cantwell might be planning to review *Witness* negatively in *Newsweek*, and asks Toledano to try to get the review assigned to someone else, without apparent success, since the review was later published much to their displeasure. In the letter, after making his plea for a reassignment of the review, Chambers goes on to say why he doesn't believe that Cantwell can review his book dispassionately, and to clarify what he means by the "stretch" about Cantwell:

I don't believe Bob can do a good review of it. By that I mean that I think the whole subject lies close to one of his personal storm centers and that whenever he approaches that field all the instruments begin to whirl around and the magnetic needle always points south. I don't think I have ever been into his story with you; he was much more involved than I have ever admitted to anyone—and am trusting you to shield him too, for he needs his job and has suffered terribly. Lest there be any misreading of this he was never involved directly in espionage. But we were close friends from 1932 [to] '40.[20]

In the published version of this letter, Toledano, writing in 1997, offers the following bracketed editorial interjection to introduce Cantwell: "book editor at *Newsweek*, who had been deep in the underground Party. Once a close friend, Chambers had used the name Lloyd Cantwell when he broke with the *apparat* and was fleeing from the GPU (KGB)." It is not clear if this is Toledano's interpretation of Chambers's letter, or if the latter provided more direct information in conversation, for it seems difficult to square the charge that Cantwell was "deep in the underground" with Chambers's own statement that he was "never directly involved in espionage." The implication seems to be that Cantwell may have aided and abetted Chambers's activities. Was this more than the well-documented financial support Cantwell had offered? Was it Chambers developing a cover story if he felt the need to smear Cantwell publicly as a spy or abettor of spies? Does it cast new light on Chambers's claim that he was delighted when Cantwell began working for *Time* because it might provide Chambers a mole in the Luce empire?

If Cantwell had been "much more involved" than the public record indicates, it certainly would have deepened the pressure he felt under in the time leading up to his breakdown. Is it possible that Cantwell worked, like Chambers, for the Communist underground? Yes. Is it likely? I think not. There is nothing in the private record to indicate such involvement, but of course one would not expect to find it. There are some sealed sections of the Robert Cantwell Papers that might conceivably offer some evidence. But I believe an underground life would have been inconsistent with the cautiousness that characterized much of Cantwell's life and career. My best supposition is that Chambers is simply trying to enlist Toledano's cooperation by leaving ambiguous the question of whether Cantwell did more than indirectly assist Chambers on occasion through such documented acts as lending him money.

In subsequent letters, Chambers and Toledano each reiterate charges that Cantwell was not in touch with reality, especially once his review of *Witness* appeared in May 1952. Chambers wrote, "Cantwell's review is truly a shocker. It seems to me that if the least responsible editors at *Newsweek* had put their heads together to devise how best to blur the meaning of the Hiss case and the book, and do the maximum disservice to both, this is what they would have come up with." The clearly angry Toledano tries to make light of the review, claiming that it "did not bother me as much as it might because I know that Cantwell has gone quietly mad; he lives in a world of dervishes."[21] Toledano's 1997 editorial notes add, "The review by Robert Cantwell was not only unintelligent but disingenuous. It was motivated largely by Cantwell's fear of being linked to Chambers and to his own Communist past—which he kept well hidden from his editors—and from a deep trauma and a discordancy of emotion. For this reason, he withdrew from those of his fellow editors who had strongly anti-Communist views. . . . Cantwell was close to a nervous breakdown and left *Newsweek* not too long afterwards."[22]

The *Witness* review in question was titled "The Chambers Story," and the title suggests precisely the tenor of Cantwell's piece—Cantwell insinuates throughout that Chambers's memoir is best approached as a work of fiction. Cantwell writes, for example, "Chambers' account of his underground life is the best of its sort in American literature, a masterpiece of casual melodrama whose dry realities and somber overtones would alone rank it, if it were a novel, with the great romantic narratives." The review is careful to work through indirection ("*if* it were a novel"), but at a time when Chambers's testimony about Hiss was at the heart of an ongoing national debate in which the (in)former was precisely accused of having made up the espionage story, the implications would indeed be "a shocker" for the Chambers camp. Cantwell ends "The Chambers Story" by pressing the fiction angle once more, hinting of his personal knowledge of the "witness," and articulating a position not dissimilar to a view of his old comrade he had expressed upon first meeting him years earlier:

> Twenty years ago, when he first entered the underground life, he had a gift for picking out of the social air phrases of common speech that sounded something like Tolstoy, perhaps a line spoken by a hitchhiker he had picked up on the road, or a waitress in a restaurant where he ate alone. His autobiography has the power of a novel, almost a very great novel, but it seems so not so much because he has organized the confused welter of happenings that make up a life as because he has organized his life along the lines of a work of fiction.[23]

Is Cantwell attacking Chambers's credibility to distract from his own disingenuousness? Or does he know as well as anyone the mix of fantasy and reality that surrounded Chambers?

Certainly Chambers and Toledano stuck to their story. Counter-claims of Cantwell's "distance from reality" are repeated in subsequent letters between the two anti-Communist crusaders. Cantwell's earlier mental breakdown no doubt provided plausibility for them to draw upon. In a commentary on Cantwell's review of some controversies surrounding T. E. Lawrence (of Arabia), Chambers writes, "I do not know enough about psychoanalytic matters to be sure of my ground. But I find myself wondering: if a quiet little man really wanted, with all his heart and soul, to be, say, Lawrence of Arabia, but failed in reality—might he not then, by a wrench of the mind, transform himself into an unreality of Lawrence, or his like; and take revenge on the reality because, all the while, he deeply senses his unreality as unreal?"[24] In a complex dance of ironies and defensiveness, Chambers is here accusing his old friend of just the kind of deluded self-importance many critics, including Cantwell, leveled against Chambers over the years. As we will see, up until his death Cantwell sought to get the last word on the matter, though as it turned out he got it only in the "privacy" of his unpublished work.

The Hiss-Chambers episode colored much of Cantwell's first return to Luceland after his breakdown. Cantwell had found his way back into the corporation only in 1949, following a decade-long absence, just when the Hiss case was emerging. Thus he may indeed have been fearful of losing his job over the events. But he held on in the once again hotly politicized world of the journal until 1954. After that, he entered another period of freelancing, then returned a third and final time to the Luce fold with *Sports Illustrated* in 1961. Cantwell stayed with the sports journal until his retirement in 1973, by which time he had become a senior editor. His strategy during all of those years following the Hiss-Chambers episode seemed to be to stay as far away as possible from politics in his published writing. Indeed, one cannot help but see a pattern of moving as far into safely nonpolitical territory as possible. Thus, the books and articles he wrote during the rest of his career were mostly divided between writing about nature and writing about sports, including biographies of an American naturalist, *Alexander Wilson: Naturalist and Pioneer* (1961), and of boxer Kid McCoy, *The Real McCoy: The Life and Times of Norman Selby* (1971). Cantwell's one attempt to write a book about some of the contemporary writers he had known—James Farrell, Erskine Caldwell, William Faulkner, and Ernest Hemingway—was published in the form of a children's introduction to "famous men of letters," thus enabling all controversial dimensions of the writing and its context to be smoothly side-stepped.[25]

Cantwell also seemed to find comfort and safety in physically and imaginatively returning to the homeland he knew before entering the complexities of New York City. Late in his life, for example, Cantwell made one foray into regional history, *The Hidden Northwest* (1972), a kind of personal travelogue that includes a section on Northwest writers, conspicuously missing from which are two fine novels by Robert Cantwell. He also made one attempt at historical fiction, a novel he planned to call *Small Boston*. The title refers to the word Northwest Indians used for white people, "bostons," and the title character is a young (hence small) "boston" boy who ventures into mid-nineteenth-century Washington state. The novel is based partly in fact (the small boston is modeled on the historical figure Jesse McCrae), and involves sympathetic portraits of a famous runaway slave who miraculously made it across the country to the Pacific Northwest, as well as sympathetic, if rather stiff, portraits of local Indians. The work, begun as early as 1953 but worked on mostly in his later years, is of little literary interest, but it shows Cantwell late in life exploring what we might now term ecological and multicultural themes, as well as relishing the imagined simplicity of an earlier time.[26]

But through all this Cantwell was apparently never able fully to let go of the 1930s. In the last years of his life, from his retirement in 1973 to his death in 1978, he thought about and began tentative work on another nonfiction novel, this one treating his own life as entangled with the strange career of Whittaker Chambers. The book never progressed much beyond an outline, but it gives a clear sense of how Cantwell looked back upon his career and the turmoil of the literary left. Research for the book, and his curiosity, led him to seek his FBI file, spurred on no doubt by passage in the mid-1970s of the Freedom of Information Act and the Privacy Act. To his dismay and anger, he found that the bureau claimed to have 20,000 pages of documents on him! Writing to the FBI's Clarence Kelly, Cantwell said that he was "at work on a book dealing in part with my literary and journalistic career and more particularly with the literary scene of the 1930s."[27] In another letter to the bureau, he protested the amount of information compiled about him, noting that several of his friends at *Time* entered the employ of the Central Intelligence Agency, though neglecting to note his own role as an informant to the FBI: "And there is surely some grave discrepancy between an official view of my work and my own knowledge of it that has resulted in ... so much material in your file." Cantwell also attempts to plead innocence by association, noting that a "number of people with whom I worked at Time became employees of the Central Intelligence Agency, including Noel Busch, Milly Schwartz, Finis Farr, and Charles Murphy. I was closely associated with the late Whittaker Chambers and in fact was instrumental in getting him a place on the staff of *Time* in 1939." So daunting was the task of getting hold of all of the material on him, Cantwell actually requested two thousand dollars in assistance from one of his former bosses at *Time* to finance his Freedom of Information inquiry.

The manuscript Cantwell refers to in his letter to the FBI now consists of notes, outlines, and hundreds of pages of FBI Freedom of Information files. Cantwell's working title for one version of the book was *Privacy*, a single word no doubt intended to echo the single-word title of Chambers's autobiography, *Witness*, and indicative also of Cantwell's sense that Chambers has invaded his "privacy." His prime recorded motive in writing the book was "to set the record straight," especially for the sake of his children, and it is clear that at the end of his life it is not primarily thirties Communists whom he blames for his troubles but the most famous anti-Communist.

In his review of *Witness* twenty-five years earlier, Cantwell had referred to the "Letter to My Children" with which Chambers began his autobiography as "unfortunate," and in his newly conceived work he gives evidence of why he found it so:

> Chambers begins *Witness* with an extensive "Letter to My Children," explaining why he became a Soviet agent, the reasons for his leaving the Communists, and his apology for the notoriety that the trial of Alger Hiss and his testimony must inevitably bring upon them. A letter to his children? What about mine? This book is then visualized as the substance of a letter to Betsy and my children, though of course in no way mentioned as such, accounting for an off-stage dispute which may or may not have concerned them personally, but which certainly affected the attitude of some persons toward them. And which quite possibly may have been a powerfully influencing factor in events in their lives of whose real source they had no knowledge whatsoever.[28]

Cantwell clearly struggled with this motivation, however, wondering if such an effort was really worth making, and noting that he did not really wish to give Chambers's "artificial(ly)" inflated story further attention, given that "other things meant so much more—illness, children, family problems in the South, the death of Calvin, constant financial trouble, disappointment with work and in other things." But he was also convinced that Chambers held some clue to the meaning of his own life story. Cantwell was clearly still bitter about and seeking to understand the fate that had befallen him and his friends: "[The] happenings of the time take on a new meaning, and the events—Calvin Fixx's heart attack, my own hospitalization—at least suggest the presence of forces inadequately portrayed in existing accounts [of the Hiss-Chambers story]. And it is possible that the corrected passages will reveal a pattern . . . identifying the villain or villains."[29] Key to this "pattern" was the fact that Chambers had used the alias "Lloyd Cantwell" in some of his underground activities and during his flight from the underground. And, as if that were not enough, Cantwell's wife's maiden name was, by coincidence, Chambers. This set off a chain of confusion that the FBI, among others, had difficulty keeping straight, and deepened the suspicions already surrounding Cantwell on the part of his former friends on the left.

Still seemingly afraid to trust his own imagination, Cantwell's notes suggest that he was approaching his subject gingerly, with strong reliance on the distance provided by the documentary dimension, and/or on a narrative voice not his own. He sketched two possible approaches to the subject of Chambers and his own life in the thirties.

The first version, the one given the tentative title *Privacy*, was imagined, á la the Filene manuscript, as a kind of nonfiction novel. As Cantwell outlined it, it would begin in the reading room of the FBI building in Washington, where he had in fact gone to look at those putative 20,000 pages of files devoted to him. He apparently never got beyond this opening scene, but he intended it to be at once factually based in the documentary evidence and complex enough to show the inadequacy of such evidence and the treachery of memory.

The second version Cantwell outlined was to be narrated in the voice of his first wife, Betsy Chambers Cantwell, noting that to do so would put the book in the voice of a "woman not interested in politics" "who'd offer a clear-eyed view of highly literate people sometimes deluded by self-importance." Conceived, it would seem, in the manner of Gertrude Stein's *Autobiography of Alice B. Toklas*, the intent was clearly to use a kind of political naïf to reveal hidden political and personal truths. Writing in his wife's voice, perhaps still bolstered by documentary footnotes, would allow a perspective different from the overly knowing, often treacherously self-justifying views he found in memoirs filled with what he calls the "genuine peril involved in retractions" (he mentions the autobiographical writings of Malcolm Cowley, Matthew Josephson, Erskine Caldwell, Edmund Wilson, Mary McCarthy, Dwight Macdonald, and Alger Hiss). "The book," he notes, "is not long. It is condensed and intense, chapter by chapter, sentence by sentence, quiet in tone, deceptively cool and unemotional, evolving slowly into melodrama before one is aware of the violence latent from the beginning." The story would start amid the narrator's southern girlhood, then introduce her cousin, Lyle Saxon, a homosexual bohemian writer whose New York literary connections eventually lead her to her future husband, Robert Cantwell. By chapter three, the narrator and her husband would be thrown into the whirlwind of literary politics, with Malcolm Cowley, Edmund Wilson, John Dos Passos, Erskine Caldwell, Matthew Josephson, Lincoln Steffens, and E. A. Filene making their appearances. But soon it becomes clear that "the center of the book is [the] recollection of Whittaker Chambers." That portrait would show Chambers as a character "whose need for being exceptional in a curious and self-impressed way leads to persistence and ruin," a man whose "conviction of his own rightness leaves wreckage all around him." Among that wreckage, apparently, was to be the sanity of the narrator's husband, Robert Cantwell, and the "conclusion would necessarily it seems to me [be] in the [mental] hospital."[30] Consistent with the style of the book, this end would be "brought in incidentally," and the reticent narrator would not directly speak of her husband's breakdown.

This proposed final book, with its fictive narrator and documentary style, seemed designed to bring together and reconcile two Cantwells, the fiction writer and the journalist. But even in plan it would end in a breakdown, and in fact it ended before it could really begin with Robert Cantwell's death on December 8, 1978.

CONCLUSION: LESSONS, LEGACIES, LITERARY LEFTS

Cantwell and the Reworking of American Literature

> The writer was convinced ... that could the subjects of biography read what was written about them, they would find, though whole libraries be studied, scarcely an interpretation they would accept, scarcely a judgment with which they would agree.
> —Robert Cantwell, "Merchant of Boston," 1934

Daniel Aaron, after years of research on literary radicalism in the thirties, including dozens of interviews and copious correspondence with participants, made the following observations concerning his pioneering study of *Writers on the Left* (1961):

> After my long stint of gathering material about living writers ... I am left with the uncomfortable feeling that my record of their lives, my explanations of their behavior and motives, are grounded on half-truths and partial evidence. At the same time, I don't think my mistakes or distortions or omissions could have been corrected in every instance by more rigorous methods of research, and I don't think the project was premature.

Sharing both Cantwell and Aaron's doubts as well as a determination to make sense of an important episode in our intellectual and cultural history, I offer some concluding remarks about the discursive site and human being "Robert Cantwell," and in doing so I want cautiously to challenge and complicate some of the formulations of other scholars upon whose rich works I have drawn throughout. Then I'll end by placing this case study into the wider context of a "reworking" of US literatures and US radical politics.

A close reading of Cantwell's critical practice complicates some of the Manichean constructions of both the anti-Communist and the revisionist critics. Cantwell can generally be linked to a group of non-Party communist critics such as Edmund Wilson, Newton Arvin, Malcolm Cowley, and James T. Farrell. But he also worked quite diligently to keep these critics in dialogue with the *New Masses* circle, worked secretly for a time on the *New Masses* staff, and for some time saw no contradiction in supporting both the *New Masses* and what quickly became its main rival, *Partisan Review*. This would seem to support Barbara Foley's caution that the later, virulent split between these two "camps" should not be projected too far back into the decade. At the same time, however, it is clear from Cantwell's correspondence, in addition to his widely quoted remarks in "Author's Field Day," that he held *New Masses* critics such as Mike Gold, Granville Hicks, Joseph Freeman, and Stanley Kunitz in generally low regard. Long before any political deviations can be attributed to him or to the other non-Party communist critics, he and his friends saw the *New Masses* critics as having only a "rudimentary" grasp of Marxism, and as tending toward formulaic and condescending critique. Again, arguing as Foley does that *New Masses* critics never developed a consistent (Party) line, that they remained deeply entrenched in "bourgeois" and empiricist aesthetic assumptions, does not absolve them of charges of dogmatism. My own reading suggests that a strong degree of dogmatism remained a constant even as the dogma frequently shifted emphasis. "Dogmatism" is clearly a relative term, however, and future discussions should perhaps shift from the discourse of "leftism" and "dogmatism" to comparative critical strategies as rooted in comparative political goals. For my part, given the aesthetico-political values I have valorized in Cantwell, I believe that revisionist James Bloom is closer to the mark in admitting that Gold often does sometimes fit the "hack" stereotype even as he also was capable of transcending such tendencies at other times.[1] We should certainly be more careful in generalizing about the work of *New Masses* critics—they are not as monolithic as many anti-Communists have sometimes made them out to be. But neither are they free from all of the charges of "leftism" leveled at them.

At the same time, it is clear that Cantwell, and presumably at least some other writers like him, had no difficulty ignoring or resisting dogmatic critical moves, and it is clear that he felt there to be a vital, alternative Marxist criticism throughout the decade. More attention and more weight needs to be given to Marxist critics who were not or were only intermittently associated with the *New Masses* group, and to those wider forces of the Cultural Front in Denning's expanded definition.[2] The general influence of *New Masses* style (a term I use not to reduce the undeniable variety of work presented in the journal but to note a widespread *perception* in the decade that there was a dominant tone) was demonstrably considerable, but it was a *general* influence; if Cantwell and his colleagues are any indication, it was not difficult for writers to embrace the broad outlines of the proletarian literary movement but resist any efforts to prescribe details of literary or critical practice.

With regard to critical theory, an evaluation of the work that Cantwell and most of his colleagues produced during the thirties is hampered by the fact that it is largely periodical criticism. The book review and the short essay are forms that call for a degree of compression that limits the development of complex themes, a fact compounded by the pressure of deadlines. Frequently Cantwell's critical judgments appear to have been intuitive and related narrowly to the specific work under review. But if this is a limitation it is also an indication of the extent to which thirties left literati sought to engage the wider public in literary-political conversation. This work appeared not only in left journals but also in such mainstream ones as the *Saturday Review*, and much of it was very much tied concretely to ongoing political activity. It is thus rather unfair and misleading to compare this journalistic criticism with the kind of academic radical criticism practiced more recently (and written mostly in the calm after a thirties-like storm of activism in the sixties).

Nevertheless, certain guiding aesthetic principles can be abstracted from Cantwell's criticism, principles that seem to have remained rather constant throughout his thirties criticism. Foremost among these is a deep respect for the perceived integrity or formal logic of a given work. As a corollary to this attitude, Cantwell insisted that social and political messages must emerge from the "natural" development of an author's story, rather than exist as an overt ideological, discursive element. He recognized that Marxism, at least as it was known to American intellectuals in the thirties, did not provide principles upon which to judge the artistry of a given work.[3] Thus Cantwell was forced to look elsewhere for such guidelines, as were virtually all Marxist critics of the decade. As I have suggested, he learned most from Henry James, who insisted, for example, that the artist must avoid the "platitude of statement," that art must represent, or embody, or dramatize ideas, not merely state them.[4] He also appears to have embraced a notion of "organic" structure to aesthetic works familiar in the writings of such contemporaries as T. S. Eliot, whose criticism was so influential on the *Partisan Review* critics (and a little later on the New Critics, whose reductive, formalistic reaction to the literary left continues to this day to inhibit our understanding of the thirties and haunts the practice of criticism—even by leftists).

By following these guidelines Cantwell was able to maintain a high degree of nonpartisanship as an evaluator of aesthetic quality while involving himself intensely in the political-literary movements of the decade (witness his emphasis on the aesthetic shortcomings of Grace Lumpkin's novels despite his strong desire to promote the literary and political movement with which she identified). Moreover, my reading of a number of other critics who embraced Marxism in the thirties—especially Edmund Wilson, Malcolm Cowley, John Chamberlain, James T. Farrell, Newton Arvin, V. F. Calverton, Horace Gregory, and Bernard Smith—suggests that blanket charges made during the thirties and since that Marxism destroyed the critical acumen of those who embraced it do not hold up. Too often, as Marxist critics themselves often noted in the thirties, the worst abuses of the *New Masses* school of critics were held up as paper tigers for anti-Marxists to denounce. Some errors of judgment by Cantwell and others are apparent in retrospect, but it remains to be proven that such lapses were more frequent among Marxists than non-Marxists, or were more frequent in the "ideological" thirties than in the less *overtly* political decades that preceded and followed the Depression era. Cantwell's own direct comments on these issues to Arvin, Farrell, and other comrades make it clear that he did perceive *New Masses* critics as problematically reductive, but that this did not invalidate the Marxist literary project and that even at its worst it was better than the barbarism masquerading as culture that he saw in the *Saturday Review* and the *New York Tribune*. The condescending review of Cantwell by Harold Strauss in the *Times* reminds us that more conservative critics could be every bit as prescriptive and reductive as some on the left.

In any event, Cantwell did not sit idly by or knuckle under to perceived abuses of legitimate radical literary energies, but instead actively resisted as critic and novelist. Cantwell understood that for Marxism or *any other ideol-*

ogy to prove useful to the artist, it must be integrated thoroughly into his or her artistic logic and sensibility. It is a suggestive coincidence that one of the most cogent essays arguing precisely this point, a piece by James Burnham titled "Marxism and Esthetics," immediately precedes Cantwell's essay on James and Lumpkin in the January 1933 issue of the *Symposium*.

In this article, Burnham observes that the logic of Marxism, or of any other social philosophy or psychological theory, differs in nature from the logic of art and must, therefore, undergo a translation in the psyche of the writer before its insights can be integrated into a work of art. He writes,

> There is no *a priori* reason why the two "logics" cannot coincide. In Dante the logic of a platonically modified thomistic Catholicism does coincide with the poetic logic.... In Proust the logic of a modified Bergsonianism does coincide with the "novel logic." But there is, on the other hand, no assurance that two different types of logic (esthetic and non-esthetic—philosophical, social), drawn from two separable—though in fact never wholly separated—fields of discourse, must coincide. Their integration cannot be imposed from without by the intellectual declaration of the artist, but only through their synthesis in the whole personality of the artist.[5]

In the wake of recent theoretical "deauthorizations," and of the decentering of subjectivity generally, this language of "whole personality" no longer seems adequate, but the basic force of this statement remains: some kind of translation process occurs in moving *any* conceptual system or ideological position into literary form. This argument, and the similar one emerging around the *Partisan Review* with its Eliot-derived notion of "aesthetic sensibility," make it clear that it is not Marxism but certain versions or articulations of allegedly Marxist ideas that limited *some* thirties writers *some* of the time.[6] Comparing this work to that of a Fredric Jameson or a Terry Eagleton is no doubt unfair, but doing so reveals that this work directed more toward "the night school" than the "graduate seminar" (to paraphrase a disparaging remark by Jameson) made some serious formulations of the complex tensions between art and politics. It is also worth noting that, while more recent theory has recapitulated these tensions and problems on a higher plane of discourse, they have not been notably more successful at resolving them.[7]

Indeed, I would endorse a remark once made by political theorist Hannah Arendt: "The conflict between politics and art . . . cannot and must not be solved."

With regard to Cantwell's literary practice as it embodies and even expands upon his theory, his exchange with Granville Hicks around the latter's review of *The Land of Plenty* is particularly instructive in bringing out some of the complexities, and perhaps contradictions, entailed by his position. Cantwell's claim to be writing "propaganda" might appear to link him with the position articulated by Foley that defends a more openly "hortatory" and "didactic" kind of fiction (as, indeed, Foley implicitly does by repeating Cantwell's propaganda remark). Hicks, by contrast, might appear, by eschewing the term "propaganda," to be avoiding leftism and dogmatism. But in fact Hicks's review of *Land of Plenty* is a near-classic example of leftism (Foley acknowledges this while also claiming that it is atypical of Hicks's position; clearly Cantwell, however, saw the review as typical of Hicks and typical precisely in its hortatory dimension). In contrast, close analysis of his criticism and fiction makes it clear that Cantwell's notion of "propaganda" did not entail the use of *overtly* didactic strategies. What is at stake, as Cantwell suggested to Farrell, is not so much a definition of propaganda as a question of "effective method." Cantwell had long maintained that novelists could be most effective as contributors to the radical movement through exploratory imaginings rather than through hortatory cheerleading. This stems both from Cantwell's sense that the novel does its best work on the plane of imagined experience (however mediated), and from his sense that didacticism required subtlety and craft, not "blunt" discursive formulation. This position is at least partly vindicated by the rise of the great sit-down strikes of the latter thirties, in which plant occupations like the one imagined in *Land of Plenty* became a key part of the strategy.

One need not call Cantwell prophetic to see that the kind of writing he was doing could have practical value to the labor movement. Cantwell's commitment to "aesthetic" quality may in part be a holdover from "bourgeois" values, but it seems to me also consistent with his position as a propagandist. He understood, though probably only partly consciously and without aid of the Gramscian concept, that since capitalist "hegemony" was maintained preponderantly by nondidactic means, it could be countered most "effectively" by nondidactic means as well, at least on the level of literary contestation. In particular he understood that one of the major inhibitors to radical action was the shame felt by workers; thus his attempt to give them (back) a sense of their own "dignity" should not be coded as "reformist" but seen as a key moment in the long process of creating revolutionary class consciousness. I would argue that any literary or political strategy that leaped over this phase was bound to fail.

Foley is certainly right to claim that to rule the "hortatory" and the explicitly "didactic" out of literature tout court is to reify the historically evolving concept of "literature." But it does not follow that, having opened up the definition, one is then led to a narrow view of literary resistance following party doctrine. Foley's argument that the literary left in the thirties was, in effect, not didactic or politically correct enough is certainly a bold reversal of virtually all previous commentary, and her analyses of the relations between doctrinal positions and generic constraints in proletarian fiction is often brilliantly illuminating. But her position assumes ultimately that a vanguard party could (and can?) identify a revolutionary direction that artists would then simply express. That is a view distinctly at odds with the views of two rather famous leaders of a vanguard party, V. I. Lenin and Leon Trotsky. Cantwell's view then, and mine now, is that the novel best serves radical change or progressive politics by theorizing independently, by testing, by exploring multiple possibilities, in short, by being part of an ongoing, democratic dialogue about political values and possibilities, not by becoming a fictionalized didactic monologue.[8]

With regard to the actual "literary production" of the thirties, Cantwell's career again suggests that we need to continue to complicate and add nuance to revisionist analysis. As even his conservative critics generally admitted, in *The Land of Plenty* Cantwell largely achieved the kind of translation of ideology into fiction that he advocated in his criticism. Translating and synthesizing his general commitment to Marxism led him to remember and reinvent his own particular past experience of class conflict in complex and illuminating ways. In so doing, he vindicated the theory behind proletarian literature, or at least one version of such theory, even as his success points up the shortcomings of many of his colleagues. But those shortcomings too have often been evaluated by inappropriate standards. The proletarian movement brought in many young people who might not otherwise have felt a literary calling at all. This meant that inevitably it brought in some whose talents did not lie in literature, or at least in Literature. But it also means that some of these efforts were exploratory ones by members of a class that had largely been excluded from the realm of literary production, and all of these efforts were made by writers who had to invent a largely nonexistent or repressed tradition of literature about working classes.[9] The reliance of some of these young proletarians on formulas has as much to do with nervous inexperience as subservience to the putative Party line. As I suggested in the opening chapter, this is partly a question of genre, of recognizing a range of writing forms that distinguish between "literature" as a relatively subtle form of "propaganda" and less stylized forms used for more time-limited purposes (akin to the distinction between Brecht and street theater).

While such dogmatic passions no doubt can ruin literary (and other) careers, literary careers have been ruined as often by failure to commit and connect as by doing so in politically formulaic ways. While historians and critics have gone to great lengths to save literature from the dogmatic distortions of the thirties, few have felt it as important to save it from, for example, the equally "formulaic" writers-workshop-(sub)urban-angst minimalism of the 1980s. That a number of formulaic proletarian novels were written in the 1930s no one should dispute. That these were somehow worse than the run-of-the-mill novels written by the majority of writers in other decades remains to be proven.

To put this more directly in terms of Cantwell's career, his first novel was more beholden to Fitzgeraldian "formulas" of romantic despair than his second was to any proletarian "formulas" of romantic revolutionism. Cantwell's second novel is inarguably an aesthetic improvement over his first, even by formalist standards, and much of that improvement can be attributed to a greater clarity of social vision that grew out of his newfound political beliefs. Cantwell's abandonment of his Filene nonfiction novel and his failure to finish another novel or any subsequent work in fiction are no doubt in part personal and idiosyncratic, and in part the result of larger social forces. Some of the blame should go to the Marxist movement of the late thirties, with its dizzying vicissitudes. Although Cantwell, despite becoming for a time virulently anti-Communist, chose not to blame political indecisiveness for foreshortening his literary career, his correspondence from the thirties and remarks by friends make it clear that it played some role. Cantwell himself singled out the Luce empire for the bulk of the blame, and surely that "bastion of capitalist literary exploitation" is also culpable—so too, Cantwell thought, was the anti-Communism of Whittaker Chambers, a different political excess, though one caught in the same spiral dance.

Part of the problem of evaluation stems from failure to be clear about the extent to which the "proletarian" novel should be submitted to standards set for evaluating "high" cultural production. Confusion on this point was rampant in the thirties, and it continues to create confusion among current interpreters. As I suggested in my introduction, much of the problem seems to me to be a failure to specify a range of kinds of radical writing to be judged by a range of aesthetic standards. By treating this work as an "emergent" workers' literature and literature about the working class, we will be both clearer about its merits and limits, and better able to understand that its development was cut short, and needs to be built upon for the future (in criticism as well as in literary production).[10] In the thirties, such a framework would have championed diverse aesthetic ideologies, including works that aspired toward the complexity of the moderns as well as works that served a more transient value through more direct links to the political scene. At its best, including in much of Cantwell's criticism, such distinctions were made, if not always as perfectly as one might have wished.

More broadly, the continuing objections to the instrumentalization of literature by more conservative scholars must be set against the massive instrumentalization of all manner of writing and culture under consumer capitalism. While some, most notably the neo-Marxists of the Frankfurt School, have used this fact to argue for a high degree of formal aesthetic abstraction as the plane of class struggle, I believe that other, more practical planes of struggle must also be employed. Distinguishing and producing a range of kinds of writing engaged in a variety of levels of cultural-political struggle seems to me a far richer strategy. Hegemony works by accretion and saturation, and counter-hegemony must be equally open to multiple modes of engagement.

Cantwell's struggle with these issues stems from the fact that he seems to have wanted to write Literature with a capital "L" and yet to contribute as directly as possible to radical change. He seems often to have been a figure caught in the middle of conflicting levels of the Cultural Front apparatus. His personal association with the proletarian movement led to ambiguous results. On the one hand, it is clear that his best work, *The Land of Plenty*, owed much of its strength to that association. On the other hand, largely self-imposed political strictures seem to have paralyzed him in the latter thirties, and the shifting political grounds eventually left him no place from which to write fiction at all. These judgments are important because in many respects Cantwell comes closest to the example of a writer of literary promise whose odyssey through the thirties proved his undoing; I do not think a great writer was lost, but I do believe a very good one lost his way.

But in this regard, to what extent can we generalize from Cantwell's case? Looking at the wider scene, a variety of experiences with the literary left are apparent. It seems clear, even on the basis of "traditional" aesthetic values, that some of the well-known writers associated with the literary left did much of their best work in the thirties, regardless of what political positions they later held. In this list I would include an established writer such as John Dos Passos, as well as various writers more contemporaneous with Cantwell, such as James T. Farrell, Edward Dahlberg, Meridel LeSueur, Nathaniel West, Josephine Herbst, Erskine Caldwell, Henry Roth, Tillie Lerner Olsen, and Richard Wright. A host of less-well-known writers with leftist sympathies also found the "Red Muse" more inspiring than any other they encountered before or after. And of course there were a few writers of stature, such as William Faulkner and Zora Neale Hurston, who seemed largely able to ignore the literary left, or, in Hurston's case, felt empowered to criticize it freely. Such writers were able to go on about their work in a separate peace, and they remind us that these other writers made a choice to go left—no literary commissars forced them into a red or pink mold. They "aligned" themselves, to borrow Denning's gloss of Raymond Williams's term, with the literary left, not out of compulsion but out of the logic of their lives and their perception of social conditions.

Reading Cantwell, and others in his various literary circles, it seems to me, does much to confirm Denning's image of a broad-based Popular Front social movement stretching far beyond any Communist Party USA (CPUSA) strategy. Cantwell's career also suggests that the split between the Third Period and Popular Front eras can be exaggerated, at least with regard to some literary leftists. Calling himself a revolutionist and a Marxist by 1931, Cantwell nevertheless never felt compelled to engage in the trashing, name calling, and reductive analysis indulged in by some on the left (and the right) during the Third Period. Conversely, during the People's Front era he remained committed to certain Third Period–style ideas regarding workers' literature (advocating, for example, histories of individual companies or industries done by or in dialogue with the relevant workers). Throughout the decade he found it quite possible to be a committed radical and yet engage in civil discourse with liberals and moderates, holding to the faith, however skeptical he became, that such dialogue was valuable. This also compelled him to try to mediate various tendencies within the literary left, attempting to get Wilson and Hicks into discussion, for example, and appreciating the *Partisan Review* position without feeling impelled to caricature publicly the *New Masses* position. In these efforts Cantwell may prove to have been unusual, but only close study of a number of other literary radical careers will tell us how deeply the positions, jealousies, and controversies of the "head boys"[11] sank into the rank and file of proletarian literati.

In choosing commitment over Jamesian withdrawal, Cantwell had accepted the gamble that his work might perish with the mass movement with which it identified itself, and this is for the most part what did occur. Cantwell identified himself and his work with a revolutionary movement with close ties to the Soviet Union, and in so doing he and his colleagues among Communists and fellow travelers tied themselves to the fate of the Soviet system. The "infantile disorder" of revolutionism, as Lenin called it in another context, that predominated in the American Communist movement in the early thirties was in part tied to a deference to Soviet wisdom as embodied in the Comintern, although the Great Depression clearly gave it a homegrown plausibility. In the People's Front era the nature of the policy to which deference was given changed drastically, but the pattern of deference did not. In the latter part of the thirties, US Communist leaders merely repeated their initial error in another form. While the Popular Front was in many respects a very fine idea, it was one pursued for dishonest, opportunistic reasons by those at the top of the Communist Party hierarchy. As a result, the fine idea was later submerged in anti-Stalinist reaction, at great cost to the possibilities for any subsequent efforts at left populism or popular leftism.[12]

But it is important to remember that the Communist and communist literary movement in the thirties was a complex pyramid in which knowledge/power moved erratically from the top down and the bottom up. Certain key elements of a knowledge/power system that started in the Kremlin, moved through the Comintern, and arrived at the top of the CPUSA hierarchy were translated into literary terms by figures such as Mike Gold, Joseph Freeman, and Granville Hicks, and then (and only then) became available as knowledge for what we might call the rank-and-file literati. Each step down this pyramid, however, entailed an element of "noise," as communication theory would have it, an element of distortion. Some of this was quite intentional, and purposely deceptive, while other elements derived indirectly from the complexity of translation (literal and figurative). This process meant that even Party-loyal left-leaning literati in fact had more freedom from bureaucratic pronouncements than has been suggested by many critics. The structure also meant that most literary leftists were kept ignorant of vitally important information held by higher levels of the hierarchy.

At the same time, partly because of the inefficiency of this structure and partly because of the intellectual independence shown by many literary leftists, the pyramid entailed considerable agency at its base. And the fact that some significant dissent (the Trotskyists merely the most obvious example) did emerge suggests that it was possible at points to see through this maze of misdirection. Thus Party members and fellow travelers are culpable to a degree for enforcing their own ignorance, and for the failure to push for a more democratic and open structure. These failures proved costly, indeed deadly. But surely most Party members and fellow travelers cannot be held accountable for crimes kept even from people in the upper reaches of the Kremlin bureaucracy.

These were not "dupes," if that term means that their work was wholly misguided; that some above or behind them had dubious motives, and at times criminal tactics, does not impugn the motives of those American radicals who had a real interest in bettering conditions for workers, for minority groups, and for women in this country. Although Party members and fellow travelers were victims of an often undemocratic and duplicitous organization, they nevertheless also contributed significantly to the elaboration of a truly democratic culture in this country.[13] The struggles for justice for blacks, against "male chauvinism," and of course for the rights of working people were all advanced by the efforts of rank-and-file Communists. Many took seriously the Popular Front slogan that Communism was 20th century Americanism. Unfortunately, few took it seriously enough to challenge the undemocratic elements on the left because they tied their radicalism too fully to ideas about the Soviet Union that were less true than they could possibly know. Thus, while Party members and fellow travelers should not be reductively characterized as "dupes," many in fact *felt* duped, and that fact too must be acknowledged and analyzed. It needs to be acknowledged because it was a major factor in the rightward drift of many thirties leftists. Revelations of the tragic history of Stalinism were devastating to those who had supported the Party.

One related great mistake of the movement in the thirties was that throughout the decade reliance on the Soviet model meant that it too often failed to raise the issue of what socialism could contribute to American society in an intelligent and reasonable manner consistent with the tradition of democratic debate in the United States. United States Communists failed so completely that most of their own sympathizers could not, at the end of the decade, dissociate Marxian socialism from the Soviet system in such a way as to make possible the continuation of a radical movement, literary or otherwise, in this country.[14]

Robert Cantwell was among those unable to dissociate Marxism from Soviet Communism at the end of the thirties, and so he abandoned not only Karl Marx but Henry James as well, at least insofar as James inspired his ambition to write prose fiction. The completion of Cantwell's odyssey through the literary left of the thirties was a sad one indeed. What is sadder still, however, is that Cantwell's total disillusionment with radicalism was a response shared by many of his colleagues in the American intelligentsia. In a kind of flip-side reaction formation, having identified socialism too fully with the Soviet Union, they came to identify democracy too exclusively with the United States. And having identified the popular too fully with the Popular Front as Communist strategy, they identified all forms of populism as the enemy. The reactive anti-Marxist bias that flourished after the collapse of the Marxian literary and political movement led to an impoverishment of intellectual life in this country for decades. Indeed, as Ellen Schrecker, among others, has documented, many more intellectual (and other) careers were destroyed or delayed by McCarthyism than had ever been destroyed by literary leftism.[15] The ideology of "the end of ideology" that developed in the forties and fifties with the active aid of many former radicals limited intellectual freedom by, among other things, restraining Americans from examining one of the most extensive literatures of cultural theory in modern scholarship, that ensemble of texts known as "Western" or "neo" Marxism.[16] It took another twenty years of intellectual activity to reverse this decline, and even with the eventual flourishing of an American neo-Marxist criticism, the lingering effects of the suppression of thirties-style engagement continue to be felt.[17] Fear of alleged thirties-style theoretical "vulgarity," and a closely related disdain of all popular culture, prevented and still prevents many on the left from engaging key arenas of the public sphere.[18]

Radicalism in the United States has, at its best, been not only democratic but also the key force in expanding the meaning of that elusive concept and giving greater substance to democracy in practice. Expanding the meaning of democracy, especially into the realm of the economy (as later radicals, from Students for a Democratic Society to the Occupy movement, have attempted) must be made a more central part of progressive struggles in this country.[19] To the degree to which neoliberalism continues to successfully deploy the rhetoric that equates democracy with "free market" capitalism, the left will continue to be marginal. Successful "American" radical democratic struggles must continue to contest largely in the terms of, even as they expose the limits of, American political rhetorics.[20] It is surely the case, as Sacvan Bercovitch and others have shown convincingly, that "the American ideology" (or the ideology of Americanism, or the American dream) has often been a powerfully hegemonic force used to absorb left energies through a counterfeit radicalism.[21] However, I believe that Bercovitch underestimates the extent to which some American radicals have been able use these rhetorics to extend rights and advance social justice. I believe that, given the inhospitable grounds for the left, for the foreseeable future the most effective strategy to reverse the hegemony of the false hope that is the American dream remains to draw out the radical energies within American political rhetorics (as the best US radical rhetoricians, from Sojourner Truth to Elizabeth Cady Stanton to Martin Luther King to the AIDS Coalition to Unleash Power, have always done). The task is to seek out and refigure those points where liberal and populist discourses open out toward more radical possibilities. If some postmodern version of radical transnationalism or "cosmopolitanism"[22] is to take root in this country, it will do so because it has been successfully translated into and grafted onto existing American discourses. This is not a cynical call for a new slogan—"radical democracy is twenty-first-century Americanism"—but rather a call to elaborate at every opportunity both the historical debt that democracy in the United States owes to radicals and a call to offer new radical solutions that speak in terms average Americans can understand.[23]

The wholesale abandonment of not only Marxism but radicalism by many thirties leftists, made possible in large part by playing the nationalist, "Americanist" trump card, accelerated a decline in representation for American workers, both literary representation as the proletarian literary movement died (part suicide, part assassination), and political representation through the labor movement (as its leaders formed a stabilizing but ultimately debilitating compromise with corporate management).[24] As Wald and others have shown, McCarthyism did not wholly stifle literary radicalism, but it did drive it largely underground. And because both radical labor and radical literature were submerged, nothing like the kind of representation in the literary canon achieved through social movement struggles by women, gay folks, and peoples of color has been achieved with regard to literature by, for, or even about American workers. Recovery of this literature, making it available in anthologies and accessible paperback editions, is well underway.[25] But there is a long distance to go to approach even the still tenuous hold gained by these other groups. Continuing the process of uncovering and recovering the thirties has an important role to play in this, particularly by continuing to disentangle the alleged literature of a party from the literatures of workers, and by getting beyond the limits imposed by generic labels such as "proletarian" to explore a range of radical writing and writings by radicals.

The failure to sustain a widely acknowledged literature by, for, or about working-class Americans has come at great cost. That women and racial and sexual minorities have, through heroic efforts, managed to open a space for their voices in the canon of American literature is a tribute to the success of a serious cultural politics backed by and entwined with movement activity and radical theory (and theory *as* movement activity). At the same time, the relative underdevelopment of working-class literary traditions and class issues in general as part of the new canon suggests how heavily the submersion of the proletarian movement weighs on the present. In turn, the lack of such an articulated tradition is complicit in the loss of much of the working class to the right over the last several decades.

The trilogy of race, class, and gender (later sexuality was added, and sometimes empire) that emerged in critical circles the late 1980s and 1990s was seldom a balanced trio. Class was often ignored or subsumed under race in much of this vital work. Redoubled efforts to bring class issues to bear more fully on the canon debates and related questions of cultural representation started a new wave of work.[26] This work obviously cannot and should not entail a revival of a proletarian movement, not least because it must not be confined to a discussion of industrial workers given the rise in importance of the service sector in the US and world economies. But taking the proletarian movement and its wider tradition of worker writing seriously must be one part of such an effort. We will also need new kinds of analysis that help to disentangle that morass called the "middle class," demonstrating ways in which that term is misused, and encouraging analyses that affiliate much of the so-called middle class with those more clearly oppressed by contemporary transnational capitalism and challenging identification upward with those oppressors. These efforts will reinforce a wider effort by progressives to articulate a new kind of public discussion of class that counters the right's use of the "middle-class tax payer" as a club against the working and underclasses, immigrants, and environmentalists.

The vital field of "working-class studies" is doing much of this necessary work.[27] We need more work like that of Laura Hapke's *Labor's Text: The Worker in American Fiction*, which analyzes the whole of US literature from the nineteenth century to the present, and Paul Lauter and Ann Fitzgerald's anthology *Literature, Class, and Culture*, which extends class-centered US literature across the centuries, examining working-class representations in the context of representations of other social classes. All of these are part of a much-needed process of reworking American literature.

The legacy of the thirties can also speak to two other, related areas of contemporary concern. As Michael Denning has pointed out, if we are to create a vital left cultural politics and political culture, we must overcome false dichotomies between "textual" and "real" politics."[28] While, as Hazel Carby notes, from a perspective close to Denning, there *is* a difference between "textually" integrating the canon of American literature and actually breaking down the vicious apartheid that continues to characterize US society, the two processes are deeply intertwined.[29] Clearly much of the success of the new right of late has come from their superior use of "textual politics," from well-placed "serious" editorials to the proliferation of talk radio shows to Fox News. It continues to amaze me that we tenured radical experts on rhetoric and media studies have done so little, with a few notable exceptions, to help develop a left rhetoric capable of challenging conservative hegemony. Perhaps the deepest irony here is that, as was revealed by that moment when an aide to George W. Bush chastised those stuck in "reality-based politics," the right has behaved like postmodern social constructionists while the left has continued to counter with empirical facts. As Stephen Duncombe has persuasively argued, the left has suffered from a curious lack of political imagination and a boring moralism that utterly fails compared to the pithy, sound-bite-worthy ideas from the right.[30]

The thirties offer interesting lessons with regard to these issues. A very "real" labor movement received substantial support from New York's literary "textual" politicos. We can acknowledge that there was in certain respects a more active mode of progressive intellectual intervention in various public spheres in the thirties than has been true of late (Cantwell's essays for the relatively conservative *Saturday Review* would be one among a myriad of possible examples), but we should not exaggerate those efforts. Thirties (or fifties or sixties) nostalgia for left-liberal "public intellectuals" will not do. But neither will complacent protection of academic privilege. We need to acknowledge both the importance and the limits of what we too glibly call "theory."[31] The new waves of literary theoretical activity during the seventies, eighties, and nineties, driven as they were by waves of social movement activity by women, the racially oppressed, and sexual radicals, can be read as in many respects a necessary corrective to some of the limited, narrowly class-centric theories proffered by *some* on the literary left in the thirties. Radical critics have learned to speak a language of "mediation" and "hegemony," to deconstruct all naive binary oppositions, to view power in complexly nuanced ways. And that is a good thing.

All of these theoretical developments entail important gains that can be turned back on the discourses of the thirties to bring forth new insights, particularly with regard to the ways in which (generally repressed) issues of race, gender, and sexuality complicated the class struggle represented in Depression writing.[32] The new theory, and the new social history that grew up alongside and entwined with it, also allows us to see that "class" itself is not a given but rather a constructed category. (An insight of Marx's that, alas, has had to be periodically relearned by his putative disciples.) In particular, literary theory and social history teach us that cultural factors often dismissed by Communist Party USA political leaders as secondary or "superstructural" in fact play a primary role in *forming* class (as with other) identities. Such a perspective allows us to see thirties literary radicalism in a new light—not as a simple *reflection* of class solidarity and class struggle but as a sometimes problematic, sometimes rich, attempt to help *create* such solidarity, not by fictionalizing slogans but by developing persuasive rhetorics that evoked very real conditions of exploitation and equally real possibilities for resistance.[33]

Among the lessons to be learned from the rise of right-wing populism since the 1960s is the necessity of engaging in popular discursive struggles; if progressives do not characterize ourselves in the popular press, then conservatives will do it for us (and to us). If there is a lesson from the thirties in this regard, it is a sense of the need to *create*, not just *critique*, culture. The métier of the recent cultural left—*analyzing* rhetorical practices—must be more fully extended to the *production* of popular progressive rhetorics. Analysis is clearly indispensable but just as clearly insufficient. But hegemony is largely performed via narrative, not analytic discourse. The universities are in fact one important site of "mass culture," but they are only one, and more progressive intellectuals must take the risk of popularity, including, as did many Cultural Front leftists, producing forms of popular literature.[34] We need not, as seems to be feared, abandon complexity; we must instead find more effective means of conveying complex analyses to audiences not trained in specialized rhetorics. It is not a question of abandoning the aesthetic joys of intellectual complexity but of redirecting some of the energy toward other, equally complex tasks. Indeed, the task of finding a rhetoric to convey progressive values to a wide audience in contemporary America is full of enough complexities to satisfy even the most ardent complicators among us!

The rapid rise of the Occupy movement in 2011 and 2012 shows a hunger for class analysis among US citizens, and should be rightly credited with reviving issues of economic justice here. But, just as surely, the rapid decline of the movement shows how much work there is to do to sustain such analyses amid current discursive struggles dominated by right-wing ideologues. Ideologically, the hardcore among the Occupy forces identify more with the anarchist tradition than with the Marxist one, as do many in the ranks of the worldwide movement against corporate globalization from which Occupy drew heavily. Anarchism has deep roots in the United States, from

Thoreau and nineteenth-century utopians to Emma Goldman to the IWW to the Student Nonviolent Coordinating Committee in the Civil Rights era to antinuclear direct-action movement of the 1970s to the Battle of Seattle activists at the turn of the twenty-first century. Antistatist libertarianism has real resonance here, but again it has been the right more than the left that has tapped into that sentiment. Decentralist politics makes more sense than ever in the wake of the disasters of centralized putatively communist states. But both in rhetoric and in practice, anarchism (or left libertarianism) in the early twenty-first century has failed as miserably as socialism to connect with ordinary folks in this country. The Occupy movement largely squandered the coalitional possibilities contained in its brilliant slogan "the 99 percent" by reenacting the ideological purism that so damaged both the Old and New Lefts. The kind of politics represented by the best aspects of the Popular Front of the thirties might have forced centrist Obama closer to becoming the "radical," "socialist" progressive the right wing ridiculously mislabeled him. Instead, after helping him defeat a more obvious representative of the 1 percent, a fragmented left has been unable to keep Obama from the embrace of Wall Street and corporate militarism.

There is no easy answer to the problems faced by progressives in the United States and around the globe today. The worldwide economic depression that began in 2008 may yet wake up "the masses" to the deep flaws in capitalism, but not without new strategic rhetorics and newly enlivened tactics. Continuing the process of reexamining the thirties left, especially its cultural arm, is important because the decade offers numerous lessons about both pitfalls and possibilities of popular leftism. A continuing dialogue between the mid-twentieth-century Cultural Front and the present is called for if critics and activists committed to social and economic justice are to understand the potential and the limits of literary and cultural radicalism.

AFTERWORD: A WORKING-CLASS HERO IS SOMETHING TO BE

About the time of Cantwell's death, a ten-year-old boy from his hometown of Aberdeen was beginning to explore the lyrical musical musings that would make him a founding figure of grunge rock. Kurt Cobain grew up a working-class kid in an Aberdeen that remained little changed from the early twentieth century. In his youth, it was still a rough-and-tumble, working-class town with few upward routes in class status. It is a sign of Cobain's time, and our current time, that his much-heralded social anger is almost never analyzed in class terms but only through the cliché of youthful rebellion. Cobain may have never developed class consciousness in any Marxist sense, but working-class experience shaped him in a myriad of ways. The failure of Cobain and millions like him to identify as working class, to recognize that "a working-class hero is something to be," however, reflects setbacks to the labor movement over the last decades of the twentieth century, and efforts by both major political parties to pretend that there is no working class in America (we are all middle class now, unless we are in abject poverty due to our own laziness). Driven largely by successful efforts to use racism as a divisive force, setting white workers against workers of color, the right wing's determined attacks on union power and cooptation of social issues to divide and conquer has led to an inability among most people to think coherently about the role of class in the everyday affairs of the United States. For this reason, among many others, recovering the legacy of the era that saw a major "laboring of American culture" is not only a historical concern but also a vitally important political endeavor today.

NOTES

NOTES TO PREFACE

1 See Michael Denning, *The Cultural Front: The Laboring of American Culture in the Twentieth Century* (London: Verso, 1996).
2 "Autobiographical Sketch of Robert Cantwell," *Wilson Bulletin for Librarians* 10 (Jan. 1936): 298.
3 In a sense, this project can be said to be a "renewed consideration" of itself, since I began work on it in 1975 as a master's thesis, put the work aside for many years, and returned to it when I saw how well it resonated with radical revisionary works of recent years.
4 Bruce Barcott, *Northwest Passages: A Literary Anthology of the Pacific Northwest* (Seattle: Sasquatch Press, 1994).
5 For too long the undeniably central New York scene was virtually the sole site of literary left analysis. This is changing through the fine work of Douglas Wixson on Midwest literary radicalism, the work of Bill Mullen on the African American left in Chicago, and the fascinating observations of Mike Davis on California's radical cultural scene. The volume *Regionalists on the Left* is an important contribution to extending these efforts to the Southeast, Deep South, Southwest, West, and, my area of concern here, the Northwest. But there is much more to be done. My efforts below to show the lingering effect in the Northwest of the Industrial Workers of the World on writers even after the rise to prominence of the CPUSA is just one point of entry for further work on what might be called the "Upper Left Coast" (Oregon and Washington, especially).
6 A biography of Cantwell does exist. Per Seyersted, *Robert Cantwell: An American Thirties Radical Writer and His Apostasy* (Oslo: Novus Press, 2004), is an exhaustively researched and richly detailed book from which I have occasionally drawn (though most of my book was written before the publication of Seyersted's). Those interested in more detail about Cantwell's entire life and work will find it in Seyersted's book. While the detailed coverage is admirable, the book is theoretically and interpretively rather thin, neither sympathetic to nor comprehending of Cantwell's complicated aesthetic and political positions in the 1930s. In particular, the biography is premised on the idea that politics and literature are anathema to one another, a view that I hope to show is quite mistaken. Seyersted and Cantwell were friends, and the book is written very much from the point of view of Cantwell in later life. It at times underplays and suggests the folly of the younger Cantwell's radicalism. Ironically, much of the evidence that Seyersted uncovers makes clear that Cantwell was careful in public to mask his more radical views, mostly out of fear of losing income, thus suggesting that we should view his commitments as even deeper than his public face reveals.
7 "The thirties" has long been a convenient code word for a larger and longer process. Recent scholarship is opening up questions leading inevitably beyond the chronological and conceptual bounds of that decade, stressing both the continuing influence of modernisms from

earlier in the century, as well as tracing various ways in which radical literary traditions managed to survive, often in somewhat submerged and changed forms, even during the terrifying decade or so from the late forties to the late fifties when McCarthyite repression and accusations of "un-American" activities were at their peak.

A number of critics, including Walter Kalaidjian, Cary Nelson, William Maxwell, and Alan Filreis, have richly documented the presence of avant-garde and high modernist aesthetic ideologies far into the era when they were purportedly submerged beneath a plethora of naïve, dogmatic naturalism. At the other end of "the thirties," Alan Wald's work on reperiodization has grown in part from genre questions, as his discovery of pop cultural radical writing shows extensive continuity into the forties and fifties, and in some cases beyond. Denning has similarly argued that the aesthetic ideologies of the Cultural Front extend far into the forties, fifties, and beyond, not only in writing and fiction film but in some neglected areas such as animation.

While these efforts to extend the literary left tradition outside the box of the 1930s are vitally important and absolutely correct, it must also be remembered that the category "the thirties" is not one simply made up by historians. Many, like Cantwell, experienced the thirties as a bounded era in their lives. As was the case of the subject of this book, many writers did in fact compartmentalize their lives with a cut-off point in 1939 or 1941. That this literary left activity, with a considerable degree of continuity with earlier moments, took place for some in later decades does not erase this other truth. Ernest Hemingway, for example, is a writer identified primarily with the 1920s Jazz Age, but in fact arguably one of his greatest works, *For Whom the Bell Tolls* (1940), is very much a product of the 1930s, not just chronologically but in ideological dynamics. Similar changes have been noted in writers identified with the Harlem Renaissance, such as Langston Hughes and Claude McKay, whose inherent radicalism found freer expression in the thirties. Important recent work has also shown more connections between the Jazz Age (read "white") and Harlem Renaissance (read "black") writers that spilled over into the thirties and beyond. Again, one exemplary figure in this regard is Ernest Hemingway. See especially Alan Wald, *Writing from the Left*, *The Responsibility of Intellectuals*, and *American Night*. Marcus Klein, building on Walter B. Rideout and Daniel Aaron, has also shown long-range continuities in American radical writing. Klein argues, for example, that literary "proletarianism" should be seen as a subcategory of modernism, not its antithesis (Marcus Klein, *Foreigners: The Making of American Literature, 1900–1940*). Cary Nelson's work on American poetry in *Repression and Recovery* offers a more variegated and complex portrait of American poetries, showing modernism and proletarianism to be far more intertwined than previous histories have suggested. Eric Homberger's book, *American Writers and Radical Politics, 1900–1939*, despite its inclusive time frame, tends to segregate eras, but certain long-range continuities can be read between the lines of its episodic chapters. See also Walter Kalaidjian, *American Culture Between the Wars: Revisionary Modernism and Postmodern Critique* (New York: Columbia University Press, 1993); William J. Maxwell, *New Negro, Old Left: African-American Writing and Communism between the Wars* (New York: Columbia University Press, 1999); Alan Filreis, *Modernism from Right to Left: Wallace Stevens, the Thirties, and Literary Radicalism* (Cambridge, UK: Cambridge University Press, 1994);

and Gary Edward Holcomb and Charles Scruggs, eds., *Hemingway and the Black Renaissance* (Columbus: The Ohio State University Press, 2012).

8   Cantwell worked in the Luce empire during and after World War II, first at *Time* and *Newsweek*, then as a writer and later senior editor at *Sports Illustrated* for twenty years, from the late fifties until his death in 1978. During that period his publications included biographies of Nathaniel Hawthorne and naturalist Alexander Wilson; much periodical writing, mostly on sports and nature; and a history/travelogue entitled *The Hidden Northwest* (Philadelphia: Lippincott, 1972). The latter volume includes some autobiographical moments, and is notable for the total absence of any discussion of labor issues amid its historical portions, including omission of *Land of Plenty* from its discussion of the literary history of the Northwest (modesty, perhaps, but more likely repudiation).

9   The Robert Cantwell Papers can be found in the Special Collections of the Knight Library, University of Oregon, Eugene, Oregon. A guide to the papers can be found online at http://nwda.orbiscascade.org/ark:/80444/xv41731.

10 Alan Wald, *Exiles from a Future Time* (Chapel Hill: North Carolina Press, 2002), xvi.

11 Denning, *The Cultural Front*.

NOTES TO CHAPTER 1

1   My own informal, "unscientific" survey of graduate students and faculty at several major research universities suggests that the caricature is still quite alive and well. Some hopeful signs that radical revision might be making headway in the general writing of literary history began to emerge by the late 1980s and have continued apace. This would include the fairly evenhanded treatment of thirties Marxist criticism in Vincent Leitch's *American Literary Criticism*, 2nd ed. (New York: Routledge, 2010), a fine essay by Paul Lauter on the proletarian novel in Emory Elliot, ed., *Columbia History of the American Novel* (New York: University Press, 1991), and a variety of other essays touching sensitively on dimensions of the literary left in the companion volume by Emory Elliot, ed., *Columbia Literary History of the United States* (New York: Columbia University Press, 1988). *The Heath Anthology of American Literature* in two volumes, edited by Paul Lauter (Belmont, CA: Wadsworth, [1989] 2013), was the first major anthology in decades to provide serious coverage of the variety of literary left writing, and has to a degree forced other major anthologies to follow suit.

2   See Philip Rahv, "Proletarian Literature: A Political Autopsy," *Southern Review* 4 (Winter 1939): 616–28.

3   The cottage industry of books dealing with the "New York intellectuals" that centered around *Partisan Review* virtually forms a subgenre of its own. The early work of James Gilbert, *Writers and Partisans: A History of Literary Radicalism in America* (New York: Wiley, 1968), has been revised and expanded by a number of significant works, including Alexander Bloom, *Prodigal Sons: The New York Intellectuals and Their World* (New York: Oxford University Press, 1986); Terry Cooney, *The Rise of the New York Intellectuals, Partisan Review, and Its Circle, 1934–45* (Madison: University of Wisconsin Press, 1986); and Neil Jumonville, *Critical Crossings: The New York Intellectuals and Postwar America* (Berkeley: University of California Press, 1991).

The best and most comprehensive of these are Alan M. Wald, *The New York Intellectuals: The Rise and Decline of the Anti-Stalinist Left from the 1930s to the 1980s* (Chapel Hill: University of North Carolina Press, 1987); and Harvey Teres, *Renewing the Left*. Teres also offers a useful summary of early *Partisan Review* aesthetics in "Remaking Marxist Criticism: *Partisan Review*'s Eliotic Leftism, 1934–1936," *American Literature* 64, no. 1 (March 1992): 127–53.

4 Aaron, *Writers on the Left: Episodes in American Literary Communism* (New York: Harcourt, Brace and World, 1961); Rideout, *The Radical Novel in the United States, 1900–1954* (Cambridge, MA: Harvard University Press, 1956).

5 See Paula Rabinowitz, *Labor and Desire: Women's Revolutionary Fiction in Depression America* (Chapel Hill: University of North Carolina Press, 1991), 19–20.

6 The collection of writing by thirties radical women, *Writing Red: An Anthology of Women Writers, 1930–1940* (New York: Feminist Press, 1987), edited by Charlotte Nekola and Paula Rabinowitz, was a landmark in the rediscovery process and is a good starting place for first-hand knowledge. The best, most comprehensive work on the gender/class matrix remains Rabinowitz's *Labor and Desire*. Other important feminist readings of thirties literature include Deborah Rosenfelt, "From the Thirties: Tillie Olsen and the Radical Tradition," *Feminist Studies* 7 (Fall 1981): 370–406, a work that did much to revive interest in Olsen; Constance Coiner, *Better Red: The Writing and Resistance of Tillie Olsen and Meridel LeSueur* (London: Oxford University Press, 1995); and Elinor Langer, *Josephine Herbst: The Story She Could Never Tell* (Boston: Little, Brown, 1984). Barbara Foley partly defends Communist Party "woman question" policy from some of these critics in chapter 6 of her *Radical Representations: Politics and Form in U.S. Proletarian Fiction, 1929–1941* (Durham, NC: Duke University Press, 1993). Other recent works that extended one or more dimensions of gender and the literary left include Suzanne Sowinska's dissertation "American Women Writers and the Radical Agenda, 1925–1940" (Ann Arbor [UMI microfilm], 1999).

7 Compare Foley, *Radical Representations*, with Rabinowitz, *Labor and Desire*.

8 Mark Naison's *Communists in Harlem During the Depression* (New York: Grove Press, 1983) was a key moment in the move toward a more balanced general picture of blacks and communism than found in previous writings by Harold Cruse, Richard Wright, or Ralph Ellison. African American leftists play a prominent role in Paul Buhle's *Marxism in the USA* (London: Zed, 1987), and are at the center of Cedric Robinson's uneven but provocative *Black Marxism* (London: Zed Books, 1983). Robin D. G. Kelly's brilliant *Hammer and Hoe: Alabama Communists during the Great Depression* (Chapel Hill: University of North Carolina Press, 1990) is very suggestive in its subtle rethinking of thirties racial cultural politics. Barbara Foley also includes an illuminating section on Communist Party racial politics in *Radical Representations*, especially chapter 5, and in her important essay "The Rhetoric of Anti-Communism in *Invisible Man*," *College English* 59, no. 5 (Sept. 1997): 530–47. Alan Wald claims that antiracist work was at the center of Communist politics in the thirties and after, and he documents this in fascinating analyses of cultural work in his *Writing from the Left: New Essays on Radical Culture and Politics* (London: Verso, 1994), most fully in part 4. See also the essays and reviews collected in part 3 of Wald's *The Responsibility of Intellectuals: Selected Essays on Marxist Traditions in Cultural Commitment* (Atlantic Highlands, NJ: Humanities Press, 1992).

Other full-length works offering complex reassessments of Communism and African Americans include William Maxwell, *New Negro, Old Left: African-American Writing and Communism between the Wars* (New York: Columbia University Press, 1999); James Smethurst, *The New Red Negro: The Literary Left and African American Poetry* (New York: Oxford University Press, 1999); and Bill Mullen, *Popular Fronts: Chicago and African American Cultural Politics, 1935–46* (Urbana-Champaign: University of Illinois Press, 1999). See also James A. Miller, "African American Writing of the 1930s: A Prologue," in Bill Mullen and Sherry Linkon, eds., *Radical Revisions: Rereading 1930s Culture* (Urbana-Champaign: University of Illinois Press, 1996), 78–90. Although focused on an earlier era, George Hutchison, *The Harlem Renaissance in Black and White* (Cambridge, MA: Harvard University Press, 1995), is very suggestive for later decades as well. Another excellent recent study is Gary Edward Holcomb, *Claude McKay, Code Name Sasha: Queer Black Marxism and the Harlem Renaissance* (Gainesville: University Press of Florida, 2009).

Writings on race in thirties literature and culture for the most part have yet to benefit fully from the theoretical insights of the "new histories of whiteness" as they reshape "white ethnicity" and "race" beginning in the 1990s with books such as David Roediger's *Wages of Whiteness* (London: Verso, 1991; revised 2007) on nineteenth-century American labor; Eric Lott's *Love and Theft* (Oxford: Oxford University Press, 1993) on the history of blackface minstrelsy; and Ruth Frankenberg's *White Women, Race Matters* (Minneapolis: University of Minnesota Press, 1993) on constructions of whiteness in American women's liberation; as well as later works such as Matthew Frye Jacobson, *Whiteness of a Different Color: European Immigrants and the Alchemy of Race* (Cambridge, MA: Harvard University Press, 1999); and David Roediger, *Working Toward Whiteness: How America's Immigrants Became White: The Strange Journey from Ellis Island to the Suburbs* (New York: Basic Books, 2006). But Alan Wald's groundbreaking essays in *Writing from the Left* on the racial ventriloquism or "cultural cross-dressing" on the left in such works as Jewish American Guy Endore's (née Samuel Goldstein) novel *Babouk* (1934) push the important work of analyzing race beyond the usual examination of other-than-white writers, and Maxwell uses some of this work, particularly Lott's, in *New Negro, Old Left*. Although not focused particularly on literary radicalism, Michael E. Staub, in *Voices of Persuasion: Politics of Representation in 1930s America* (New York: Cambridge University Press, 1994), explores thirties racial politics via ethnographic and documentary writing, with illuminating chapters treating Native Americans and Zora Neale Hurston's African American folk studies.

9   Among the important works on writers of color other than African Americans are two books by E. San Juan, Jr., *Carlos Bulosan and the Imagination of Class Struggle* (Quezon City, Philippine: University of Philippines Press, 1972), and *The Philippine Temptation: Dialectics of Philippines-U.S. Literary Relations* (Philadelphia: Temple University Press, 1996).

10 Suzanne Sowinska, "Writing Across the Color Line: White Women Writers and the 'Negro Question' in the Gastonia Novels," in Mullen and Linkon, *Radical Revisions*.

11 See Wald, *Writing from the Left*.

12 On McWilliams, see especially Michael Denning, *The Cultural Front: The Laboring of American Literature in the Twentieth Century* (London: Verso, 1996).

13 Gay/lesbian/bisexual/queer studies have only begun to turn toward the thirties and the literary left as a terrain to explore, but with figures such as Langston Hughes, Kenneth Fearing, Muriel Rukeyser, Claude McKay, Newton Arvin, Lorraine Hansberry, and dozens of others to examine, this promises to be an illuminating project. An excellent example is Gary Holcomb, *Claude McKay, Code Name Sasha: Queer Black Marxism and the Harlem Renaissance* (Gainesville: University Press of Florida, 2009). See also Alan Wald, *American Night: The Literary Left in the Cold War Era* (Chapel Hill: University of North Carolina Press, 2012), especially chapter 4. Isaac Julien's brilliant filmic evocation/analysis of Langston Hughes's sexuality in "Looking for Langston" has set the model for future treatments as it moves richly between present concerns and various possible constructions of the past (Isaac Julien, "Looking for Langston," British Film Institute, 1989). The Communist roots of important homophile activists are noted in John D'Emilio's groundbreaking history *Sexual Politics, Sexual Communities*, 2nd ed. (Chicago: University of Chicago Press, 1998). D'Emilio's equally groundbreaking essay "Capitalism and Gay Identity" suggests an important line of convergence with Marxist thought. The latter essay is most easily accessible in the wide-ranging *Lesbian and Gay Studies Reader* (New York: Routledge, 1993), edited by Henry Abelove et al. Kevin Mumford's *Interzones: Black/White Sex Districts in Chicago and New York in the Early Twentieth Century* (New York: Columbia University Press, 1997) is suggestive with regard to the race/sexuality intersection. And George Chauncey's magisterial *Gay New York: Gender, Urban Culture, and the Making of the Gay World, 1890–1940* (New York: Basic Books, 1994) is rich in information about the context in which many gay male Communists would have lived, and is a model for other urban gay histories. Also useful in extending the story to include lesbians is Eric Garber, "A Spectacle in Color: The Lesbian and Gay Subculture of Jazz Age Harlem," in Martin Duberman et al., eds., *Hidden from History: Reclaiming the Gay and Lesbian Past* (New York: New American Library, 1989). Sherry Wolf's *Sexuality and Socialism: History, Politics, and LGBT Liberation* (Chicago: Haymarket Press, 2009) surveys with a long view the relation between the left and queerness. And Kevin Floyd brilliantly theorizes this connection in *The Reification of Desire: Toward a Queer Marxism* (Minneapolis: University Minnesota Press, 2009).

14 See David Bergman, "F. O. Matthiessen: The Critic as Homosexual," *Raritan* 7, no. 4 (1990): 62–82; and the novel by Mark Merlis, *American Studies: A Novel* (New York: Penguin, 1994), with its central character based upon Matthiessen. For a brilliant reading of the novel, see Nishant Shahani, *Queer Retrosexualities* (Bethlehem, PA: Lehigh University Press, 2012).

15 See Maxwell, *New Negro, Old Left*.

16 See Holcomb, *Claude McKay, Code Name Sasha*.

17 I draw the concept of "emergent" (along with its related concepts, "dominant" and "residual") from the work of Raymond Williams. See *Marxism and Literature* (London: Oxford University Press, 1981).

18 See T. V. Reed, *Fifteen Jugglers, Five Believers: Literary Politics and the Poetics of American Social Movements* (Berkeley: University of California Press, 1992).

19 Lisa Lowe, *Immigrant Acts: On Asian American Cultural Politics* (Durham, NC: Duke University Press, 1996), 157–58.

20 See Denning, *Cultural Front*, xix–xx.
21 George Lipsitz, *Rainbow at Midnight: Labor and Culture in the 1940s* (Urbana-Champaign: University of Illinois Press, 1990).
22 Julia Mickenberg, *Learning from the Left: Children's Literature, the Cold War and Radical Politics in the United States* (New York: Oxford University Press, 2006).
23 See especially Walter Kalaidjian, *American Culture between the Wars: Revisionary Modernism and Postmodern Critique* (New York: Columbia University Press, 1993); Cary Nelson, *Repression and Recovery: Modern American Poetry and the Politics of Cultural Memory, 1910–1945* (Madison: University of Wisconsin Press, 1989), and *Revolutionary Memory: Recovering the Poetry of the American Left* (New York: Routledge, 2001); and John Lowney, *History, Memory, and the Literary Left: Modern American Poetry, 1935–1968* (Iowa City: University of Iowa Press, 2006).
24 See Denning, *Cultural Front*.
25 See Rita Barnard, *The Great Depression and the Culture of Abundance: Kenneth Fearing, Nathaniel West and Mass Culture in the 1930s* (New York: Cambridge University Press, 1995); and Denning, *Cultural Front*.
26 See June Howard, *Form and History in American Literary Naturalism* (Chapel Hill: University of North Carolina Press, 1985); Amy Kaplan, *The Social Construction of American Realism* (Chicago: University of Chicago Press, 1988); and Paula Rabinowitz, *They Must Be Represented: The Politics of Documentary* (London: Verso, 1994).
27 A comprehensive overview of this ongoing revisionary project is provided in Wald's *Writing from the Left*, most broadly in chapters 5 and 7, and scattered through Wald's historical trilogy are the names of dozens of writers he and others have been rescuing from Cold War burial.
28 I have written as if the revisionist cause was being driven by a united class of actors, but in fact that is far from the truth. Very significant differences of style and substance exist across a range of scholars who have worked and are working to undo stereotyped images of, and open up new perspectives on, the cultural left. Positions range from figures such as Marcus Klein (who extends the liberal anticommunism of a Daniel Aaron) to scholars such as Alan Wald and Harvey Teres (whose sympathies seem closest to the arguments of independent communists and Trotskyists such as James T. Farrell and the *Partisan Review* group in its early year) to Paula Rabinowitz (who revalues women writers on the left and reviews the gendered structure of all thirties writing using a combination of feminist, Marxist, and poststructuralist theory) to figures such as Barbara Foley and James Murphy (who seem virtually to be neo-Stalinists and critical defenders of the CPUSA cultural leadership) to cultural historian Douglas Wixson (who speaks on behalf of a strand of grassroots anarchocommunist "worker-writers" nourished by but highly critical of the Communist Party's literary critics) to a critic such as Michael Denning (whose sweeping reconsideration of the left recasts the much-maligned Popular Front as a broad, worker-based left-liberal, multicultural counterhegemonic social movement). At their worst, these differences threaten to devolve into retro reruns of the sectarianism that mars some thirties writing itself. At its best, and fortunately the best predominates, this range of perspectives provides a sympathetic survey and complementary angles of analysis that give a new and richer voice to the best of left literature and

criticism. In a rather ungenerous survey of her fellow revisionists at the beginning of *Radical Representations*, Foley suggests that they are all victims (dupes?) of anti-Stalinist propaganda. Some of her claims are certainly worth arguing about point by point, but her overall analysis simply asserts a set of political values far more tolerant of Stalinist politics than those she is critiquing. She couches much of this critique in terms of fact, but in actuality the issues she raises primarily concern political judgment. Foley sees the CPUSA literary cup as half-full, while the critics she attacks see it as half-empty. She argues that the CP critics were on the right track but did not carry it through rigorously, while those more enamored of liberalism, the Trostky-inspired opposition, or independent Marxists, see the CPUSA hierarchy as on the wrong track altogether. While this style of argument colors Foley's entire book, it does not keep it from making stunning new contributions to the field that can be of use to critics with a variety of political positions. My point is that the epithet anti-Stalinist, like the epithet Stalinist, is too thin of a concept on which to hinge an argument. We need instead an open engagement over differing political values and strategies.

29 Useful works treating particular writers and critics include two books by Alan Wald, *James T. Farrell: The Revolutionary Socialist Years* (New York: New York University Press, 1978), and *The Revolutionary Imagination: The Poetry and Politics of John Wheelwright and Sherry Mangan* (Chapel Hill: University of North Carolina Press, 1983); E. San Juan, Jr., *Carlos Bulosan and the Imagination of Class Struggle*; Michel Fabre, *The Unfinished Journey of Richard Wright* (New York: Morrow, 1973); Townsend Luddington, *John Dos Passos* (New York: Dutton Adult, 1980); Elinor Langer, *Josephine Herbst: The Story She Could Never Tell* (Boston: Little, Brown, 1984); Janice R. MacKinnon and Stephen R. MacKinnon, *Agnes Smedley: The Life and Times of an American Radical* (Berkeley: University of California Press, 1986); Arnold Rampersand, *The Life of Langston Hughes*, 2nd ed., 2 vols. (London: Oxford University Press, 2001); Cary Nelson and Jefferson Hendricks, *Edwin Rolfe: A Biographical Essay and Guide to the Rolfe Archive at the University of Illinois* (Urbana-Champaign: University of Illinois Press, 1990); Constance Coiner, *Better Red: The Writing and Resistance of Tillie Olsen and Meridel LeSueur* (London: Oxford University Press, 1994); and Leonard Wilcox, *V. F. Calverton: Radical in the American Grain* (Philadelphia: Temple University Press, 1992).

30 Denning, xvi, 9.

31 Contrary to some reviewers, Denning makes clear that shifting to this wider focus in no way denies the "Communist party its due"; Denning, *Cultural Front*, 6. It is a sad commentary on the sectarian imagination that some folks would apparently rather give the CPUSA full credit for a relatively small movement than give it partial credit for a far larger one.

32 Denning, *Cultural Front*, 5. Emphasis in original.

NOTES TO CHAPTER 2

1 Class discord in a Washington mill town in the early twentieth century is brilliantly portrayed in Norman Clark's classic study *Mill Town: A Social History of Everett Washington* (Seattle: University of Washington Press, 1970). For an equally rich study that throws light on the kind of environment in which Cantwell grew up, see William G. Robbins, *Hard Times in Paradise: Coos Bay, Oregon, 1850–1986* (Seattle: University of Washington Press, 1988). A

richly informative work that directly focuses on political discord in the area is "Red Harbor: Class, Violence and Community in Gray's Harbor, Washington," a PhD dissertation by Aaron Goings available online at http://libcom.org/files/redharbor.pdf. Two decades after Cantwell's death, another angry young artist from Aberdeen representing a later generation of rebels, grunge rocker Kurt Cobain, cut short his career through suicide. For the context of Cobain's life and a portrait of the largely unchanged nature of Aberdeen today, see the special issue of *Rolling Stone* 683 (June 2, 1994), especially Mikal Gilmore's essay on Cobain's relation to his hometown, "The Road to Nowhere," 44–46, 53.

2 Little Falls, which later became Vader, is located a few miles southwest of Chehalis. In 1968, a group of real estate promoters from Seattle, noting the superb view, gave the place yet a third name, Enchanted Hills, apparently in hopes of attracting an upper-middle-class clientele in search of gracious country living. See Cantwell, *The Hidden Northwest* (Philadelphia: Lippincott, 1972), 209. The information on the early days of Little Falls is taken from the *Longview* (Washington) *Daily News*, February, 7, 1976.

3 Cantwell, *Hidden Northwest*, 210–11.

4 Herbert Hunt and Floyd C. Kaylor, *Washington: West of the Cascades*, vol. 2 (Charleston, SC: Nabu, 2010), 666–67.

5 Cantwell, *Hidden Northwest*, 211; Cantwell, "Autobiographical Sketch of Robert Cantwell," *Wilson Bulletin for Librarians* 10 (1936): 298

6 *Polk's Gray's Harbor Country Directory* (Seattle 1923–24), 98.

7 Cantwell, "A Town and Its Novels," *New Republic* (Feb. 19, 1936): 51.

8 Mrs. Anne Cotton, interview with author, April 1, 1976, Aberdeen, Washington; Mrs. Ed Van Syckle, interview with author, April 1, 1976, Aberdeen, Washington. The former is a historian and librarian in Aberdeen, the latter a high school classmate of Cantwell's.

9 Weatherwax High senior class, eds., *The Quinault, 1923–24* (Aberdeen, WA: Quick Print Co., 1924); Mrs. Ed Van Syckle, interview with author, April 1, 1976, Aberdeen, Washington.

10 Cantwell, "Autobiographical Sketch."

11 A company film of Harbor Plywood made during the years Cantwell worked there and including the clipper machine that he worked on can be found at https://www.youtube.com/watch?v=yrisN16mJX0. Accessed January 8, 2013.

12 *Polks Gray's Harbor County Directory* (Seattle, 1928–29), 104.

13 Cantwell, *Laugh and Lie Down* (New York: Farrar and Rinehart, 1931), xii.

14 Ibid., 11.

15 Calvin Fixx to Cantwell, July 1, 1929, Robert Cantwell Papers, Knight Library Special Collections, University of Oregon (hereafter cited as Cantwell Papers).

16 Fixx to Cantwell, October 5, 1935, Cantwell Papers.

17 Fixx to Cantwell, ca. 1925, Cantwell Papers.

18 References to these works are scattered throughout the Fixx-Cantwell correspondence, but the works themselves apparently have not survived.

19 See, for example, Fixx to Cantwell, January 14, 1929, Cantwell Papers. Keene Wallis (1898–1968) was a minor poet and essayist; Alfred Kreymborg (1883–1966) was an American modernist poet, novelist, playwright, and, most importantly, literary editor and anthologist (including editing *American Caravan*, where Cantwell's first story appeared).

20 See Cantwell to Betsy Cantwell, August 22, 1942, Cantwell Papers.
21 Fixx to Cantwell, June 7, 1926, Cantwell Papers.
22 Fixx to Cantwell, March 3, 1929, Cantwell Papers.
23 The best study of Wobbly activity in the region remains Robert L. Tyler, *Rebels of the Woods: The I.W.W. in the Pacific Northwest* (Eugene: University of Oregon Press, 1967). For a more thorough and perceptive treatment of IWW ideology, see Melvyn Dubofsky, *We Shall Be All: A History of the IWW* (New York: Quadrangle Press, 1969).
24 Written in 1934, the story was published in 1935 in the anthology *Proletarian Literature in the United States*, edited by Granville Hicks, Mike Gold, Isidor Schneider, and Joseph North (New York: International, 1935).
25 Fixx to Cantwell, August 1928, Cantwell Papers. Cantwell, autobiographical sketch.
26 Fixx to Cantwell, March 13, 1929, Cantwell Papers. Malcolm Cowley, reviewing the *New American Caravan*, ed. Van-Wyck Brooks, Alfred Kreymborg, and Lewis Mumford (New York: Macauley, 1929), called Cantwell's story "the best in the volume: it is the aftermath of a love affair treated in the analytical manner which one associates with Henry James and yet with a certain lyricism." *New Republic* (Nov. 6, 1929): 326.
27 Fixx to Cantwell, September 2, 1929, Cantwell Papers.
28 Cantwell to editor, *New York Times Book Review* (May 13, 1934): 23.
29 Cantwell to Carl Haverlin, September 29, 1954, Cantwell Papers. Seyersted, *Robert Cantwell*, 24.
30 Cantwell, *Laugh and Lie Down*, xi.
31 Ibid., 41.
32 Ibid., xxx.
33 Ibid., 173.
34 Ibid., 191–92.
35 Unsigned review, *New York Times Book Review* (Oct. 18, 1931): 6.

NOTES TO CHAPTER 3

1 See T. S. Matthews, *Name and Address: An Autobiography* (New York: Simon and Schuster, 1969), 248–86.
2 Jack Conroy, "Robert Cantwell's *Land of Plenty*," in *Proletarian Writers of the Thirties*, ed. David Madden (Carbondale, IL: Southern Illinois University Press, 1968), 77.
3 Malcolm Cowley, letter to author, Robert Cantwell Papers, Knight Library Special Collections, University of Oregon (hereafter referred to as Cantwell Papers).
4 Edmund Wilson, *The American Jitters: A Year of the Slump* (New York: Scribners, 1932), 297.
5 On the continuities, see especially Daniel Aaron, *Writers on the Left: Episodes in American Literary Communism* (New York: Harcourt Brace, 1961); Marcus Klein, *Foreigners: The Making of American Literature, 1900–1940* (Chicago: University of Chicago Press, 1981); and Cary Nelson, *Repression and Recovery: Modern American Poetry and the Politics of Cultural Memory, 1910–1945* (Madison: University of Wisconsin Press, 1989).
6 Michael Gold, "Thornton Wilder: Prophet of the Genteel Christ," *New Republic* (Oct. 22, 1930): 266–67.

7   Michael Gold, "Towards Proletarian Art," *Liberator* 4 (Feb. 1921): 20–24.
8   Bohemian radical Floyd Dell had used the term two years earlier, but it is widely thought that it was Gold's usage that stuck, and it was surely Gold who did the most to keep the idea of proletarian art alive during the left doldrums of the twenties.

   Significant (somewhat differing) accounts of the development of proletarian literary theory can be found in Barbara Foley, *Radical Representations: Politics and Form in U.S. Proletarian Fiction, 1929–1941* (Durham, NC: Duke University Press, 1993); James Bloom, *Left Letters: The Culture Wars of Michael Gold and Joseph Freeman* (New York: Columbia University Press, 1992); Eric Homberger, *American Writers and Radical Politics, 1900–1939: Equivocal Commitments* (London: MacMillan, 1986); James P. Murphy, *The Proletarian Moment* (Urbana: University of Illinois Press, 1991); Walter Rideout, *The Radical Novel in the United States, 1900–1954* (Cambridge, MA: Harvard University Press, 1956); Lawrence H. Schwartz, *Marxism and Culture: The CPUSA and Aesthetics in the 1930s* (Port Washington, NY: Kennikat Press, 1980); Adam Fischer, "Formula for Utopia: The American Proletarian Novel, 1930–1939" (PhD diss., University of Massachusetts, 1974); David Peck, "The Development of an American Marxist Literary Criticism: The Monthly *New Masses*" (PhD diss., Temple University, 1968); Jon Christian Suggs, "The Influence of Marxist Aesthetics on American Fiction, 1929–1940" (PhD diss., University of Kansas, 1978); Arthur D. Casciato, "Citizen Writers: A History of the League of American Writers, 1935–1942" (PhD diss., University of Virginia, 1986,); and Mary E. Papke, "An Analysis of Selected Marxist Criticism, 1920–1941: From Dogma to Dynamic Strategies," *Minnesota Review* 13 (Fall 1979): 41–69.
9   See Aaron, *Writers on the Left*, 216–30.
10 Michael Gold, untitled editorial, *New Masses* 4 (July 1928): 2.
11 On the John Reed Clubs, see Homberger, "Proletarian Literature and the John Reed Clubs," in his *American Writers and Radical Politics*. Aaron sketches their activities well in *Writers on the Left*, and Malcolm Cowley vividly evokes the atmosphere of the clubs in "A Remembrance of the Red Romance, Part 2," *Esquire* 61 (April 1964): 78–81.
12 Foley, *Radical Representations*. James T. Farrell, in his famous attack on what we might call "prolitcrit," was able, by simply cataloguing the definitions of proletarian literature in circulation in 1936, to summarize the confusion the term engendered. But read against the grain of Farrell's satirical intent, this excerpt reveals just how varied the criticism and the literature were: "It seems to me there are the following possible definitions of proletarian literature: it can be defined as creative literature written by a member of the industrial proletariat, regardless of the author's political orientation; as creative literature that reveals some phase of the experience of the industrial proletariat, regardless of the political orientation of the author; as creative literature written by a member of the industrial proletariat who is class-conscious in the Marxist sense and a member of the proletarian vanguard; as creative literature written by a class-conscious member of the proletariat and treating solely (or principally) of some phase of the life of that group; as creative writing about that group within the proletariat regardless of the author's class status or his group status within his class; as creative literature written to enforce, through its conclusions and implications, the views of the proletarian vanguard; or as creative literature combining these features in differing combinations." James T. Farrell, *A Note on Literary Criticism* (New York: Vanguard Press, 1936), 86–87. For the purposes of this

study, I use the term "proletarian" to describe any thirties novel written by a self-declared Marxist and apparently meant to have a radicalizing effect on its readers.

13. Indeed, Schwartz, in *Marxism and Culture*, details a variety of ways in which Comintern literary and other policy was frequently in asymmetrical relation to practices in the United States, partly due simply to an inefficient mechanism of linguistic and cultural translation, and partly due to limits set on information leaving the Soviet Union, even to friendly outsiders. See also Foley, *Radical Representations*, chapters 2–4, and Murphy, *Proletarian Moment*.

14. See Douglas Wixson, *Worker-Writer in America: Jack Conroy and the Tradition of Midwestern Literary Radicalism, 1898–1990* (Urbana-Champaign: University of Illinois Press, 1994), especially chapters 8–10.

15. Aaron, *Writers on the Left*, 236–47; Fischer, "Formula for Utopia," 105–11; and Foley, *Radical Representations*, chapters 3 and 4.

16. I am referring to the (in)famous "Author's Field Day," *New Masses* (July 3, 1934): 27–28.

17. As James Bloom has shown, even Mike Gold, who fits the stereotype of literary commissar as well as any one, produced work, in both his novel/autobiography *Jews Without Money* and his criticism, that was far more complex than his oft-cited literary prescriptions would suggest. Gold had after all written futurist plays in the twenties and was more than passingly familiar with avant-garde trends. See especially chapter 1 of Bloom, *Left Letters*. On Farrell, see Alan Wald, *James T. Farrell: The Revolutionary Socialist Years* (New York: New York University Press, 1978); on Richard Wright, see Michel Fabre, *The Unfinished Quest of Richard Wright* (New York: Morrow, 1973).

18. Alfred Kazin, *Starting Out in the Thirties* (Boston: Little, Brown, 1965), 15.

19. Foley considers this a weakness of the proletarian literary movement, one sign that it was too attached to "bourgeois" literary values. While this may be true from the perspective of Leninist party discipline, to so argue is to out of hand rule out a variety of kinds of actually existing working-class literature from which even a Leninist might learn.

20. See Bloom, *Left Letters*, chapter 4. I would argue that both this oft-quoted phrase and Gold's famous attack on Wilder may stem as much from homophobia as from antimodernism. I offer this observation as another small contribution to the ongoing development of queer theorization of the thirties.

21. On the bohemian radicals of the teens and twenties, see Leslie Fishbein, *Rebels in Bohemia: The Radicals of "The Masses," 1911–1917* (Chapel Hill: University of North Carolina Press, 1982); Edward Abrams, *The Lyrical Left: Randolph Bourne, Alfred Steiglitz, and the Origins of Cultural Radicalism in America* (Charlottesville: University Press of Virginia, 1986); Casey Nelson Blake, *Beloved Community: The Cultural Criticism of Randolph Bourne, Van Wyck Brooks, Waldo Frank, and Lewis Mumford* (Chapel Hill: University of North Carolina Press, 1990); the early chapters of James Gilbert, *Writers and Partisans: A History of Literary Radicalism in America* (New York: Wiley, 1968); and Homberger, *American Writers and Radical Politics*.

22. Murphy, in *The Proletarian Moment*, makes the strongest claim for appreciation of modernism among the literary Communists of the thirties. He even argues, though less convincingly, that the Communist Party political bureaucracy was favorably disposed toward modernist techniques. See also Foley, *Radical Representations*, especially 54–63. Alan Wald dissents with

many of Murphy's claims in his review of *Proletarian Moment*. See Wald, "Literary 'Leftism' Reconsidered," *Science and Society* 57, no. 2 (Summer 1993): 214–22, reprinted in Wald, *Writing from the Left: New Essays on Radical Culture and Politics* (London: Verso, 1994). Wald explores the issues of modernism and proletarianism from a different angle in *The Revolutionary Imagination: The Poetry and Politics of John Wheelwright and Sherry Magnan* (Chapel Hill: University of North Carolina Press, 1983); and Cary Nelson greatly broadens this project in his examination of poetry in *Repression and Recovery*.

23 As with "proletarian literature," I use "Marxist literary criticism" as a broadly inclusive term. I designate as Marxist any critics who either declare themselves to be Marxist, or who centrally employ a Marxist vocabulary as part of their critical apparatus.

24 See Edmund Wilson, *The Shores of Light* (New York: Farrar, Straus and Young, 1952); Malcolm Cowley, *Think Back on Us: A Contemporary Chronicle of the 1930s*, ed., with an introduction, by Henry Dan Piper, 2 vols. (Carbondale: Southern Illinois University Press, 1967), especially 47–50, 78–83; and Malcolm Cowley, *Dream of the Golden Mountain: Remembering the 1930s* (New York: Viking, 1980). On Phillips and Rahv, see Alan Wald, *The New York Intellectuals: The Rise and Decline of the Anti-Stalinist Left from the 1930s to the 1980s* (Chapel Hill: University of North Carolina Press, 1987).

25 The views of Marx and Engels on literature can be gleaned from the following works: Lee Baxandall and Stefan Morawski, eds., *Marx and Engels on Literature and Art: A Selection of Writings* (Milwaukee: Telos Press, 1973); Maynard Solomon, ed., *Marxism and Art: Essays Classic and Contemporary* (New York: Knopf, 1974); Georg Lukács, "Marx and Engels on Aesthetics," in *Writer and Critic* (London: Merilin, 1970); and Fredric Jameson, "Introduction," in *Marxist Esthetics*, by Henri Arvon, trans. from French by Helen Lane (Ithaca, NY: Cornell University Press, 1973).

26 Leon Trotsky, *Literature and Revolution*, trans. Rose Strunsky (Ann Arbor: University of Michigan Press, 1960), especially chapter 7. Trotsky denies in this work that the proletariat will ever produce a culture wholly separate from that of the bourgeoisie, but will instead contribute through political struggle leading to a postrevolutionary classless literature. By 1930, however, the existence of a body of literature called "proletarian" already seemed to contradict this view.

27 See Harvey Teres, "Remaking Marxist Criticism: *Partisan Review*'s Eliotic Leftism, 1934–1936," *American Literature* 64, no. 1 (March 1992): 127–53.

28 See Michael Denning, *The Cultural Front: The Laboring of American Literature in the Twentieth Century* (London: Verso, 1996), 5, 57–58.

29 Originally an unsigned editorial in the *New Republic* (Nov. 26, 1930): 31–32, the essay was included as Edmund Wilson, "The Economic Interpretation of Wilder," in his collection *Shores of Light*.

30 In addition to Wilson, *Shores of Light*, 498–99, see Granville Hicks, "The Fighting Decade," *Saturday Review of Literature* 11 (July 6, 1940): 4.

31 Aaron, *Writers on the Left*, 248–86.

32 Malcolm Cowley, letter to author, n.d., Cantwell Papers.

33 Cowley, "A Remembrance of the Red Romance," *Esquire* 61 (March 1964): 127.

34 Alfred Kazin, *Starting Out in the Thirties*, 12–13.
35 Matthew Josephson, *Infidel in the Temple* (New York: Knopf, 1967), 178, 144.
36 Cantwell, "The Wreck of the Gravy Train," *New Republic* (Jan. 6, 1932): 218.
37 Aaron, *Writers on the Left*, 448.
38 Ibid., 214.
39 Quoted in Josephson, *Infidel*, 144.
40 Ibid.
41 Cowley, "Remembrance of the Red Romance," 127.
42 Cantwell, "Dramatist's Raw Material," *New Republic* 75 (June 28, 1933): 187–88.
43 Josephson, *Infidel*, 144; Cowley, letter to author, March 10, 1977.
44 T. S. Matthews, quoted in Per Seyersted, *Robert Cantwell: An American Thirties Radical Writer and His Apostasy* (Oslo: Novus Press, 2004), 30–31.
45 Josephson, *Infidel*, 144.
46 Cantwell to editor, *New Republic* (Aug. 24, 1932): 48.
47 Josephson, *Infidel*, 174.
48 Ibid., 175.
49 Ibid., 177.
50 Ibid., 178.
51 Cowley, letter to author, n.d., Cantwell Papers.
52 See Foley, *Radical Representations*, chapter 4.
53 See, for example, Cantwell, "Mr. Eliot's Sunday Afternoon," *New Republic* (Sept. 14, 1932): 132–33.
54 Walter Benjamin, "The Author as Producer," in *Reflections* (New York: Schocken, 1986), 220–38, 221.
55 Cantwell, "No Landmarks," *Symposium* 4 (Jan. 1933): 70–85.
56 Ibid. 72.
57 Ibid.
58 Ibid.
59 Ibid.
60 Ibid. 76.
61 See Fredric Jameson, "Introduction," in Avron, *Marxist Esthetics*, xxi–xxii.
62 Cantwell, "No Landmarks," 79.
63 For a summary of these disputes, see Foley, *Radical Representations*, chapters 3 and 4. Adam Fischer also discusses this debate in detail in "Formula for Utopia," 70–157.
64 Cantwell, "No Landmarks," 80.
65 Ibid., 81.
66 Ibid., 82.
67 See Rideout, *Radical Novel*, 174.
68 Cantwell, "No Landmarks," 82.
69 Ibid., 83.
70 Ibid., 84.
71 Cantwell, "Four Novelists of Tomorrow," *New Republic* (Mar. 8, 1933): 108.

72 Ibid.
73 Ibid.
74 Ibid., 109.
75 Cantwell, review of Caldwell's *Tobacco Road*, in *Symposium* 3 (Apr. 1932): 256–60.
76 Cantwell, "Some Recent Novels," *New Republic* (Feb. 8, 1933): 356.
77 Cantwell, "The Influence of James Joyce," *New Republic* 77 (Dec. 27, 1933): 200.
78 Ibid., 200–201.
79 Ibid., 201.
80 Ibid.
81 Ibid.
82 Cantwell to Newton Arvin, November 15, 1933, Cantwell Papers.
83 See Rabinowitz, *Labor and Desire: Women's Revolutionary Fiction in Depression America* (Chapel Hill: University of North Carolina Press, 1991), for an extended analysis of the intersections of masculinity and proletarianism.
84 For a more complicated reading of the positions of Gold and Freeman, see Bloom, *Left Letters*.
85 John Dos Passos, "The *New Masses* I'd Like," *New Masses* 1 (June 1926): 20.
86 See, Foley, *Radical Representations*, 143–46.
87 Cantwell to James T. Farrell, June 12, 1934, Cantwell Papers.
88 Cantwell's observations on the limits of Farrell's position are confirmed by Wald's claim that Farrell "never fully embraced Marxist philosophy" but instead remained to a large degree a pragmatist in the Dewey-Mead tradition. Wald, *James T. Farrell*, 148.

NOTES TO CHAPTER 4

1 Cantwell, "Can You Hear Their Voices?" *New Republic* (Oct. 18, 1933): 286.
2 Commentary on the novel can be found in the following sources: Harry T. More, "Preface," *Land of Plenty*; Walter B. Rideout, *The Radical Novel in the United States, 1900–1954* (Cambridge, MA: Harvard University Press, 1956); Barbara Foley, *Radical Representations: Politics and Form in U.S. Proletarian Fiction, 1929–1941* (Durham, NC: Duke University Press, 1993); Jack Conroy, "Robert Cantwell's Land of Plenty," and Frederick J. Hoffman, "The Aesthetics of the Proletarian Novel," both in *Proletarian Writers of the Thirties*, ed. David Madden (Carbondale: Southern Illinois University Press, 1968); Jack Saltzman, "Robert Cantwell," in *Contemporary Novelists*, ed. by James Vinson (London: St. James Press, 1976); Merrill Lewis, *Robert Cantwell* (Boise, ID: Boise State University, 1985); Richard Pells, *Radical Visions and American Dreams: Culture and Social Thought in the Depression Years* (New York: Harper & Row, 1973); Kenneth Ledbetter, "The Idea of the Proletarian Novel in the United States, 1927–1939" (PhD diss., University of Illinois, 1963); Adam Fischer, "Formula for Utopia: The American Proletarian Novel, 1930–1939," (PhD diss., University of Massachusetts, 1974); Cheryl Davis, "A Rhetorical Study of Selected Proletarian Novels of the 1930s," (PhD diss., University of Utah, 1976); Calvin Harris, "Twentieth Century American Political Fiction: An Analysis of Proletarian Fiction," (PhD diss., University of Oregon, 1979); Joel Wingard, "Towards a Workers' America: The Theory and Practice of the Proletarian Novel, 1937–39," (PhD diss., Louisiana State University, 1979) .

3. See Rideout, *Radical Novel*, 174–80; and Foley, *Radical Representations*, chapter 10.
4. See Cantwell, "A Town and Its Novels."
5. "Mentor figure" is a term used by Foley to describe a stock character especially prevalent in the proletarian bildungsroman. See *Radical Representations*, chapter 9.
6. On the dime novel as allegory and site of working-class struggle, see Michael Denning, *Mechanic Accents* (New York: Verso, 1987).
7. Text citations refer to the original 1934 edition and are given as page numbers in parentheses following quoted or paraphrased material. The novel was reprinted in 1971 by Southern Illinois University Press with a preface by Harry T. Moore, and reprinted once more by Pharos Press in 2013, with a preface by Jess Walter.
8. Ledbetter, "Idea of the Proletarian Novel," 45.
9. Cantwell, autobiographical sketch, *Wilson Library Bulletin,* January 1936.
10. Vin Garl's Finnish extraction is not an arbitrary detail but reflects Cantwell's understanding that Finns were especially active in the radical movement in the Northwest. See, for example, Paul Hummasti, "Finnish Radicals in Astoria, Oregon, 1904–1940: A Study in Immigrant Socialism" (PhD diss., University of Oregon, 1975), 128–53.
11. Foley, *Radical Representations*, 366.
12. Ledbetter, "Idea of the Proletarian Novel," 51.
13. See Foley, *Radical Representations*, 366, 394. For Foley's general reading of gender in thirties radicalism, see the chapter 6 of her study. For a more critical reading of sexism in the Communist movement and the proletarian novel, see Rabinowitz, *Labor and Desire: Women's Revolutionary Fiction in Depression America* (Chapel Hill: University of North Carolina Press, 1991).
14. This is the famous talk back to the critics symposium mentioned in my introduction. Cantwell, "Author's Field Day: A Symposium on Marxist Criticism," *New Masses* (July 3, 1934): 27.
15. Cantwell to Farrell, June 12th, 1934, Robert Cantwell Papers, Special Collection, University of Oregon Library, Eugene, Oregon (hereafter referred to as Cantwell Papers).
16. Cantwell, "Authors' Field Day."
17. Ibid.
18. Hicks had by this time replaced Mike Gold as the major interpreter of the proletarian novel, and thus his comments may be viewed as the orthodox critical position.
19. *Granville Hicks in the* New Masses, ed. Jack Alan Robbins (Port Washington, NY: Kennikat, 1974), 80.
20. Granville Hicks, review, *New Masses* (July 3, 1934): 32.
21. See chapter 2.
22. John Dos Passos, review, *New Republic* (May 16, 1934): 25.
23. Jack Conroy, review, *Partisan Review* (June–July 1934): 52–53.
24. Jack Conroy, "Robert Cantwell's *Land of Plenty*," 74–84.
25. Louis Kronenberger, review, *Nation* (June 13, 1934): 679. See also Horace Gregory, review, *Books* (April 29, 1934): 6.
26. Harold Strauss, review, *New York Times Book Review* (April 29, 1934): 7.
27. Cantwell to editor, *New York Times Book Review* (May 13, 1934): 25.

28 Ibid., 23.
29 Geoffrey Stone, review, *Commonweal* (Aug. 17, 1934): 23
30 John Dos Passos, *New Republic* (May 16, 1934): 25.
31 One could also explain this "failure" (again by certain "humanistic" cum New Critical standards) as resting in the general limits of Cantwell's literary gifts, not his ideological beliefs, since the same "flaw" mars the characterization in his pre-Marxist *Laugh and Lie Down*. This is a personal opinion, but one shared by several critics of Cantwell's first novel. See, for example, Horace Gregory, *Books* (Nov. 8, 1931): 21.
32 Louis Kronenberger, review, *Nation* (June 13, 1934): 679. Henry Seidel Canby expressed a similar opinion in *Saturday Review*: "Once the modern novelist takes up the class struggle one eye or the other goes blind. Mr. Cantwell's workers are convincing. . . . But when he brings in the bourgeoisie (to whom presumably he belongs), the faint paranoia, so familiar to readers of class fiction, begins." Henry Seidel Canby, *Saturday Review* (May 5, 1934): 677.
33 Cantwell to James T. Farrell, June 12, 1934, Cantwell Papers.
34 Unsigned review, *Time* (April 30, 1934): 69. The reviewer for *Forum* expressed a similar sense of *The Land of Plenty* having surpassed its genre: "This excellent novel of class discord in a Pacific Coast lumber mill exhibits none of the crudities too often associated with proletarian fiction. Mr. Cantwell is a subtle and exciting writer, no trafficker in bald blacks and whites. . . . There is nothing doctrinaire about this book. Mr. Cantwell writes of actual, individualized workers and owners. He writes of them so well that it is not necessary for him to tag his moral." E. H. Waltor, review, *Forum* (July 1934): 5.
35 Strauss, *New York Times Book Review* (April 29, 1934): 7.
36 Clifton Fadiman, review, *New Yorker* (May 1934): 27.
37 Robbins, *Granville Hicks in the* New Masses, 276.
38 See especially Fischer, "Formula for Utopia," chapters 4 and 5.
39 Cantwell to Farrell, June 12, 1934, Cantwell Papers.
40 In addition to Hicks's review, the *New Masses*' view is expressed by Joseph Freeman in his preface to the influential collection *Proletarian Literature in the United States*, ed. Granville Hicks et al., 39–57 (New York: International, 1935), in which he singles out Cantwell (and Josephine Herbst) for special mention (10), and *Partisan Review* editors Wallace Phelps and Philip Rahv list Cantwell as among four breakthrough proletarian novelists in their 1934 essay "Problems and Perspectives in Revolutionary Literature" (3).
41 Calvin Fixx to Cantwell, November 4, 1934, Cantwell Papers. Conroy in the *Partisan Review* found the character quite believable and predicted, correctly, that "bourgeois" critics would not recognize him as such.
42 Published in the seminal anthology *Proletarian Literature in the United States*, this story brilliantly fictionalizes the aftermath of the Centralia massacre of members of the IWW in 1917. While this setting somewhat distances the story from the immediate issues of the thirties, it resonates with the time period in suggesting not revolutionary progress (like *Land of Plenty*, it has a downbeat ending) but the rise of fascism as a possible scenario if the calls for justice by workers were not heeded. The story reprises Cantwell's preferred perspective technique, alternating between the viewpoint of a young boy scout and that of one of the hounded Wobblies he encounters in the woods. See *Proletarian Literature in the United States*, 39–57.

43 Cantwell, *Land of Plenty*, 1.
44 Conroy, "Robert Cantwell's *Land of Plenty*," 83–84.
45 See Rideout, *Radical Novel*, 235.
46 Cantwell, "What the Working Class Reads," *New Republic* (July 17, 1935): 274–76.
47 John Scott Bowman, "The Proletarian Novel in America," quoted in Rideout, *Radical Novel*, 237.
48 For more on the history of Northwest radical politics, see Jeffery Johnson, *"They Are All Red Out Here": Socialist Politics in the Pacific Northwest, 1895–1925* (Norman: University of Oklahoma Press, 2008), and for Cantwell's home region, Aaron Goings, "Red Harbor: Class Violence and Community in Gray's Harbor, Washington," PhD diss., Central Washington University, 2005.
49 "Communism in Washington State," http://depts.washington.edu/labhist/cpproject/index.shtml, accessed September 15, 2011.
50 In the early twenty-first century, in what may or may not be an example of Marx's famous claim that tragic history repeats itself as farce, a revived IWW union organized the workers of Washington state's most (in)famous retailer, Starbucks.
51 The best resources on IWW culture are Joyce L. Kornbluh, ed., *Rebel Voices: An I.W.W. Anthology* (Ann Arbor: University of Michigan Press, 1964), and Salvatore Salerno, *Red November, Black November: Culture and Community in the Industrial Workers of the World* (Albany: State University of New York Press, 1989).
52 On Paterson Strike Pageant, see http://historymatters.gmu.edu/d/5649/, accessed September 15, 2011.
53 Cantwell, "A Town and Its Novels," *New Republic* (Feb. 19, 1936): 51.
54 See Brian Teague Beckwith, "A Town and Its Novelists," in *On the Harbor*, ed. Brian Teague Beckwith and John C. Hughes (Las Vegas: Stephens Press, 2005), 88–95.
55 Fixx to Cantwell, March 3, 1929, Cantwell Papers.
56 International Labor Defense, *Night Riders in Gallup* (New York: International Labor Defense, 1935).
57 Alan Wald, "Revising the Barricades: Scholarship about the US Cultural Left in the Post–Cold War Era," 101–22, in *Socialist Cultures East and West: A Post–Cold War Reassessment* (Westport, CT: Praeger, 2002), edited by Dubravka Juraga and M. Keith Booker, 168n14. On the Weatherwax siblings, see also Sara Halprin, *Seema's Show: A Life on the Left* (Albuquerque: University of New Mexico Press, 2005).
58 Clara Weatherwax, *Marching! Marching!* (New York: International Press, 1935), ix.
59 See Jon Christian Suggs, "*Marching! Marching!* and the Idea of the Proletarian Novel," in Janet Casey, *The Novel and the American Left* (Iowa City: University of Iowa Press, 2004), 163.
60 John G. Wright, "Prize Novel," *New International* 3, no. 1 (February 1936): 30.
61 Of later critics writing about *Marching! Marching!* the most interesting is Paula Rabinowitz's elegant feminist reading of a dialectic of "feminine desire" and "masculine labor" in the novel in her work *Labor and Desire*. And Jon Christian Suggs has carefully placed the novel in the wider context of proletarian literature in his essay "*Marching! Marching!* and the Idea of the Proletarian Novel."

62 Foley, *Radical Representations*.
63 Ben Cochrane and William Dean Coldiron, *Disillusion* (Portland: Binfords & Mort, 1941).
64 Murray Morgan, *Viewless Winds* (New York: Dutton, 1949).

NOTES TO CHAPTER 5

1 Cantwell to Ernest Hemingway, October 21, 1950, Robert Cantwell Papers, Special Collection, University of Oregon Library, Eugene, Oregon (hereafter referred to as Cantwell Papers).
2 Cantwell, "The Merchant of Boston," (biography of E. A. Filene), unpublished manuscript, Robert Cantwell Papers, Knight Library Special Collections, University of Oregon (hereafter cited as Cantwell Papers).
3 Steffens met Filene in 1908 when the latter hired the journalist to rake the muck of Boston on behalf of the city's Good Government Association. As the two reformers summered together at Marblehead and floated about on Filene's yacht, they formed a lifelong friendship that even weathered Steffen's move to the far left in the thirties. See Justin Kaplan, *Lincoln Steffens: A Biography* (New York: Simon and Schuster, 1974), 166–67, 171, 174–75, 314, 316.
4 Kaplan, *Lincoln Steffens*, 314.
5 Cantwell, "Merchant of Boston," 8.
6 Cantwell, "Merchant of Boston," 5.
7 Quoted by Cantwell in "Merchant," 8. Taken from Lenin's "An Open Letter to E. A. Filene and the Progressive Capitalists."
8 Cantwell, "Merchant of Boston," 14.
9 All previous and subsequent citations refer to the second of the named versions of the manuscript. The first "auto/biographical" manuscript suffers from an inability to overcome the essential banality of its subject and from Cantwell's self-censoring efforts to submerge his own views. I have corrected obvious typographical errors in his manuscript.
10 Cantwell, "Merchant of Boston," 7–8.
11 Ibid., 9.
12 Kaplan, *Lincoln Steffens*, 166; Cantwell, "Merchant of Boston," 128.
13 Cantwell, "Merchant of Boston," 17.
14 Ibid., 20.
15 Ibid., 45.
16 Ibid., 40.
17 Ibid., 22.
18 Ibid., 30.
19 Ibid., 47.
20 Ibid., 86.
21 Quoted in Kaplan, *Lincoln Steffens*, 314.
22 Cantwell, "Merchant of Boston," 75, 86.
23 Ibid., 86.
24 Ibid., 86.
25 Ibid., 110.

26 Ibid.
27 Ibid., 112.
28 Cantwell to Newton Arvin, January 14, 1934, Cantwell Papers.
29 Cantwell, "Merchant of Boston," 186.
30 Kaplan, *Lincoln Steffens*, 316.
31 Lincoln Steffens, *The Letters of Lincoln Steffens*, vol. 2, *1920–1936*, Ella Winter and Granville Hicks, eds. (New York: Praeger, 1938), 976.
32 Cantwell, "Merchant of Boston," 125. Cantwell can be accused of mythicizing his own past a bit here as well.
33 Ibid., 139–41. Cantwell writes that the myth of the self-made man was a "keystone" in "the attempt of capitalists to find a moral basis for their wealth and power to exploit, to convince themselves and their employees . . . that capital represented previous sacrifices."
34 Ibid., 215–16.
35 Ibid., 223.
36 Ibid., 231. For a diametrically opposed view of Filene's career, one which is precisely the kind of testimonial Cantwell believed Filene secretly desired, see "'There Ain't No Such Person': An Inquiry into the Meaning of E. A. Filene," written anonymously by a former "associate" of Filene's and published in *Speaking of Change: A Selection of Speeches and Articles by Edward A. Filene* (Washington, DC: National Home Library Association, 1939). A perusal of this tome suggests that, while Cantwell's view of Filene was unduly harsh, it was not substantially inaccurate. I cannot judge his financial thought, but this sample of what might be called Filene's aesthetic theory suggests a good deal about the origins of Cantwell's contempt:

"When we get to discussing the question 'what is beauty?' all of us—even our artists—seem to get bewildered.

Why do we call a lion or a tiger beautiful? And why do we think of a hippopotamus as anything but?

It isn't because we would rather meet a lion or tiger, or because the thought of such a meeting stirs pleasant memories. I venture the guess that it is because the lion and the tiger are streamlined, while the hippopotamus is not. Anything shaped like that, we know, cannot use his power most effectively. Just one look convinces us that the hippopotamus requires too much gas per mile.

We simply cannot separate beauty from fitness. We may love the flaming red of the sunset, but we do not want to see it on our noses. Green may be our favorite color; but if the baby turned green we'd think it awful." (from a radio address, station KEX, Portland, Oregon, August 24, 1934, in *Speaking of Change*, 161).
37 Ibid., 140.
38 Cantwell to Newton Arvin, November 15, 1933, Cantwell Papers. Evidence from other letters makes it clear that "N.M." refers to *New Masses*. The magazine was being reorganized at this time under a new editorial staff. Cantwell is being purposely cryptic in this letter because, as he later wrote to Arvin, he was unsure about the Filene project. The short story he alludes to was probably "Hills around Centralia," his story about the Centralia "massacre" of IWW members, later published in *Proletarian Literature in the United States* (1935), which was

edited by Granville Hicks, Joseph Freeman, and other members of the *New Masses* staff.
39 William Leuchtenberg, *Franklin D. Roosevelt and the New Deal, 1932–1940* (New York: Harper, 1973), argues that 1934 was the peak of radical enthusiasm. See chapter 5, "Waiting for Lefty."
40 For works detailing these developments, see notes in the "introduction" above.
41 Cantwell to Newton Arvin, January 31, 1934, Cantwell Papers.
42 Ibid.
43 Cantwell, "Outstanding Books of the Year," *New Outlook* 162, no. 6 (Dec. 1933): 57.
44 Cantwell, "New Outlook on Books," *New Outlook* 163, no. 4 (Apr. 1934): 56.
45 Cantwell, "Outstanding Books of the Year," *New Outlook* 165, no. 1 (Jan. 1935): 53.
46 Steffens, *Letters of Lincoln Steffens*, 980.
47 Ibid.
48 Ibid., 982.
49 Cantwell to James T. Farrell, June 12, 1934, Cantwell Papers.
50 Cantwell, "The Little Magazine," *New Republic* (July 25, 1934): 297.
51 See Irving Bernstein's classic account *The Turbulent Years: A History of the American Worker, 1933–1941* (Boston: Houghton-Miflin, 1970), and Charles P. Larrowe, *Harry Bridges* (Chicago: Lawrence Hill and Co., 1977). Cantwell's coverage of the San Francisco events is discussed in greater detail in Seyersted, *Robert Cantwell*, 121–46.
52 Cantwell, "San Francisco: Act One," *New Republic* (July 25, 1934): 280.
53 Anne Loftis, *Witnesses to the Struggle: Imaging the 1930s California Labor Movement* (Reno: University of Nevada Press, 1998), 83–84.
54 Cantwell, "War on the West Coast," *New Republic* (Aug. 1, 1934): 308, 310. Obed Brooks, in the *Partisan Review* (April–May 1935): 31, makes an interesting allusion to Cantwell's coverage of the general strike: "Sensibility comes only after the assimilation and practice of ideas. When men as a result of experience or willful penetration become completely aware of new relationships in experience, when Marxism is intuitive and perceptive, sensibility will take care of itself, there will be no problem of where it can be legitimately borrowed. We see promise of this in work like Marx's *Eighteenth Brumaire*, Dimitroff's speeches, Cantwell's articles on the San Francisco strike, Spender's poem 'Vienna.'"
55 "The Press as Strikebreaker," *New Republic* (Aug. 8, 1934): 33 (unsigned editorial written by Cantwell).
56 Cited in Loftis, *Witnesses to the Struggle*, 85.
57 Quoted in Loftis, *Witnesses to the Struggle*, 85.
58 Cantwell to T. S. Mathews, Cantwell Papers.
59 Cantwell to John Dos Passos, n.d., Cantwell Papers.

NOTES TO CHAPTER 6

1 Michael Denning, *The Cultural Front: The Laboring of American Literature in the Twentieth Century* (London: Verso, 1996).
2 Per Seyersted, *Robert Cantwell: An American Thirties Radical Writer and His Apostasy* (Oslo: Novus Press, 2004), 110.

3 For a brief summary of Communist Party gains in the mid- to late thirties, see William Leuchtenberg, *Franklin Roosevelt and the New Deal, 1932-1940* (New York: Harper, 1973), 281–83.
4 For the relationship between Comintern policy and the American literary left, see Aaron, *Writers on Left: Episodes in American Literary Communism* (New York: Harcourt, Brace and World, 1961), 287–300.
5 These quotations and the list of signatories are taken from Henry Hart, ed., *American Writers' Congress* (New York: International Publishers, 1935), 10–11.
6 Hart, *American Writers' Congress*, 13. This quotation is from a "fraternal" message sent to the American Congress by the International Union of Revolutionary Writers.
7 Cantwell, "Better News from California," *New Republic* (May 22, 1935): 41–42.
8 Many of the papers delivered at the Congress were reprinted in Hart, *American Writers' Congress*. For a discussion of the first Writers' Congress, see Aaron, *Writers on Left*, 300–8.
9 Cantwell to Malcolm Cowley, n.d. Cantwell Papers, Knight Library Special Collections, University of Oregon (hereafter cited as Cantwell Papers).
10 Cantwell to Ernest Hemingway, October 21, 1950, Cantwell Papers.
11 T. S. Matthews, *Name and Address: An Autobiography* (New York: Simon and Schuster, 1960), 228–29.
12 Matthews, *Name and Address*, 228. Matthew Josephson to author, September 5, 1977.
13 Whittaker Chambers, *Witness* (New York: Random House, 1952), 85–86. The complexities of possible motives, and Cantwell's possible knowledge of Chambers's deeper motives, are discussed in the next chapter.
14 All *Time* writers wrote anonymously during this period, and although it is generally possible to discern from the staff list in the magazine whether Cantwell or Matthews is the reviewer, Cantwell's friend Calvin Fixx, who was hired as an assistant, also wrote reviews. Cantwell's distinctive style makes identification somewhat easier, but never foolproof. In any event, Cantwell seems to have steered clear of controversial subjects, in part, no doubt, because Luce and his staff or editors were judicious in their efforts to maintain a Luce version of "objectivity."
15 Cantwell, "The Return of Henry James," *New Republic* (Dec. 12, 1934): 121.
16 Cantwell, "Return of Henry James," 121.
17 John Dos Passos, *The Fourteenth Chronicle: Letters and Diaries of John Dos Passos*, ed. Townsend Ludington (Boston: Gambit, 1973), 464. This letter in holograph forms part of the Cantwell Papers as well. Cantwell and Dos Passos corresponded off and on from 1934. In a letter to the author (March 25, 1977), Cantwell refers to Dos Passos as his "close friend and benefactor" in the thirties.
18 Dos Passos, *Fourteenth Chronicle*, 463, 464.
19 Louis Adamic, "What the Proletariat Reads: Conclusions Based on a Year's Study among Hundreds of Workers throughout the United States," *Saturday Review of Literature* (Dec. 1, 1934): 321–22. Adamic found that 99.5 percent of American workers had not read a proletarian novel or exhibited any other signs of class consciousness.
20 Cantwell, "What the Working Class Reads," *New Republic* (July 17, 1935): 274.
21 Ibid., 274.

22 See Harvey Teres, "Remaking Marxist Criticism: *Partisan Review's* Eliotic Leftism, 1934–1936," *American Literature* 64, no. 1 (March 1992): 127–53"; Alan Wald, *The New York Intellectuals: The Rise and Decline of the Anti-Stalinist Left from the 1930s to the 1980s* (Chapel Hill: University of North Carolina Press, 1987); and Cooney, *Rise of the New York Intellectuals* (Madison: University of Wisconsin Press, 1986).
23 Cantwell, "What the Working Class Reads," 275–76.
24 Ibid., 276.
25 Ibid., 276.
26 Cantwell, "A Sign for the Future," *New Republic* (Oct. 23, 1935): 305.
27 Ibid., 305
28 Cantwell to James T. Farrell, June 12, 1934; Farrell to Cantwell, April 30, 1934, Cantwell Papers.
29 Cantwell, "A Town and Its Novels," *New Republic* (Feb. 19, 1936): 51–52. In October of 1935, Cantwell's friend Fixx was in Aberdeen and wrote to Cantwell that he saw "an astonishing healthy growth of class-consciousness" there, and that "the roots go deep into trade unions that have won out." Fixx to Cantwell, October 5, 1935, Cantwell Papers. That Cantwell was not wrong in imputing a good deal of militancy to Gray's Harbor workers is revealed by the history of CIO activity there in the mid- to late thirties. Violent conflicts were endemic to the organizing drive in the lumber industry there and elsewhere in the state. See John Blanchard and Dorothy Terrill, *Strikes in the Pacific Northwest, 1927–1940: A Statistical Analysis* (Portland, OR: Northwest Regional Council, 1942), 8–9.
30 Cantwell's friend James Farrell, however, amusedly noted a certain reticence in the piece (and in Cantwell generally): "No decent young critics review for the New Republic. Except for Bob Cantwell. And Bob is well mannered in his criticism, and rather than not be well mannered, as in his review of 'Marching! Marching!', he will write about geography." Cited in Seyersted, *Robert Cantwell*, 194.
31 Cantwell, "Ten Great Strikes," *New Republic* (March 25, 1936): 201.
32 Ibid., 202.
33 Cantwell to Farrell, June 13, 1934, Cantwell Papers.
34 James T. Farrell to Cantwell, Jan. 29, 1936, Cantwell Papers.
35 Ibid.
36 Cantwell to Farrell, February 3, 1934, Cantwell Papers.
37 Cantwell, letter to *Partisan Review and Anvil* (Feb. 1936): 31.
38 Quoted in Walter B. Rideout, *The Radical Novel in the United States, 1900–1954* (Cambridge, MA: Harvard University Press, 1956), 243.
39 Rideout, *Radical Novel*, 297–98.
40 Cantwell, "Fiction for the Millions," *New Republic* (Dec. 22, 1937): 204. This idea is similar to a proposition put forth by Mike Gold in 1929, but never acted upon, to assign one proletarian writer to study and write about each major American industry.
41 "Fiction for the Millions," 203.
42 Cantwell, "Upton Sinclair," *New Republic* (Feb. 24, 1937): 71. Reprinted in Malcolm Cowley, ed., *After the Genteel Tradition* (New York: Norton, 1937). Cowley's anthology also includes a Cantwell essay on Sinclair Lewis, originally published as "Sinclair Lewis," *New Republic* (Oct. 21, 1936): 298–301. Cantwell treats Lewis's novels as chronicles of the decay of middle-class

life in America, but as was true of his treatment of *A Sign for Cain*, he remains vague about the nature, causes, or precise symptoms of decline. Nevertheless, he concludes, "Lewis drew a revolutionary picture of American middle-class life without coming to revolutionary conclusions about it, unlike Upton Sinclair, who leaped to revolutionary conclusions and then filled in the picture."

43. All three of these writers, along with Cantwell's friend John Chamberlain, were "renegades" who, having attended the First Writers' Congress in 1935, boycotted the second, more tepid reformist Writers' Congress of 1937. See Aaron, *Writers on Left*, 319–24, 462.
44. For a brief description of the evolution of Dos Passos's opinions from 1937 to the end of the decade, see *The Fourteenth Chronicle*, 493–501.
45. See "Contributors," *New Republic* (Feb. 24, 1937): 189. The novel was also listed as "completed" in "Contributors," *New Republic* (Apr. 27, 1938): 378. Unfortunately, no manuscript of the novel exists among the Cantwell Papers.
46. John Chamberlain, "Literature," in Harold Stearns, ed., *America Now: An Inquiry into Civilization in the United States* (New York: Library Guild of America, 1938), 37.
47. See Matthews, *Name and Address*, 215–25.
48. Cantwell to Hemingway, October 21, 1950, Cantwell Papers.
49. Cantwell to Anna Koontz, July 9, 1938, Cantwell Papers.
50. Cantwell to Weldon Keys, January 6, 1939, Cantwell Papers.
51. See Cantwell, "The Communists and the CIO," *New Republic* (Feb. 23, 1938): 63–66.
52. Cantwell, "Communists and the CIO," 66.
53. Matthews, *Angels Unaware* (New York: Ticknor and Fields, 1985). 169–70.
54. Cantwell, "The Future of American Journalism," *New Republic* (Nov. 8, 1939): 41.
55. Cantwell, "A Warning to Pre-War Novelists," *New Republic* (June 23, 1937): 178, 179.
56. Ibid., 180.

NOTES TO CHAPTER 7

1. Per Seyersted, *Robert Cantwell: An American Thirties Radical Writer and His Apostasy* (Oslo: Novus Press, 2004), 110–11.
2. John Chamberlain, *A Life with the Printed Word* (Washington, DC: Regenery, 1982), 43.
3. Cantwell to T. S. Matthews, February 3, 1936, Robert Cantwell Papers, Knight Library Special Collections, University of Oregon (hereafter cited as Cantwell Papers).
4. Diary, 1939, Cantwell Papers.
5. See Chamberlain, *Life with the Printed Word*, 68, 97; see as well testimony in the freedom of information act FBI records in the Cantwell Papers.
6. Chamberlain, *Life with the Printed Word*, 149.
7. FBI file, Cantwell Papers (capitalization in original).
8. See T. S. Matthews, *Name and Address: An Autobiography* (New York: Simon and Schuster, 1960).
9. Cowley to author, April, 1977, Cantwell Papers; Granville Hicks, "Writers in the Thirties," in *As We Saw the Thirties*, ed. Rita James Simon (Urbana-Champaign: University of Illinois Press, 1969).

10 Quoted in Carol Brightman, *Writing Dangerously: Mary McCarthy and Her World* (Boston: Mariner Books, 1994), 227.
11 McCarthy, who can't be said to have liked many people, liked Cantwell, and had in common with him both a Northwest birth and a love of literary conversation. She thought him one of the few proletarian writers who wrote with real style. See, McCarthy, *Intellectual Memoirs: New York, 1936–38* (New York: Harcourt Brace, 1992), 7; and Brightman, *Writing Dangerously*, 108, 134, 139, and 224–27.
12 Josephson to author, March 1977, Cantwell Papers.
13 Cantwell to Hemingway, October 21, 1950, Cantwell Papers.
14 Ibid.
15 See, for example, Josephson to author, March 1977, Cantwell Papers.
16 Cantwell Papers.
17 "The Future of American Journalism," *New Republic* (Nov. 8, 1939): 39–41.
18 Ralph de Toledano, *Notes from Underground: The Whittaker Chambers–Ralph de Toledano Letters, 1949–1960* (Washington, DC: Regnery, 1997), 56–57.
19 Whittaker Chambers, *Witness* (New York: Random House, 1952), 85–86.
20 Toledano, *Notes from Underground*, 57–58.
21 Ibid.
22 Ibid., 79.
23 "The Chambers Story," *Newsweek* (May 26, 1952): 101–2.
24 Toledano, *Notes from Underground*, 171–72.
25 Published as Cantwell, *Famous American Men of Letters* (New York: Dodd-Mead, 1956).
26 "Small Boston," Cantwell Papers.
27 Book outline, ca. 1977, Cantwell Papers.
28 Ibid.
29 The manuscript of *Privacy* can be found in the Cantwell Papers.
30 Ibid.

NOTES TO CONCLUSION

1 James Bloom, *Left Letters: The Culture Wars of Michael Gold and Joseph Freeman* (New York: Columbia University Press, 1992). Clearly these judgments cannot simply be sorted out empirically; they are largely a matter of definition, degrees of tolerance for certain kinds of rhetoric, and, most importantly, differing political philosophies.
2 With regard to Cantwell, Malcolm Cowley's influence was particularly important. Cowley has been the subject of a biography, Hans Bak, *Malcolm Cowley: The Formative Years* (Athens: University of Georgia Press, 1993), but that work stops at the end of the twenties, with the thirties treated only tangentially and condescendingly in the epilogue.
3 Georg Lukács, Stefan Morawski, and a host of others after them have made elaborate efforts to extrapolate a Marxian aesthetic from Marx's and Engel's own scattered aesthetic comments, but to do so they have utilized a number of texts by Marx, Hegel, and others that were not available to American Marxists in the thirties. For a description of what which texts by Marx,

Engels, and Lukács were available to thirties leftists, and when, see Barbara Foley, *Radical Representations: Politics and Form in U.S. Proletarian Fiction, 1929–1941* (Durham, NC: Duke University Press, 1993), especially chapter. 4.

4 Henry James, *The Art of the Novel: Critical Prefaces*, with an introduction by Richard P. Blackmur (New York: Scribner, 1962), xi.

5 James Burnham, "Marxism and Esthetics," *Symposium* 4 (Jan. 1933): 27–28.

6 See Harvey Teres, "Remaking Marxist Criticism": *Partisan Review's* Eliotic Leftism, 1934–1936," *American Literature* 64, no. 1 (March 1992): 127–53, for an elaboration of this concept of "sensibility" as developed by Wallace Phelps/William Phillips and Philip Rahv.

7 See, for example, Terry Eagleton's *Ideology of the Aesthetic* (London: Verso, 1990); and the sometimes tortured turns of Michael Sprinker's attempt to fashion an Althusserian Marxist aesthetic in *Imaginary Relations: Aesthetics and Ideology in the Theory of Historical Materialism* (London: Verso, 1987).

8 Foley is a bit oblique about some of this. If her point is that overtly didactic "literature" can be one among a number of literary strategies for the left, then I have no quarrel with her (indeed I have argued in favor of this position in my book *Fifteen Jugglers, Five Believers*). If, however, she sees this as the main or only strategy for progressives, then I think she badly misunderstands our current literary-political context, which seems to me a conservative one calling for a far more Popular Front-like strategy. In addition to my work, see Rita Felski's *Beyond Feminist Aesthetics* (Cambridge, MA: Harvard University Press, 1989) for a rich argument about the need for a range of literary strategies for contemporary radicals, in her case with special relevance to the creation of feminist "counter publics."

9 See Douglas Wixson's rich evocation of the attempt by Jack Conroy and other midwestern "worker-writers" to sustain such a tradition, *Worker-Writer in America: Jack Conroy and the Tradition of Midwestern Literary Radicalism, 1898–1990* (Urbana-Champaign: University of Illinois Press, 1994).

10 I take the term "emergent" from Raymond Williams's tripartite staging of cultural formations as residual (declining but still present), dominant, and emergent (newly arising). Emergent formations are inevitably less sophisticated and fulsome than formations that have existed previously. They "emerge" into full power only over time. See Raymond Williams, *Marxism and Literature* (London: Oxford University Press, 1981).

11 This derisive phrase is Josephine Herbst's way of noting both the masculinism and elitism of elements on the literary left. Quoted in Paula Rabinowitz, *Labor and Desire: Women's Revolutionary Fiction in Depression America* (Chapel Hill: University of North Carolina Press, 1991), 4.

12 For a perceptive study that illuminates the strengths and weaknesses of the popular front culture with regard to music, see Robbie Lieberman, *"My Song Is My Weapon": People's Songs, American Communism, and the Politics of Culture* (Chicago: University of Chicago Press, 1989).

13 Richard Flacks, in his excellent history of American radicalism, *Making History: The American Left and the American Mind* (New York: Columbia University Press, 1991), elaborates on this crucial distinction, arguing that, despite its internally undemocratic form, the Com-

munist movement was nevertheless in many ways an important force in furthering the long tradition of radical democratic struggle in the United States.

14 This analysis is based on reading in new histories of communism cited in my introduction, as well as the work of James Weinstein, who elaborates the nature of the failure of the Communist Party in *Ambiguous Legacy: The Left in American Politics* (New York: New Viewpoints, 1975), and to Richard Flacks's analysis in *Making History*.

15 Ellen W. Schrecker, *No Ivory Tower: McCarthyism and the Universities* (London: Oxford University Press, 1986).

16 See Robert Sklar, "The Problem of an American Studies 'Philosophy': A Bibliography of New Directions," *American Quarterly* 23 (Aug. 1975): 245–62, for an early analysis of the cost of this process; Michael Denning, "'The Special American Conditions': Marxism and American Studies," *American Quarterly* 38 (1986): 356–80. See also the essays collected in Donald Pease, ed., *Revisionary Interventions into the Americanist Canon* (Durham, NC: Duke University Press, 1994), especially Pease's introduction; Gregory Jay, "Ideology and the New Historicism," in *Revisionary Interventions into the Americanist Canon*, ed. Donald Pease (Durham, NC: Duke University Press, 1994); and Donald Pease and Robyn Wiegman, eds., *The Futures of American Studies* (Durham, NC: Duke University Press, 2002), for elaborations of the ongoing harm done by US anti-Marxism and Marxism's continuing usefulness in synthesis with poststructuralism and other postmodern theoretical developments.

17 See Jay, "Ideology and the New Historicism," as it analyzes the way in which "consensus" history and new critical anti-ideological moves reassert themselves in many recent American versions of (not always so) New Historicism.

18 For an analysis of the deleterious effects of the left's failure for many years to engage in the crucial struggle over popular culture and popular pleasures, see Andrew Ross, *No Respect: Intellectuals and Popular Culture* (London: Routledge, 1989), especially chapters 1 and 2.

19 For a call for radical democracy rooted in a synthesis of neo-Gramscian and poststructuralist analysis, see Ernesto Laclau and Chantal Mouffe's classic *Hegemony and Socialist Strategy* (London: Verso, 1986). For a similar, less abstruse argument more rooted in American radical traditions, see Richard Flacks, *Making History: The American Left and the American Mind* (New York: Columbia University Press, 1991).

20 A classic example of this from the thirties is Kenneth Burke's "prematurely Popular Frontist" argument for substituting the word "people" for "worker" in Communist rhetoric. Burke was immediately denounced as "protofascist" for suggesting this idea at the American Writers Congress in 1935. For an important, Burke-derived neo-Marxist critical position, see Frank Lentricchia's *Criticism and Social Change* (Chicago: University of Chicago Press, 1985).

21 See, for example, Sacvan Bercovitch, "The Problem of Ideology in American Literary History," *Critical Inquiry* 12, no. 4 (1986): 631–53.

22 "Cosmopolitan intellectual" is Bruce Robbins's term for figures such as Edward Said and Gayatri Spivak, who attempt to inhabit a space at once in the First and in the Third worlds, or rather a space that attempts to undo such inadequate concepts. Bruce Robbins, *Secular Vocations: Intellectuals, Professionalism, Culture* (London: Verso, 1993).

23 This is one of the contributions of Michael Kazin's *American Dreamers: How the Left Changed*

a Nation (New York: Knopf, 2011). It does the important work of crediting the left for much positive change in the United States—for which they too seldom get (and too seldom claim) credit.

24 The most illuminating general analysis of this moment remains Stanley Aronowitz's *False Promises: The Shaping of American Working Class Consciousness* (Durham, NC: Duke University Press, 1992).

25 For a summary of this ongoing work, see Alan Wald, "Revising the Barricades: Scholarship about the US Cultural Left in the Post–Cold War Era," in *Socialist Cultures East and West: A Post–Cold War Reassessment*, ed. Dubravka Juraga and M. Keith Booker (Westport, CT: Praeger, 2002), 101–22, as well as several essays in *Writing from the Left* and the introduction to *Exiles from a Future Time: The Forging of the Mid-Twentieth Century Literary Left* (Chapel Hill: University of North Carolina Press, 2002). The best of the "new canon" anthologies, *The Heath Anthology of American Literature*, 2 vols., 6th ed. (Boston: Cenage, 2010), under the general editorship of Paul Lauter, goes the furthest of any major textbook in covering the long worker-writer tradition.

26 For a provocative collection of literary class analyses that I wish had been more influential, see the volume edited by Wai-chee Dimock and Michael T. Gilmore, *Rethinking Class: Literary Studies and Social Formations* (New York: Columbia University Press, 1994).

27 Laura Hapke, *Labor's Text: The Worker in American Fiction* (New Brunswick, NJ: Rutgers University Press, 2000); Paul Lauter and Ann Fitzgerald, *Literature, Class, and Culture: Anthology* (New York: Longman, 1999); and Janet Zandy, ed., *What We Hold in Common: An Introduction to Working Class Studies* (New York, 2001). See also the Working Class Studies Association at http://www.wcstudies.org.

28 Michael Denning argues cogently against both these rhetorical moves in his essay "The Academic Left and the Rise of Cultural Studies," *Radical History* 54 (Fall 1992): 21–47.

29 Hazel Carby, "The Multicultural Wars." *Radical History* (Fall 1992): 48–63.

30 Stephen Duncombe, *Dream: Re-imagining Progressive Politics in an Age of Fantasy* (New York: The New Press, 2007).

31 For a rich study of "what counts as theory," see the first chapter of Katie King, *Theory in Its Feminist Travels* (Bloomington: University of Indiana Press, 1994).

32 Once, again, Rabinowitz's *Labor and Desire*, a study of "women's revolutionary fiction in Depression America," is a highly suggestive work. See also Constance Coiner's *Better Red: The Writing and Resistance of Tillie Olsen and Meridel LeSueur* (London: Oxford University Press, 1994). For a perceptive reading of Richard Wright's literary work as an exploration of the race/class nexus in the United States and as a critique of CPUSA policy, see Cedric Robinson, *Black Marxism* (London: Zed Books, 1983), chapter 11. And for a nuanced reading of the role of black Southern culture in transforming a Communist-inspired sharecroppers union in the thirties, see Robin D. G. Kelly's *Hammer and Hoe: Alabama Communists during the Great Depression* (Chapel Hill: University of North Carolina Press, 1990).

33 Developing an analysis of how the proletarian novel functioned in this way is part of the project of Foley in *Radical Representation*. But, as I have suggested throughout, I am far less enamored than Foley of the idea that a unified, centralized party-led approach to such an effort was or should in the future be desirable. Indeed, that would be a disaster.

34 A fascinating study in this regard is Julia Mickenberg's, *Learning from the Left: Children's Literature, the Cold War, and Radical Politics in the United States* (New York: Oxford University Press, 2006), a book that details how radical writers nurtured in the thirties produced progressive children's literature well into the Cold War era, keeping alive an alternative vision that among other things influenced the sixties generation of activists.

BIBLIOGRAPHY

PRIMARY SOURCES

Manuscript Sources

Arvin, Newton. Papers. Mortimer Rare Book Room, Smith College Library.

Cantwell, Robert. Papers. Special Collections, University of Oregon Knight Library, Eugene, Oregon. An inventory of the collection is available from the manuscripts librarian, or online at http://nwda.orbiscascade.org/ark:/80444/xv41731.

Cowley, Malcolm. Papers. Yale University Library.

Josephson, Matthew. Papers. Yale University Library.

Published Fiction by Robert Cantwell, 1929–39

"Hanging by My Thumbs." In *New American Caravan* edited by Van-Wyck Brooks, Alfred Kreymborg, and Lewis Mumford, 184–98. New York: Macauley, 1929.

"Hills around Centralia." In *Proletarian Literature in the United States* edited by Granville Hicks et al., 39–57. New York: International, 1935.

"The Land of Plenty." *New Republic* (Oct. 12, 1932): 228–32.

The Land of Plenty. New York: Farrar and Rhinehart, 1934.

The Land of Plenty. Carbondale: Southern Illinois University Press, 1971.

The Land of Plenty. Logansport, IN: Pharos Press, 2013.

Laugh and Lie Down. New York: Farrer and Rhinehart, 1931.

"The Wreck of the Gravy Train." *New Republic* (Jan. 6, 1932): 216–18.

Critical Essays, Book Reviews, and Reportage by Robert Cantwell, 1929–39

The list that follows is not meant to be comprehensive but rather aims to include Cantwell's most important literary-political pieces as well as a sampling of his nonpolitical criticism. Persons wishing to gain a fuller picture of Cantwell's work as a book reviewer should also consult the monthly review column of the *New Outlook*, which carried Cantwell's byline from October 1932 until April 1935.

"America and the Writers' Project." *New Republic* (Apr. 26, 1939): 323–25.

"Author's Field Day: A Symposium on Marxist Criticism." *New Masses* (July 3, 1934): 27–28.

"The Autobiographers." *New Republic* (Apr. 27, 1938): 354–56.

"Autobiographical Sketch of Robert Cantwell." *Wilson Bulletin for Librarians* 10 (1936): 298.

"Better News from California." *New Republic* (May 22, 1935): 41–42.

"Both Monologues." *New Republic* (June 26, 1935): 199. Review of *Grandsons* by Louis Adamic, and *Talk United States* by Robert Whitcomb.

"Brightness Falls from the Air: A Literary Sermon." *New Republic* (Aug. 5, 1936): 375–77. On James Joyce.

"Can You Hear Their Voices?" *New Republic* (Oct. 18, 1933): 285–86.
"The Communists and the C.I.O." *New Republic* (Feb. 23, 1938): 63–66.
"Dramatists' Raw Material." *New Republic* (June 28, 1933): 187–88. On the "Bonus March".
"Effective Propaganda." *Nation* (Dec. 19, 1932): 372–73. On Grace Lumpkin's *To Make My Bread*.
"The End of a Tradition." *New Republic* (March 30, 1932): 188.
"The Esthetics of Plunder." *New Republic,* March 14, 1934, 135–36. Review of Matthew Josephson's *The Robber Barons*.
"Exiles." *New Republic* (Dec. 13, 1933): 136–37. Review contrasting Kay Boyle and Jack Conroy.
"Faulkner's Thirteen Stories." *New Republic* (Oct. 21, 1931): 271.
"Fiction for the Millions." *New Republic* (Dec. 22, 1937): 203. Review of Upton Sinclair's *The Flivver King*.
"Four Novelists of Tomorrow." *New Republic* (March 8, 1933): 108–9. Review of novels by James Farrell, Albert Harper, Meyer Levin, and M. K. Rawlings.
"Four Novels—Not without Propaganda." *New Republic* (April 12, 1933): 252.
"The Future of American Journalism." *New Republic* (Nov. 8, 1939): 39–41.
The Hidden Northwest. Philadelphia: Lippincott, 1972.
"The Influence of James Joyce." *New Republic* (Dec. 27, 1933): 200–201.
"Journalism—Magazines." In *America Now: An Inquiry into Civilization in the United States*, edited by Harold E. Stearns, 345–55. New York: Literary Guild of America, 1938.
"The King Is Naked." *New Republic* (May 20, 1936): 35–38. Review of three current biographies of William Randolph Hearst.
"Lawrence's Last Novel." *New Republic* (Dec. 24, 1930): 171.
"Lincoln Steffens' Voice." *New Republic* (Nov. 18, 1936): 81. Review of *Lincoln Steffens Speaking* by Lincoln Steffens.
"The Literary Life in California." *New Republic* (August 22, 1934): 49. Letter on persecution of literary radicals in California.
"Mr. Eliot's Sunday Afternoon." *New Republic* (Sept. 14, 1932): 132.
"No Landmarks." *Symposium* 4 (Jan. 1933): 70–85. New York: Harper and Row, 1937. (On Henry James and Grace Lumpkin.)
"Poet of the Irish Revolution." *New Republic* (Jan. 24, 1934): 313–14. Review of Sean O'Faolain's novel *A Nest of Simple Folk*.
"Prologue to Fascism." *New Republic* (Feb. 14, 1934): 22–23. Review of *Man of Good Will* by Jules Romain.
"The Return of Henry James." *New Republic* (Dec. 12, 1934): 119–21.
"The Revolution in Here!" *New Republic* (Aug. 24, 1932): 48.
"The Rover Boy on Wall Street." *New Republic* (July 12, 1933): 239.
"San Francisco: Act One." *New Republic* (July 25, 1934): 280–82.
"A Season's Run." *New Republic* (Dec. 11, 1935): 149–53. General overview of fiction in 1935.
"Sign for the Future." *New Republic* (Oct. 23, 1935): 305. Review of *A Sign for Cain* by Grace Lumpkin.
"Sinclair Lewis." *New Republic* (Oct. 21, 1936): 298–301. Reprinted in *After the Genteel Tradition*, edited by Malcolm Cowley, 112–19. New York: W. W. Norton, 1937.

Speaking of Change: A Selection of Speeches and Articles by Edward A. Filene. Washington, DC: National Home Library Association, 1939.
"Sympathetic to Revolt." *New Republic* (March 25, 1931): 159.
"Ten Great Strikes." *New Republic* (March 25, 1936): 201–2. Review of *American Labor Struggles* by Samuel Yellen.
"*Tobacco Road*." Review. *Symposium* 3 (Apr. 1932): 256–60.
"Toward a Better Death." *New Republic* (Oct. 2, 1935): 221–22.
"A Town and Its Novels." *New Republic* (Feb. 19, 1936): 51–52.
"Upton Sinclair." *New Republic* (Feb. 24, 1937): 69–71. Reprinted in *After the Genteel Tradition*, edited by Malcolm Cowley. New York: W. W. Norton, 1937.
"A Warning to Pre-War Novelists." *New Republic* (June 23, 1937): 177–80.
"War on the West Coast: The Gentlemen of San Francisco." *New Republic*, August 1, 1934, 308–10.
"What the Working Class Reads." *New Republic* (July 17, 1935): 274–76.

SECONDARY SOURCES

Aaron, Daniel. "The Treachery of Recollection: The Inner and the Outer History." In *Essays on History and Literature*, edited by Robert H. Bremner, 3–27. Columbus: The Ohio State University Press, 1966.

———. *Writers on the Left: Episodes in American Literary Communism*. New York: Harcourt, Brace and World, 1961.

Aaron, Daniel, and Robert Bendiner, eds. *The Strenuous Decade: A Social and Intellectual Record of the 1930s*. New York: Doubleday, 1973.

Abrams, Edward. *The Lyrical Left: Randolph Bourne, Alfred Stieglitz, and the Origins of Cultural Radicalism in America*. Charlottesville: University Press of Virginia, 1986.

Adamic, Louis. "What the Proletariat Reads: Conclusions Based on a Year's Study among Hundreds of Workers throughout the United States." *Saturday Review of Literature* (Dec. 1, 1934): 321–22.

Aronowitz, Stanley. *False Promises: The Shaping of American Working Class Consciousness*. Durham, NC: Duke University Press, 1992.

Bak, Hans. *Malcolm Cowley: The Formative Years*. Athens: University of Georgia Press, 1993.

Barcott, Bruce, ed. *Northwest Passages: A Literary Anthology of the Pacific Northwest*. Seattle: Susquatch Press, 1994.

Barnard, Rita. *The Great Depression and the Culture of Abundance: Kenneth Fearing, Nathaniel West and Mass Culture in the 1930s*. New York: Cambridge University Press, 1995.

Baxandall, Lee, and Stefan Morawski, eds. *Marx and Engels on Literature and Art: A Selection of Writings*. Milwaukee: Telos Press, 1973.

Beckwith, Brian Teague. "A Town and Its Novelists." In *On the Harbor*, edited by Beckwith and John C. Hughes, 88–95. Las Vegas: Stephens Press, 2005.

Benjamin, Walter. "The Author as Producer." In *Reflections*, edited by Peter Demetz, 220–38. New York: Schocken, 1986.

Bercovitch, Sacvan. "The Problem of Ideology in American Literary History." *Critical Inquiry* 12, no. 4 (1986): 631–53.

Bernstein, Irving. *The Turbulent Years: A History of the American Worker, 1933–1941*. Boston: Houghton-Mifflin, 1970.

Bérubé, Michael. *Public Access: Literary Theory and American Cultural Politics*. London: Verso, 1994.

Blake, Casey Nelson. *Beloved Community: The Cultural Criticism of Randolph Bourne, Van Wyck Brooks, Waldo Frank, and Lewis Mumford*. Chapel Hill: University of North Carolina Press, 1990.

Blake, Fay. *The Strike in the American Novel*. Metuchen, NJ: Scarecrow Press, 1972.

Blanchard, John, and Dorothy Terrill. *Strikes in the Pacific Northwest, 1927–1940: A Statistical Analysis*. Portland, OR: Northwest Regional Council, 1942.

Bloom, Alexander. *Prodigal Sons: The New York Intellectuals and Their World*. New York: Oxford University Press, 1986.

Bloom, James. *Left Letters: The Culture Wars of Michael Gold and Joseph Freeman*. New York: Columbia University Press, 1992.

Bové, Paul. *Intellectuals in Power*. New York: Columbia University Press, 1986.

Bowman, John Scott. "The Proletarian Novel in America." PhD diss., Pennsylvania State College, 1939.

Brightman, Carol. *Writing Dangerously: Mary McCarthy and Her World*. Boston: Mariner Books, 1994.

Brown, Edward J. *The Proletarian Episode in Russian Literature, 1928–1932*. New York: Columbia University Press, 1953.

Brown, Michael, et al., eds. *New Studies in the Politics and Culture of U.S. Communism*. New York: Monthly Review Press, 1993.

Buhle, Paul. *Marxism in the USA*. London: Zed, 1987.

Burnham, James. "Marxism and Esthetics." *Symposium* 4 (Jan. 1933): 27–28.

Calmer, Alan. "Portrait of the Artist as Proletarian." *Saturday Review* 16 (July 31, 1937): 17–20.

Carby, Hazel. "The Multicultural Wars." *Radical History* (Fall 1992): 48–63.

Casciato, Arthur D. "Citizen Writers: A History of the League of American Writers, 1935–1942." PhD diss., University of Virginia, 1986.

Casey, Janet, ed. *The Novel and the American Left*. Iowa City: University of Iowa Press, 2004.

Chamberlain, John. *A Life with the Printed Word*. Washington, DC: Regenery, 1982.

———. "Literature." In *America Now: An Inquiry into Civilization in the United States*, edited by Harold Stearns, 36–47. New York: Library Guild of America, 1938.

Chambers, Whittaker. *Witness*. New York: Random House, 1952.

Chauncey, George. *Gay New York: Gender, Urban Culture, and the Making of the Gay World, 1890–1940*. New York: Basic Books, 1994.

Clark, Norman. *Mill Town: A Social History of Everett Washington*. Seattle: University of Washington Press, 1970.

Coiner, Constance. *Better Red: The Writing and Resistance of Tillie Olsen and Meridel LeSueur*. London: Oxford University Press, 1995.

———. "Literature and Resistance: The Intersection of Feminism and the Communist Left in Meridel LeSueur and Tillie Olsen." In *Left Politics and the Literary Profession*, edited by Lennard J. Davis and M. Bella Mirabella, 162–85. New York: Columbia University Press, 1990.

———. "'Pessimism of the Mind, Optimism of the Will': Literature of Resistance." PhD diss., University of California, Los Angeles, 1987.

Colman, Louis. *Lumber*. New York: Little, Brown, and Co., 1931.

Conroy, Jack. "Robert Cantwell's *Land of Plenty*." In *Proletarian Writers of the Thirties*, edited by David Madden, 74–84. Carbondale: Southern Illinois University Press, 1968.

Conroy, Jack, and Curt Johnson, eds. *Writers in Revolt: The Anvil Anthology, 1933–1940*. New York: Lawrence Hill and Co., 1973.

Cooney, Terry. *The Rise of the New York Intellectuals, Partisan Review, and Its Circle, 1934–45*. Madison: University of Wisconsin Press, 1986.

Cowley, Malcolm, ed. *After the Genteel Tradition*. New York: Norton, 1937.

———. *Dream of the Golden Mountain: Remembering the 1930s*. New York: Viking, 1980.

———. *Exile's Return*. New York: W. W. Norton, 1934.

———. "A Remembrance of the Red Romance." *Esquire* 61 (Mar. 1964): 124–29, and *Esquire* 62 (Apr. 1964): 78–81.

———. *Think Back on Us: A Contemporary Chronicle of the 1930s*. Carbondale: Southern Illinous University Press, 1967.

Davis, Cheryl. "A Rhetorical Study of Selected Proletarian Novels of the 1930s." PhD diss., University of Utah, 1976.

Davis, Mike. *City of Quartz*. London: Verso, 1990.

Day, William R. "The Politics of Art: A Reading of Selected Proletarian Novels of the 1930s." PhD diss., Drew University, 1983.

Demilio, John. *Sexual Politics, Sexual Communities*. 2nd ed. Chicago: University of Chicago Press, 1998.

Denning, Michael. "The Academic Left and the Rise of Cultural Studies." *Radical History* 54 (Fall 1992): 21–47.

———. *The Cultural Front: The Laboring of American Literature in the Twentieth Century*. London: Verso, 1996.

———. *Mechanic Accents*. London: Verso, 1987.

———. "'The Special American Conditions': Marxism and American Studies." *American Quarterly* 38 (1986): 356–80.

Dimock, Wai-chee, and Michael T. Gilmore, eds. *Rethinking Class: Literary Studies and Social Formations*. New York: Columbia University Press, 1994.

Dolinar, Brian. *The Black Cultural Front: Black Writers and Artists of the Depression Generation*. Jackson: University Press of Mississippi, 2012.

Dos Passos, John. *The Fourteenth Chronicle: Letters and Diaries of John Dos Passos*. Edited with a biographical narrative by Townsend Ludington. Boston: Gambit, 1973.

———. "The *New Masses* I'd Like." *New Masses* 1 (June 1926): 20.

Duberman, Martin, et al., eds., *Hidden from History: Reclaiming the Gay and Lesbian Past*. New York: New American Library, 1989.

Dubofsky, Melvyn. *We Shall Be All: A History of the IWW*. New York: Quadrangle Press, 1969.

Duncombe, Stephen. *Dream: Re-imagining Progressive Politics in an Age of Fantasy*. New York: The New Press, 2007.

Eagleton, Terry. *Ideology of the Aesthetic*. London: Verso, 1990.

Fabre, Michel. *The Unfinished Quest of Richard Wright*. New York: Morrow, 1973.

Farrell, James T. *A Note on Literary Criticism*. New York: Columbia University Press, 1992.

Felski, Rita. *Beyond Feminist Aesthetics*. Cambrdige, MA: Harvard University Press, 1989.

Filler, Louis, ed. *The Anxious Years: America in the 1930s*. New York: Capricorn, 1963.

Filreis, Alan. *Modernism from Right to Left: Wallace Stevens, the Thirties, and Literary Radicalism*. Cambridge, UK: Cambridge University Press, 1994.

Fischer, Adam. "Formula for Utopia: The American Proletarian Novel, 1930–1939." PhD diss., University of Massachusetts, 1974.

Fishbein, Leslie. *Rebels in Bohemia: The Radicals of "The Masses," 1911–1917*. Chapel Hill: University of North Carolina Press, 1982.

Flacks, Richard. *Making History: The American Left and the American Mind*. New York: Columbia University Press, 1991.

Floyd, Kevin. *The Reification of Desire: Toward a Queer Marxism*. Minneapolis: University of Minnesota Press, 2009.

Foley, Barbara. *Radical Representations: Politics and Form in U.S. Proletarian Fiction, 1929–1941*. Durham, NC: Duke University Press, 1993.

———. "The Rhetoric of Anti-Communism in *Invisible Man*." *College English* 59, no. 5 (Sept. 1997): 530–47.

Folsom, Franklin. *Days of Anger, Days of Hope: A Memoir of the League of American Writers, 1937–1942*. Boulder: University of Colorado Press, 1994.

Frankenberg, Ruth. *White Women, Race Matters*. Minneapolis: University of Minnesota Press, 1993.

Gilbert, James B. *Writers and Partisans: A History of Literary Radicalism in America*. New York: Wiley, 1968.

Gilmore, Mikal. "The Road to Nowhere." *Rolling Stone* 683 (June 2, 1994): 44–46, 53.

Glenn, Robert William. "Rhetoric and Poetics: The Case of Leftist Fiction and Criticism in the 1930s." PhD diss., Northwestern University, 1971.

Goings, Aaron. "Red Harbor: Class, Violence, and Community in Gray's Harbor, Washington." PhD diss., Central Washington University, 2005. Available at http://libcom.org/files/redharbor.pdf.

Goldstein, Malcolm. *The Political Stage: American Drama and the Great Depression*. Oxford: Oxford University Press, 1974.

Hapke, Laura. *Labor's Text: The Worker in American Fiction*. New Brunswick, NJ: Rutgers University Press, 2000.

Harris, Calvin. "Twentieth-Century American Political Fiction: An Analysis of Proletarian Fiction." PhD diss., University of Oregon, 1979.

Hart, Henry, ed. *American Writers' Congress*. New York: International Publishers, 1935.

Hedges, Elaine. "Introduction." In Meridel LeSeur, *Ripening: Selected Work of Meridel LeSeur, 1927–80*, edited by Elaine Hedges, 1–29. New York: Feminist Press, 1982.
Heller, David P. *Hope Among Us Yet: Social Criticism and Social Solace in Depression America*. Athens: University of Georgia Press, 1987.
Hemingway, Andrew. *Artists on the Left: American Artists and the Communist Movement, 1926–1956*. New Haven: Yale University Press, 2002.
Hicks, Granville. "The Fighting Decade." *Saturday Review of Literature* 11 (July 6, 1940): 3–5.
———. *Part of the Truth*. New York: Harcourt, Brace and World, 1965.
———. *Where We Came Out*. New York: Viking, 1954.
———. "Writers in the Thirties." In *As We Saw the Thirties*, edited by Rita James Simon, 76–101. Urbana-Champaign: University of Illinois Press, 1969.
Hicks, Granville, Mike Gold, Isidor Schneider, and Joseph North, eds. *Proletarian Literature in the United States*. New York: International, 1935.
Hoffman, Frederick J. "Aesthetics of the Proletarian Novel." In *Proletarian Writers of the Thirties*, edited by David Madden, 184–93. Carbondale: Southern Illinois University Press, 1968.
Holcomb, Gary Edward. *Claude McKay, Code Name Sasha: Queer Black Marxism and the Harlem Renaissance*. Gainesville: University Press of Florida, 2009.
Holcomb, Gary Edward, and Charles Scruggs, eds. *Hemingway and the Black Renaissance*. Columbus: The Ohio State University Press, 2012.
Homberger, Eric. *American Writers and Radical Politics, 1900–1939: Equivocal Commitments*. London: MacMillan, 1986.
Howard, June. *Form and History in American Literary Naturalism*. Chapel Hill: University of North Carolina Press, 1985.
Howe, Irving, and Lewis Coser. *The American Communist Party: A Critical History*. Boston: Beacon, 1957.
Hummasti, Paul. "Finnish Radicals in Astoria, Oregon, 1904–1940: A Study in Immigrant Socialism." PhD diss., University of Oregon, 1975.
Hunt, Herbert, and Floyd C. Kaylor. *Washington: West of the Cascades*. Vol. 2. Charleston, SC: Nabu, 2010.
Hutchison, George. *The Harlem Renaissance in Black and White*. Cambridge, MA: Harvard University Press, 1995.
Irr, Caren. *Sburbs of Dissent: Cultural Politics in the United States and Canada during the 1930s*. Durham, NC: Duke University Press, 1998.
Jacobson, Matthew Frye. *Whiteness of a Different Color: European Immigrants and the Alchemy of Race*. Cambridge, MA: Harvard University Press, 1999.
James, Henry. *The Art of the Novel: Critical Prefaces*. With an introduction by Richard P. Blackmur. New York: Scribner, 1962.
Jameson, Fredric. "Introduction." In *Marxist Esthetics*, by Henri Arvon. Translated from French by Helen Lane. Ithaca, NY: Cornell University Press, 1973.
———. *Marxism and Form*. Princeton, NJ: Princeton University Press, 1973.
Jay, Gregory. "Ideology and the New Historicism." In *Revisionary Interventions into the Americanist Canon*, edited by Donald Pease, 211–42. Durham, NC: Duke University Press, 1994.

Johnson, Jeffery. *"They Are All Red Out Here": Socialist Politics in the Pacific Northwest, 1895–1925*. Norman: University of Oklahoma Press, 2008.

Josephson, Matthew. *Infidel in the Temple*. New York: Knopf, 1967.

Julien, Isaac. "Looking for Langston." Film. London: British Film Institute, 1989.

Jumonville, Neil. *Critial Crossings: The New York Intellectuals and Postwar America*. Berkeley: University of California Press, 1991.

Kalaidjian, Walter. *American Culture between the Wars: Revisionary Modernism and Postmodern Critique*. New York: Columbia University Press, 1993.

Kaplan, Amy. *The Social Construction of American Realism*. Chicago: University of Chicago Press, 1988.

Kaplin, Justin. *Lincoln Steffens: A Biography*. New York: Simon and Schuster, 1974.

Kazin, Alfred. *On Native Grounds: An Interpretation of Modern American Literature*. New York: Harcourt, Brace and World, 1942.

———. *Starting Out in the Thirties*. Boston: Little, Brown, 1965.

Kazin, Michael. *American Dreamers: How the Left Changed a Nation*. New York: Knopf, 2011.

Kelly, Robin D. G., *Hammer and Hoe: Alabama Communists during the Great Depression*. Chapel Hill: Univerisity of North Carolina Press, 1990.

Kempton, Murray. *Part of Out Time: Some Monuments and Ruins of the Thirties*. New York: Dell, 1955.

King, Katie. *Theory in Its Feminist Travels*. Bloomington: University of Indiana Press, 1994.

Klehr, Harvey. *The Heyday of American Communism*. New York: Basic Books, 1984.

Klehr, Harvey, et al. *The Secret World of American Communism*. New Haven: Yale University Press, 1995.

———. *The Soviet World of American Communism*. New Haven: Yale University Press, 1998.

Klein, Marcus. *Foreigners: The Making of American Literature, 1900–1940*. Chicago: University of Chicago Press, 1981.

Kornbluh, Joyce L., ed. *Rebel Voices: An I.W.W. Anthology*. Ann Arbor: University of Michigan Press, 1964.

Kriegel, Leonard. *Edmund Wilson*. Carbondale: Southern Illinois University Press, 1971.

Kutulas, Judy. *The Long War: The Intellectual People's Front and Anti-Stalinism, 1930–1940*. Durham, NC: Duke University Press, 1995.

Lacey, Candida. "Engendering Conflict: American Women and the Making of Proletarian Fiction." PhD diss., University of Sussex, 1986.

———. "Striking Fictions: Women Writers and the Making of a Proletarian Realism." *Women's Studies International Forum* 9.4 (1986): 373–84.

Langer, Elinor. *Josephine Herbst: The Story She Could Never Tell*. Boston: Little, Brown, 1984.

Larrowe, Charles P. *Harry Bridges*. Chicago: Lawrence Hill and Co., 1977.

Laclau, Ernesto, and Chantal Mouffe. *Hegemony and Socialist Strategy*. London: Verso, 1986.

Lasch, Christopher. *The Agony of the American Left*. New York: Random House, 1966.

Lauter, Paul. "American Proletarianism." In *The Columbia History of the American Novel*, edited by Emory Elliot and Cathy Davidson, 331–56. New York: University Press, 1991.

———. *Canons and Contexts*. New York: Oxford University Press, 1991.

Lauter, Paul, ed. *The Heath Anthology of American Literature*. 6th edition. Boston: Cenage, 2010.

Lauter, Paul, and Ann Fitzgerald, eds. *Literature, Class, and Culture: Anthology*. New York: Longman, 1999.

Ledbetter, Kenneth. "The Idea of the Proletarian Novel in America, 1927–1939." PhD diss., University of Illinois, 1963.

Lentriccia, Frank. *Criticism and Social Change*. Chicago: University of Chicago Press, 1985.

Leuchtenberg, William. *Franklin D. Roosevelt and the New Deal, 1932–1940*. New York: Harper, 1973.

Lewis, Merrill. *Robert Cantwell*. Boise, ID: Boise State University, 1985.

Lieberman, Robbie. *"My Song Is My Weapon": People's Songs, American Communism, and the Politics of Culture*. Chicago: University of Illinois Press, 1989.

Lipsitz, George. *Rainbow at Midnight: Labor and Culture in the 1940s*. Urbana-Champaign: University of Illinois Press, 1990.

Loftis, Ann. *Witnesses to the Struggle: Imaging the 1930s California Labor Movement*. Reno: University of Nevada Press, 1998.

Lott, Eric. *Love and Theft*. Oxford: Oxford University Press, 1993.

Lowe, Lisa. *Immigrant Acts: On Asian American Cultural Politics*. Durham, NC: Duke University Press, 1996.

Lowney, John. *History, Memory, and the Literary Left: Modern American Poetry, 1935–1968*. Iowa City: University of Iowa Press, 2006.

Lukács, Georg. "Marx and Engels on Aesthetics." In *Writer and Critic and Other Essays*, edited by Arthur Khan, 61–88. New York: New York Author's Guild, 2005.

Lyons, Eugene. *The Red Decade: The Stalinist Penetration of America*. Indianapolis: Bobbs-Merrill, 1941.

MacKinnon, Janice R., and Stephen R. MacKinnon. *Agnes Smedley: The Life and Times of an American Radical*. Berkeley: University of California Press, 1988.

Madden, David, ed. *Proletarian Writers of the Thirties*. Carbondale: Southern Illinois University Press, 1968.

Matthews, T. S. *Angels Unaware*. New York: Ticknor and Fields, 1985.

———. *Name and Address: An Autobiography*. New York: Simon and Schuster, 1960.

Maxwell, William J. *New Negro, Old Left: African-American Writing and Communism between the Wars*. New York: Columbia University Press, 1999.

McCarthy, Mary. *Intellectual Memoirs: New York, 1936–38*. New York: Harcourt Brace, 1992.

Merlis, Mark. *American Studies: A Novel*. New York: Penguin, 1996.

Merod, Jim. *The Political Responsibility of the Critic*. Ithaca: Cornell University Press, 1987.

Mickenberg, Julia. *Learning from the Left: Children's Literature, the Cold War, and Radical Politics in the United States*. New York: Oxford University Press, 2006.

Milibrand, Ralph, et al., eds. *Socialist Register 1984: The Uses of Anti-Communism*. London: Merlin, 1984.

Mullen, Bill. *Popular Fronts: Chicago and African-American Cultural Politics, 1935–46*. Urbana-Champaign: University of Illinois Press, 1999.

Mullen, Bill, and Sherry Linkon, eds. *Radical Revision: Rereading 1930s Culture.* Urbana-Champaign: University of Illinois Press, 1996.

Mumford, Kevin. *Interzones: Black/White Sex Districts in Chicago and New York in the Early Twentieth Century.* New York: Columbia University Press, 1997.

Murphy, James P. *The Proletarian Moment.* Urbana: University of Illinois Press, 1991.

Naison, Mark. *Communists in Harlem During the Depression.* New York: Grove Press, 1983.

Nekola, Charlotte, and Paula Rabinowitz, eds. *Writing Red: An Anthology of Women Writers, 1930–1940.* New York: Feminist Press, 1987.

Nelson, Cary. *Repression and Recovery: Modern American Poetry and the Politics of Cultural Memory, 1910–1945.* Madison: University of Wisconsin Press, 1989.

———. *Revolutionary Memory: Recovering the Poetry of the American Left.* New York: Routledge, 2001.

Nelson, Cary, and Jefferson Hendricks. *Edwin Rolfe: A Biographical Essay and Guide to the Rolfe Archive at the University of Illinois.* Urbana-Champaign: University of Illinois Library Press, 1990.

North, Joseph, ed. *The New Masses: An Anthology of the Thirties.* New York: International Publishers, 1969.

O'Neill, William L., ed. *Echoes of Revolt: The Masses, 1911–1917.* Chicago: Quadrangle, 1966.

Papke, Mary E. "An Analysis of Selected American Marxist Criticism, 1920–1941: From Dogma to Dynamic Strategies." *Minnesota Review* 13 (Fall 1979): 41–69.

Pearson, Norman Holmes. "The Nazi-Soviet Pact and the End of a Dream." In *America in Crisis,* edited by Daniel Aaron, 327–63. New York: Knopf, 1952.

Pease, Donald, ed. *Revisionary Interventions into the Americanist Canon.* Durham, NC: Duke University Press, 1994.

Pease, Donald, and Robyn Wiegman, eds. *The Futures of American Studies.* Durham, NC: Duke University Press, 2002.

Peck, David. "The Development of an American Marxist Literary Criticism: The Monthly *New Masses.*" PhD diss., Temple University, 1968.

———. "The New Marxist Criticism." *Massachusetts Review* 14 (Summer 1973): 639–41.

———. "Salvaging the Marxist Criticism of the Thirties." *Minnesota Review* 4 (Summer 1975): 59–84.

Pells, Richard H. *Radical Visions and American Dreams: Culture and Social Thought in the Depression Years.* New York: Harper and Row 1973.

Penrod, John. "American Literature and the Great Depression." PhD diss., University of Pennsylvania, 1954.

Rabinowitz, Paula. *Labor and Desire: Women's Revolutionary Fiction in Depression America.* Chapel Hill: University of North Carolina Press, 1991.

———. *They Must Be Represented: The Politics of Documentary.* London: Verso, 1994.

———. "Women and U.S. Literary Radicalism," In *Writing Red,* edited by Charlotte Nekola and Paula Rabinowitz, 1–16. New York: Feminist Press, 1987.

Rahv, Philip. "Proletarian Literature: A Political Autopsy." *Southern Review* 4 (Winter 1939): 616–28.

Rampersand, Arnold. *The Life of Langston Hughes.* 2nd ed. 2 vols. London: Oxford University Press, 2001.

Redding, Arthur. *Turncoats, Traitors, and Fellow Travellers: Culture and Politics of the Early Cold War.* Jackson: University of Mississippi Press, 2008.

Reed, T. V. *Art of Protest: Culture and Activism from the Civil Rights Movement to the Streets of Seattle.* Minneapolis: University of Minnesota Press, 2005.

———. *Fifeen Jugglers, Five Believers: Literary Politics and the Poetics of American Social Movements.* Berkeley: University of California Press, 1992.

Rideout, Walter B. *The Radical Novel in the United States, 1900–1954.* Cambridge, MA: Harvard University Press, 1956.

Robbins, Bruce, ed. *Intellectuals: Aesthetics, Politics, Academics.* Minneapolis: University of Minnesota Press, 1990.

———. *Secular Vocations: Intellectuals, Professionalism, Culture.* London: Verso, 1993.

Robbins, Jack Alan, ed. *Granville Hicks in the* New Masses. Port Washington, NY: Kennikat, 1974.

Robbins, William G. *Hard Times in Paradise: Coos Bay, Oregon, 1850–1986.* Seattle: University of Washington Press, 1988.

Robinson, Cedric. *Black Marxism.* London: Zed Books, 1983.

Roediger, David. *Wages of Whiteness.* London: Verso, 1991.

———. *Working Toward Whiteness: How America's Immigrants Became White: The Strange Journey from Ellis Island to the Suburbs.* New York: Basic Books, 2006.

Rosenfelt, Deborah. "From the Thirties: Tillie Olsen and the Radical Tradition." *Feminist Studies* 7 (Fall 1981): 370–406.

———. "Getting into the Game: Women Writers and the Radical Tradition." *Women's Studies International Forum* 9, no. 4 (1986): 363–72.

Ross, Andrew. *No Respect: Intellectuals and Popular Culture.* London: Routledge, 1989.

Salerno, Salvatore. *Red November, Black November: Culture and Community in the Industrial Workers of the World.* Albany: State University of New York Press, 1989.

Saltzman, Jack. "Robert Cantwell." In *Contemporary Novelists*, edited by James Vinson, 244–45. London: St. James Press, 1976.

Salzman, Jack, ed. *Years of Protest: A Collection of American Writing in the 1930s.* With Barry Wallerstein. New York: Bobbs and Merrill, 1967.

Salzman, Jack, and Leo Zenderer, eds. *Social Poetry of the 1930s.* New York: Burt and Franklin and Co., 1978.

Samuelson, Joan Wood. "Patterns of Survival: Four American Women Writers and the Proletarian Novel." PhD diss., The Ohio State University, 1982.

San Juan, Jr., E. *Carlos Bulosan and the Imagination of Class Struggle.* Quezon City, Phillipines: University of Phillipines Press, 1972.

———. *The Philippine Temptation: Dialectics of Philippines-U.S. Literary Relations.* Philadelphia: Temple University Press, 1996.

Schachner, E. A. "Revolutionary Literature in the United States." *Windsor Quarterly* (Spring 1934): 27–64.

Schrecker, Ellen W. *No Ivory Tower: McCarthyism and the Universities.* London: Oxford University Press, 1986.
Schwartz, Lawrence H. *Marxism and Culture: The CPUSA and Aesthetics in the 1930s.* Port Washington, NY: Kennikat Press, 1980.
Seyersted, Per. *Robert Cantwell: An American Thirties Radical Writer and His Apostasy.* Oslo: Novus Press, 2004.
Shahani, Nishant. *Queer Retrosexualities.* Bethlehem, PA: Lehigh University Press, 2012.
Shulman, Robert. *The Power of Politcal Art: The 1930s Literary Left Reconsidered.* Chapel Hill: University of North Carolina Press, 2000.
Sklar, Richard. "The Problem of an American Studies 'Philosophy': A Bibliography of New Directions." *American Quarterly* 23 (Aug. 1975): 245–62.
Smethurst, James. *The New Red Negro: The Literary Left and African American Poetry.* New York: Oxford University Press, 1999.
Smith, Bernard. *Forces in American Criticism.* New York: Harcourt, Brace and World, 1939.
Solomon, Maynard, ed. *Marxism and Art: Essays Classic and Contemporary.* New York: Knopf, 1974.
Spivak, Gayatri. *In Other Worlds.* New York: Routledge, 1987.
——. *The Postcolonial Critic.* New York: Routledge, 1991.
Sprinker, Michael. *Imaginary Relations: Aesthetics and Ideology in the Theory of Historical Materialism.* London: Verso, 1987.
Staub, Michael E. *Voices of Persuasion: Politics of Representation in 1930s America.* New York: Cambridge University Press, 1994.
Steffens, Lincoln. *The Letters of Lincoln Steffens.* Vol. 2, *1920–1936.* Edited with an introduction by Ella Winters and Granville Hicks. New York: Praeger, 1938.
Stott, William. *Documentary Expression and Thirties America.* New York: Oxford University Press, 1973.
Suggs, Jon Christian. "The Influence of Marxist Aesthetics on American Fiction: 1929–1940." PhD diss., University of Kansas, 1978.
——. "Introduction." In *Marching! Marching!,* by Clara Weatherwax. Detroit: Omni Graphics, 1990.
——. "*Marching! Marching!* and the Idea of the Proletarian Novel," in *The Novel and the American Left,* edited by Janet Casey, 163–72 (Iowa City: University of Iowa Press, 2004).
——, ed. *American Proletarian Culture.* Detroit: Gale Research. 1993.
Suleiman, Susan. *Authoritarian Fictions: The Ideological Novel as a Literary Genre.* New York: Columbia University Press, 1983.
Susman, Warren. "The Culture of the Thirties." In *Culture as History,* edited by Warren Susman, 150–83. Washington, DC: The Smithsonian Institution Press, 2003.
Sutton, Walter. *Modern American Criticism.* Englewood Cliffs, NJ: Prentice Hall, 1936.
Swados, Harvey, ed. *The American Writer and the Great Depression.* New York: Bobbs-Merrill, 1966.
——. "Cantwell Redivivus." *Novel* 6 (Fall 1972): 92–94.

Szalay, Michael. *New Deal Modernism: American Literature and the Invention of the Welfare State*. Durham, NC: Duke University Press, 2000.

Tannenhaus, Sam. *Whittaker Chambers*. New York: Random House, 1997.

Teres, Harvey. "Remaking Marxist Criticism: *Partisan Review's* Eliotic Leftism, 1934–1936." *American Literature* 64, no. 1 (March 1992): 127–53.

Toledano, Ralph de. *Notes from Underground: The Whittaker Chambers–Ralph de Toledano Letters, 1949–1960*, edited and annotated by Ralph de Toledano. Introduction by Terry Teachout. Washington, DC: Regnery: 1997.

Trotsky, Leon. *Literature and Revolution*. Trans. by Rose Strunsky. Ann Arbor: University of Michigan Press, 1960.

Tyler, Robert. *Rebels of the Woods: The I.W.W. in the Pacific Northwest*. Eugene: University of Oregon Press, 1967.

Urgo, Joseph R. "Proletarian Literature and Feminism: The Gastonia Novels and Feminist Protest." *Minnesota Review* 24 (Spring 1985): 64–84.

Wald, Alan. *American Night: The Literary Left in the Cold War Era*. Chapel Hill: University of North Carolina Press, 2012.

———. *Exiles from a Future Time: The Forging of the Mid-Twentieth Century Literary Left*. Chapel Hill: University of North Carolina Press, 2002.

———. *James T. Farrell: The Revolutionary Socialist Years*. New York: New York University Press, 1978.

———. *The New York Intellectuals: The Rise and Decline of the Anti-Stalinist Left from the 1930s to the 1980s*. Chapel Hill: University of North Carolina Press, 1987.

———. *The Responsibility of Intellectuals: Selected Essays on Marxist Traditions in Cultural Commitment*. Atlantic Highlands, NJ: Humanities Press, 1992.

———. "Revising the Barricades: Scholarship about the US Cultural Left in the Post–Cold War Era," in *Socialist Cultures East and West: A Post–Cold War Reassessment*, edited by Dubravka Juraga and M. Keith Booker, 101–22 (Westport, CT: Praeger, 2002).

———. *The Revolutionary Imagination: The Poetry and Politics of John Wheelwright and Sherry Magnan*. Chapel Hill: University of North Carolina Press, 1983.

———. *Trinity of Passion: The Literary Left in the Anti-Fascist Crusade*. Chapel Hill: University of North Carolina Press, 2007.

———. *Writing from the Left: New Essays on Radical Culture and Politics*. London: Verso, 1994.

Warren, Frank. *Liberals and Communism: The "Red Decade" Revisited*. Bloomington: Indiana University Press, 1956.

Weatherwax, Clara. *Marching! Marching!* New York: International Press, 1935.

Weatherwax High Senior Class. *The Quinault, 1923–24*. Aberdeen, WA: Quick Print Co.,1924.

Weinstein, James. *Ambiguous Legacy: The Left in American Politics*. New York: New Viewpoints, 1975.

Werth, Barry. *The Scarlet Professor: Newton Arvin: A Literary Life Shattered by Scandal*. New York: Anchor, 2002.

Wilcox, Leonard. *V. F. Calverton: Radical in the American Grain*. Philadelphia: Temple University Press, 1992.

Williams, Raymond. *Marxism and Literature*. London: Oxford University Press, 1981.
Wilson, Edmund. *The American Jitters: A Year of the Slump*. New York: Scribners, 1932.
———. *Shores of Light*. New York: Farrar, Straus and Young, 1952.
Wingard, Joel. "Towards a Workers' America: The Theory and Practice of the American Proletarian Novel." PhD diss., Louisiana State University, 1979.
Wixson, Douglas. *Worker-Writer in America: Jack Conroy and the Tradition of Midwestern Literary Radicalism, 1898–1990*. Urbana-Champaign: University of Illinois Press, 1994.
Wolf, Sherry. *Sexuality and Socialism: History, Politics, and LGBT Liberation*. Chicago: Haymarket Press, 2009.
Zandy, Janet, ed. *What We Hold in Common: An Introduction to Working Class Studies*. New York: The Feminist Press, 2001.

INDEX

A

Aaron, Daniel, 5, 159, 180n7, 185n28, 189n11
Aberdeen, WA, ix, 178, 187n1; Cantwell adolescence there, 23, 24; Cantwell's description of, 23–4, 90–1; ethnic and class tensions within, 23–4; as inspiration for *The Land of Plenty*, xv, 96, 130; and labor movement, 201n29; and literary left, 90–6; as site for proletarian novels, 90, 92, 96, 130. *See also* Cantwell, Robert, literary criticism of: "A Town and Its Novels"
Adamic, Louis, 27, 125, 126, 127, 200n19
aesthetics and the literary left, 11–16. *See also* Marxist literary criticism
Agee, James, 99
AIDS Coalition to Unleash Power (ACT UP), 172
Algren, Nelson, 120
Althusser, Louis, 61
American Caravan, 30, 187n19. See also *New American Caravan*
American Federation of Labor (AF of L), 71, 95, 113, 116–17
Anarchism, 67, 176–7
Anderson, Sherwood, 37, 40, 45
Arendt, Hannah, 164
Arvin, Newton, 10, 40, 45, 50, 59, 160, 162, 184n13; Cantwell's letters to, 103, 106–7, 108; views of Moscow trials, 137

B

Balzac, Honoré 52
Barcott, Bruce: on *The Land of Plenty*, x
Beard, Charles, 122
Benjamin, Walter, 51
Bercovitch, Sacvan, 172

Bloom, James, 160, 190n17
"Bohemian" radicalism, 40, 190n21
Bourdieu, Pierre, 11–13
"bourgeois" aesthetics, xiv; as barrier to development of proletarian art 50, 82–3, 190n19; Cantwell's views of, 50, 52, 59–61, 127–8, 164–5; radical engagement with, xiv, 39–40, 43, 160; radical opposition to, 36, 43
Bridges, Harry, 111, 114, 132
Brooks, Obed, 199n54
Brooks, Van Wyck, 37
Bulosan, Carlos, 8, 9, 93; *America Is in the Heart*, 93
Burke, Kenneth, 120, 205n20
Burnham, James: "Marxism and Esthetics," 163
Busch, Noel, 156

C

Cagney, James, 116
Caldwell, Erskine, 39, 45, 120, 168; autobiographical writing of, 158; Cantwell's views of, 57–8, 109; as figure in *Famous American Men of Letters* (Cantwell), 154–5; *God's Little Acre*, 58
Calverton, V. F., 40, 162
Canby, Henry Seidel, 83; Cantwell's views of, 133; review of *The Land of Plenty* (in *Saturday Review*), 195n32; review of *Marching! Marching!* (Weatherwax) (in *Saturday Review*), 95
Cantwell, Charles (Harry), brother, 20, 30
Cantwell, Charles James, Jr., father, 20, 21–2; death of, 25, 26
Cantwell, Charles James, Sr., grandfather, 21

Cantwell, Elizabeth Ann, daughter, 142
Cantwell, Elizabeth (Betsy) Chambers, spouse, 30–1, 45, 48, 98, 115, 143, 149, 156; Dupee's views of, 145; Josephson's views of, 146; as narrator in Cantwell's unpublished manuscript, 157
Cantwell, Frances Dorothy, sister, 20, 30, 47
Cantwell, James (Jim), brother, 20, 25, 29–30, 113; remarks on IWW, 28, 91
Cantwell, Joan, daughter, 47, 115, 142
Cantwell, Mary Elizabeth, daughter, 142
Cantwell, Nina, mother, 20, 21, 25, 30, 47
Cantwell, Robert (b. Lloyd Emmett Cantwell): adolescence of, 26; and CPUSA, 116, 118–19, 150, 151; as "critical fellow traveler," xii, 19, 42, 116, 140; descriptions of, 43–4; disillusion with the left after Nazi-Soviet Pact (1939), 139–40, 142, 144–5, 147, 150; education of, 25; extramarital affair of, 148; FBI file on, 150, 155–6, 157; as FBI informant, 149–50, 155; financial insecurity of, 30, 47, 49, 118, 142–3, 149, 157; and First Writers' Congress, 120, 121–2, 125; lost early writings of, 187n18; marriage to Betsy Chambers, 30–1, 45, 98, 115, 145, 146, 149; mental breakdown of, xvi, xvii, 145, 146, 148, 152–3, 154; on "organic" art, 49, 51, 84, 111, 162; persona as revolutionary writer, 44; possible extent of radicalism, 150–2, 179n6; Robert Simmons (Cantwell pseudonym), 50, 107. *See also* Cantwell, Robert, fiction by; Cantwell, Robert, literary criticism by; Cantwell, Robert, nonfiction work by; Cantwell, Robert, unfinished manuscripts of
Cantwell, Robert, fiction by: "Hanging by My Thumbs" (1929), 30; "Hills Around Centralia" (1935), 29, 87, 188n24, 195n42, 198n38; "Homage to Fletcher Henderson," 27; "The Wreck of the Gravy Train" (1932), 44. See also *The Land of Plenty*; *Laugh and Lie Down*
Cantwell, Robert, literary criticism by: "The Chambers Story" (1952), 151, 152–3, 156; "Four Novelists of Tomorrow" (1933), 56–7; "The Influence of James Joyce" (1933), 58–9, 64; "No Landmarks" (1933), 51–4, 63, 163; remarks in "Author's Field Day: A Symposium on Marxist Criticism" (1934), 160, 194n14; "The Return of Henry James" (1934), 123–4; "A Sign for the Future" (1935), 128–9, 202n42; "Sinclair Lewis" (1936), 201n42; "Ten Great Strikes" (1936), 131–2; "A Town and Its Novels" (1936), 130–1, 201n30; "Upton Sinclair" (1937), 136, 201n42; "What the Working Class Reads" (1935), 27, 125–8
Cantwell, Robert, nonfiction work by: *Alexander Wilson: Naturalist and Pioneer* (1961), 154, 181n8; "Background of War" (1939), 144, 145; "Better News from California" (1935), 121; *Famous American Men of Letters* (1956), 154–5; "The Future of American Journalism" (1939), 145, 150; *The Hidden Northwest* (1972), 155, 181n8; *Nathaniel Hawthorne* (1948), 149, 181n8; "The Press as Strikebreaker" (1934), 115; *The Real McCoy: The Life and Times of Norman Selby* (1971), 154; "The Revolution is Here!" (1932), 46–7; "San Francisco: Act One" (1934), 111–12; "War on the West Coast" (1934), 112–13
Cantwell, Robert, unfinished manuscripts of: *Enchanted City* (non-extant planned novel on San Francisco General Strike), 125, 132, 138, 139, 202n45; *Privacy* (unfinished nonfiction novel on Whittaker Chambers and the 1930s written in voice of Betsy Chambers Cantwell,), 155, 156–8; *Small Boston* (unfinished historical novel), 155. See also *Merchant of Boston*
Carby, Hazel, 174
Carlisle, WA, 23

224 INDEX

Carlisle, William, Jr., 22, 23
Carlisle, William, Sr., 22
Carlisle-Pennell Lumber Co., 22
Celine, Ferdinand: Cantwell's views of, 109
Census of Manufactures (1931), 87
Centralia Massacre, 23, 29, 71, 92, 114, 195n42, 198n38. *See also* Cantwell, Robert, fiction by: "Hills around Centralia"; Industrial Workers of the World (IWW)
Central Intelligence Association (CIA), 155, 156
Chamberlain, John, 43, 108, 143, 162, 202n43; on Cantwell's inability to finish third novel, 138; later anti-Communism of, 144; as partial inspiration for "Portrait of the Intellectual as a Yale Man" (McCarthy), 146
Chambers, Whittaker, 10, 97–8, 107; alleged underground work of, 48–9, 115; on Cantwell's mental instability, 154; on Cantwell's radicalism, 150–2; on Cantwell's review of *Witness* (in *Newsweek*), 152; Cantwell's unfinished nonfiction novel about, xvii, 155–6, 157–8; conversion to anti-Communism, xi, xvii, 142, 144–5, 167; and CPUSA, 118, 139, 145; as FBI informant, xvii, 149–50; as figure in *The Enchanted City* (Cantwell), 132; friendship with Cantwell, 48–9, 115, 122–3, 129, 139, 143, 149, 156; Josephson's description of, 47–8; as reviewer for *Time*, 139, 148; *Witness*, 150, 151, 152–3; views of *Laugh and Lie Down*, 49. *See also* "The Chambers Story" (Cantwell's review of *Witness*); Hiss-Chambers controversy
Chambers of Commerce, 106
Chase, Stuart: Cantwell's response to, 46–7, 109
Chauncey, George, 184n13
Chehalis, WA, 23, 187n2
Cobain, Kurt, 178, 187n1
Cochrane, Ben: *Disillusion*, 96

Coldiron, William Dean: *Disillusion*, 96
Colman, Louis, 45, 90; friendship with Cantwell, 28; *Lumber*, xv, 28, 90, 91–2, 96, 130; *Night Riders in Gallup*, 92
Commonweal: review of *The Land of Plenty*, 82
Communist International (Comintern), 38, 119, 121, 170; deference to Soviet wisdom, 169; and proletarian literature, 38, 190n13, 200n4; Second International, 136; "Third Period" of, 37, 119, 135, 168–9. *See also* International Union of Revolutionary Writers; Popular Front
Communist Party USA (CPUSA), xvi, 3, 4–5, 28, 40, 114, 160, 176, 179n5; and 1930s public relations, 119; and 1932 election, 45; failure of, 205n14; gains in 1930s, 200n3; and gender, 7, 182n6; and John Reed Clubs, 38; and labor movement in Washington State, 89; in *The Land of Plenty*, 78; and the leftist literary movement, xii, 6, 36–8, 40–1, 42, 45, 49, 62, 87, 94, 120, 185n28; in *Marching! Marching!* (Weatherwax), 93, 95, 96; and New Deal, 120; and *New Masses*, 36, 37, 135; and Popular Front, 18, 42, 118, 119–20, 168, 169; and race, 8–9. *See also* Cantwell, Robert: and CPUSA; Chambers, Whittaker: and CPUSA; Communist International (Comintern)
Congress of Industrial Organizations (CIO), 18, 114, 139; activity in Gray's Harbor, 201n29; rise of, 119, 135
Conroy, Jack, 90, 204n9; review of *The Land of Plenty* (in *Partisan Review*), 81, 87–8, 195n41
Corey, Lewis, (Louis Fraina): Cantwell's views of, 109; *The Decline of American Capitalism*, 109
Coser, Lewis, xiii
Coughlin, Charles, 107
Cowell, Henry, 93

Cowley, Malcolm, ix, xi, 45, 50, 108, 158, 160, 189n11; Cantwell's letters to, 121–2; on Cantwell's move to the right, 145; on Filene biography, 98; friendship with Cantwell, 46, 49, 98, 203n2; on John Reed Clubs, 189n11; and leftist criticism, 39, 40, 162; as partial inspiration for "Portrait of the Intellectual as a Yale Man" (McCarthy), 146; recollections of Cantwell, 43; review of "Hanging by My Thumbs" (Cantwell) (in *New Republic*), 188n26; on *Viewless Winds* (Murray), 96; views of Moscow trials, 137

Cullen, Countee, 8, 11

Cultural Front, 9, 16, 161, 176, 177; and Cantwell's career, xiii, 167–8; and literary production, 176; and music, 15; and periodization, 180n7. *See also* Popular Front

"Culture and the Crisis" (pamphlet), 45

Cummings, E. E., 27

D

Dahlberg, Edward, 39, 58, 168; Cantwell's views of, 109

Daily Worker, 96, 125

Darcy, Sam, 114, 132

Davis, Rebecca Harding, 66

Debs, Eugene, 89

Dell, Floyd, 189n8

Denning, Michael, ix, 17–18, 168; "aesthetic ideologies" vs. "cultural politics," 14; on components of the literary left, 39; on Cultural Front, 9, 161, 180n7; on dime novels, 194n6; on "fellow travelers," xii, 18, 42; on Popular Front, xvi, 15, 18, 42, 118, 168, 185n28, 186n31; on "textual" vs. "real" politics, 174, 206n28

Dietz (worker at Harbor Plywood): on *The Land of Plenty*, 85–7

dime novels, 66, 194n6

Dineson, Isaak: Cantwell's views on, 109

Dos Passos, John, ix, x, 37, 158, 168, 202n43–4; advice to Cantwell, 124–5; Cantwell's letters to, 117, 129–30; and CPUSA, xvi; on Filene biography, 98; and literary left, 39, 40, 45, 120; move to far right, 137; relationship with Cantwell, 200n17; review of *The Land of Plenty* (in *New Republic*), 81, 82; and Spanish Civil War, 137; views of Moscow trials, 137; views on proletarian literature, 61, 124, 135

Dreiser, Theodore, 40, 45, 120

Duncombe, Stephen, 175

Dupee, F. W., 10, 145

DuPont Corporation, 118, 143

E

Eastman, Max, 3

Eliot, T.S., 50, 109, 162, 163

Ellison, Ralph, 8, 182n8

Endore, Guy (b. Samuel Goldstein), 10; *Babouk*, 183n 8

End Poverty in California. *See under* Sinclair, Upton

Engels, Frederick, 41, 131, 191n25, 203n3

ethnicity and the literary left, 8–9, 183n8

Everett, Wesley, 29

F

Fadiman, Clifton, 43, 45; review of *The Land of Plenty* (in *New Yorker*), 84

Farr, Finis, 156

Farrar and Rinehart, 30, 138

Farrell, James T., ix, x–xi, 185n28, 190n17, 202n43; Cantwell's letters to, 62–3, 79, 83–4, 85, 110, 130; Cantwell's views of, 56, 62–3, 79, 109, 193n88; as figure in *Famous American Men of Letters* (Cantwell), 154–5; *Gas-House McGinity*, 56; and leftist literary criticism, 3–4, 40, 41, 50, 132–4, 162; and literary left, xvi, 39, 120, 160, 168; *A Note on Literary Criticism*, 3–4, 41; on proletarian literature, 189n12; reluctance to embrace Marxism, 62–3, 193n88; remarks on "A Town and Its Novels" (Cantwell), 201n30; views of Moscow trials, 137

Faulkner, William, 58, 96, 168; *As I Lay Dying*, 67; as figure in *Famous American Men of Letters* (Cantwell), 154–5

Fearing, Kenneth, 15, 184n13

Federal Bureau of Investigation (FBI), 115, 157; Cantwell as informant for, 149–50, 155; Chambers as informant for, xvii, 149–50; file on Cantwell, 150, 155–6, 157

Federal Emergency Relief Administration, 115

fellow traveling xii, 18; critical fellow traveling, xii, 19, 42

Filene, E.A., xv; Cantwell's impressions of, 99–101, 104–6, 144, 198n36; Cantwell's unpublished ghostwritten autobiography of, 98–9, 122; career as emblematic of capitalism, 97, 98; character of, 98, 100, 198n36; childhood of, 104; decision to fire Cantwell, 102; as figure in *The Enchanted City* (Cantwell), 132; first meeting with Cantwell, 99–100; friendship with Steffens, 197n3; Lenin's comment on, 98; reform efforts of, 97, 100, 101, 105, 106; relations with Cantwell, 103–4; self-image of, 97, 110; speeches of, 101, 102; Steffens's views of, 101; tensions with Cantwell, 103; Twentieth Century Fund founded by, 106. See also *Merchant of Boston*

First Writers' Congress, 120–1, 125, 128, 202n43

Fitzgerald, F. Scott, 31, 58; on bourgeois culture, 36; as influence on Cantwell, 72, 166; views of Cantwell, ix

Fixx, Calvin, 85; abandonment of Communism, 144; and CPUSA, 118; death of, 148, 157; early encouragement of Cantwell, 26, 27, 29, 30; at *Time*, 144, 148, 200n14

Foley, Barbara, 186n28: on "bourgeois" aesthetics, 50, 60–1, 62, 82–3, 190n19; and categories of proletarian novels, 70, 92, 96; on Communist Party racial politics, 8, 182n 8; on divisions among leftist critics, 160; on gender and the left, 7, 182n6, 194n13; on *The Land of Plenty*, 65, 73, 75–6, 96; on literary didacticism, 41, 164, 165, 204n8, 206n33; on Marxist literary criticism, 49–50; on the "mentor figure," 194n5; on proletarian literary theory, 189n8; on proletarian literature, 38; on proletarian writers, 66, 190n19

Ford, Henry, 135, 136. See also Sinclair, Upton: *The Flivver King*

Fortune, 123, 144

Forum: review of *The Land of Plenty*, 195n34

Frank, Waldo, 40

Frankfurt School, 167

Freedom of Information Act, 155

Freeman, Joseph, 193n84; Cantwell's views of, 160; and the literary left, 61, 135, 170; mention of Cantwell in preface to *Proletarian Literature in the United States*, 195n40. See also *New Masses*

G

gender and the literary left, 6–8, 60; in critical methodologies, 173–4, 175; and experiences of oppression, 39; racial dynamics of, 10; studies of, 7, 182n6, 185n28, 194n13. See also *The Land of Plenty*: gender and sexuality in

genre and the literary left, 14–16

Gilmore, Mikal, 187n1

Gold, Michael, 190n17; Cantwell's views of, 133, 160; founding of John Reed Clubs, 37, 38; and Gold-Wilder controversy, 42–3, 60, 190n20; on modernism, 39–40; and the proletarian literary movement, 36–8, 42–3, 61, 170, 189n8, 193n84, 194n18, 201n40; "Thornton Wilder: Prophet of the Genteel Christ," 36, 42–3. See also *New Masses*

Goldman, Emma, 177

Gregory, Horace, 162

H

Hapke, Laura, 174
Harbor Plywood Corp., 27, 29, 66, 85, 86, 87, 96
Harlem Renaissance, 11, 180n7
Harper, Albert: Cantwell's review of *Union Square* (in *New Republic*), 56–7
Hart, Henry, 128
Hearst, William Randolph, 140, 150
Hemingway, Ernest, x: Cantwell's letters to, 97, 146–8, 149; as figure in *Famous American Men of Letters* (Cantwell), 154–5; *For Whom the Bell Tolls*, 180n 7; views of Cantwell, ix, 31
Herald Tribune, 60, 133
Herbst, Josephine, 7, 39, 168, 195n40, 204n11
Hicks, Granville, 108, 169, 170: on Cantwell's shift to the right, 145; Cantwell's views of, 133, 160; Dos Passos's views of, 125; editorship of *New Masses*, 107; Farrell's views of, 132–3; and leftist literary criticism, 61, 164; and leftist literary movement, 38, 85, 194n18; review of *The Land of Plenty* (in *New Masses*), 80, 84, 87, 164; and Writers' Congress manifesto, 120. See also *New Masses*
Hill, Joe, 89
Hiss, Alger, xvii, 48, 149, 153; autobiographical writing of, 158; trial of, 150, 156. See also Hiss-Chambers controversy
Hiss-Chambers controversy, xvii, 151, 152, 153, 154, 156, 157
Hitler, Adolf, 119, 139–40
Hitler-Stalin Pact (1939). See Nazi-Soviet Pact (1939)
Holcomb, Gary Edward, 11, 183n8, 184n13
Hoquiam, WA, 66
House Un-American Activities Committee, xvii, 18
Howard, June, 16
Howe, Irving, xiii
Hughes, Langston, 8, 11, 114, 120, 180n7, 184n13; as figure in *The Enchanted City* (Cantwell), 132
Hunger March (1932), 46
Hurston, Zora Neale, 168, 183n8

I

Industrial Workers of the World (IWW), 40, 44, 114; and anarcho-syndicalism, 67, 177; beliefs of, 28, 188n23; Cantwell's uncle's involvement with, 29; critical studies of, 188n23; cultural production of, 89; decline of, 28; influence on Cantwell, 29, 44; Jim Cantwell's remarks on, 28, 91; John Reed's involvement with, 89–90; in *The Land of Plenty*, 66, 70–1, 78; and "Little Red Song" book, 89; in *Lumber* (Colman), 92; in *Marching! Marching!* (Weatherwax), 95; methods of, 28, 89; and Pacific Northwest culture, 23, 24, 28–9, 89–90, 91, 179n 5, 196n50. See also Centralia Massacre; Paterson Strike Pageant
International Bureau of Revolutionary Literature, 38
International Labor Defense organization, 92
International Longshoreman's Association (ILA), 111, 112, 114. See also San Francisco General Strike (1934)
International Union of Revolutionary Writers, 38, 121
Intrator, Mike, 49, 129

J

James, Henry, x, 60, 126, 140; aesthetic style of, 51–3, 54–6, 123–4, 141, 161–2; as "bourgeois" predecessor, 50; Cantwell's abandonment of, 171; Cantwell's admiration for, 12, 35; *Julia Bride*, 51, 53; on "organicism," 49, 51; "The Turn of the Screw," 52. *See also* Cantwell, Robert, literary criticism of: "No Landmarks," and "The Return of Henry James"

Jameson, Frederic, 62, 163
Jazz Age, 27, 34, 43, 180n7
John Reed Clubs, 41, 42, 49, 114, 189n11; elimination of, 120, 135; establishment of, 37–8
Johnson, Hugh, 112, 113
Josephson, Matthew, 45, 46; account of Cantwell's breakdown, 146, 148; autobiographical writing of, 158; Cantwell's views of, 109; recollection of Cantwell, 43–4, 47–8; recollection of Chambers, 47–8; *The Robber Barons*, 109
Joyce, James, x, 95; aesthetic style of, 51, 58–9, 60; as "bourgeois" predecessor, 50; Cantwell's views of, 12, 27, 58–9, 61, 64, 109, 124; *Finnegans Wake*, 59; "The Influence of James Joyce" (Cantwell), 58–9, 61, 64; *Ulysses*, 27, 58–9, 71

K

Kahlo, Frida, 93
Kaplan, Amy, 16
Kaplan, Justin, 104
Kazin, Alfred, 39; recollection of Cantwell, 43
Kazin, Michael, 205n23
Kelly, Clarence, 155
Kelly, Robin D. G., 182n8
Keys, Weldon, 139
King, Martin Luther, 172
Kreymborg, Alfred, 27, 187n19
Kronenberger, Louis, 84; review of *The Land of Plenty* (in *Nation*), 81, 83
Kunitz, Joshua, 133
Kunitz, Stanley, 160

L

"laboring of American culture," ix, xiii, 96, 139, 178
labor movement, 175; in American Northwest, xv, 23, 95, 130–1, 179n5, 194n10, 196n48, 196n50; decline of, 173, 178; in *The Land of Plenty*, 70–1; in *Lumber* (Colman), 28, 91–2; in *Marching! Marching!* (Weatherwax), 94–6. See also American Federation of Labor (AF of L); Congress of Industrial Organizations (CIO); Industrial Workers of the World (IWW); San Francisco General Strike (1934)

The Land of Plenty (Cantwell) (1934), x, xiv–xv, 97, 147, 164; Aberdeen as inspiration for, xv, 96, 130; and allegory, 44, 66, 67, 77, 78; Canby's review of, 195n32; Cantwell's autocritiques of, 78, 79–80, 82, 85, 130; and class consciousness, 69–73, 76, 77, 78; climax of, 74–5, 195n42; compared to *Laugh and Lie Down*, 166; critical response to, 80–8, 164–5, 195n40; Dos Passos's views of, 81, 125; editions of, 194n7; Foley's views of, 65, 75–6, 96; gender and sexuality in, 76–8; as "nonhortatory propaganda," 65, 78–9, 80–1, 82, 83, 84, 85, 86, 87, 88; omission from *The Hidden Northwest* (Cantwell), 155, 181n8; as proletarian novel, 63, 64–6, 86, 167–8; race and ethnicity in, 76; readership of, 87–8; Rideout's views of, 65; sales of, 88, 128; scholarly commentary on, 193n2; Steffens's views of, 110; structure of, 66–8, 70–1. See also Cantwell, Robert, literary criticism of: "A Town and Its Novels"

Laugh and Lie Down (Cantwell) (1931), xiv, 25–6, 30, 31–4, 46; autobiographical elements of, 31, 72; Chambers's views of, 49; characterization in, 195n31; debate over possible Marxist tendencies in, 49, 81; style of, 166, 195n31
Lauter, Paul, 174, 181n1
Lawrence, T. E., 154
League of American Writers, 120–1
League of Professional Groups for Foster and Ford, 45
Lenin, Vladimir, 62, 90, 105, 165, 169: comment on Filene, 98

LeSueur, Meridel, 7, 168
Levin, Meyer: Cantwell's views of, 56; *The New Bridge*, 56
Lewis, Sinclair: Cantwell's essay on, 201n42
Liberator, 36
Lipsitz, George, 15
Little Falls, WA (later Vader, then Enchanted Hills) (Cantwell birthplace), 20, 21, 187n2
Locke, Alain, 8, 11
London, Jack, 66
Long, Huey, 107
Lowe, Lisa 9, 13
Luce, Henry, 122, 138, 144; Cantwell's working relationship with, xvi–xvii, 144, 147, 148; empire of, 123, 142, 145, 146, 152, 154, 166–7, 181n8, 200n14; and Josephson's account of Cantwell's breakdown, 146, 148; and offer of severance package to Cantwell, 149. See also *Fortune*; *Time*
Lukács, Georg, 41, 203n3
lumber industry: in American Northwest, 20, 22, 89, 201n29; in *The Land of Plenty*, 81, 87; in *Lumber* (Colman), 92
Lumpkin, Grace, 45, 49; Cantwell's views of, 53–6, 128–9, 162; *A Sign for Cain*, 128–9, 202n42; *To Make My Bread*, 51, 53–6, 128. See also Cantwell, Robert, literary criticism of: "No Landmarks" and "A Sign for the Future"
Lyons, Eugene, 4

M

Macdonald, Dwight, 146; autobiographical writing of, 158
Malraux, André, 139; Cantwell's views of, 109, 136
Marx, Karl, 24, 48, 62, 91, 171, 175; aesthetic criticism of, 41, 52, 191n25, 203n3; *The Eighteenth Brumaire of Napoleon Bonaparte*, 114, 199n54
Marxist literary criticism, x, xiii, 3–4, 12, 35–6, 40–3, 49–50; and anti-Marxist criticism, 6; Cantwell's views of, 35, 49–51, 57, 59, 61–3, 78–82, 121–2, 132–4, 160–3; as a term, 191n23
Matthews, T. S., 27, 116, 122, 138, 139, 143, 145, 200n24
Matthiessen, F. O., 10, 184n14
Maxwell, William, 8, 11, 180n7
McCarthy, Mary, ix; autobiographical writing of, 158; on Luce's literary influence, 146; opinion of Cantwell, 146, 203n11; "Portrait of the Intellectual as a Yale Man," 146
McCarthyism, ix, xvii, 4, 48, 146, 149, 180n7; impact on literary radicalism, 5, 171, 173
McKay, Claude, 8, 11, 180n7, 184n13
McWilliams, Carey, 10
Melville, Herman: *Moby Dick*, 51, 55
Merchant of Boston (Cantwell) (unpublished), xv, 159: Cantwell's decision to write, 98; Cantwell's research for, 99–102, 104–5, 110; Cantwell's vision for, 99, 111; choice of Cantwell as writer for, 98; dissolution of project, 102–3, 117, 122; Filene's vision for, 97; impact on Cantwell, 147; impact of Popular Front era on, 122; manuscripts for, 98–9, 197n9; unpublished ghostwritten autobiography version of, 98–9, 122
Mickenberg, Julia, 15, 207n34
modernism, xiv, 179n7; and aesthetics, 14, 15; and proletarian writers, 39–40, 41, 94, 127, 167, 180n7, 190n22
Moore, Marianne, 27
More, Paul Elmer, 126
Morgan, Murray: *Viewless Winds*, 96
Moscow Trials (1936–8), 119, 137, 138
Murphy, James P., 185n28, 190n22

N

Nation, ix; review of *The Land of Plenty*, 81
National Recovery Administration, 100, 112

naturalism (literary), 15, 16, 66, 180n7
Nazi-Soviet Pact (1939), 4, 147; and Cantwell's shift from the left, xvi, 139–40, 142, 144
Nekola, Charlotte, 7, 182n6
Nelson, Cary, 15, 180n7, 188n5, 191n22
New American Caravan, 188n26
New Criticism, 49, 162, 195n31, 205n17
New Deal, 109, 115, 120, 122
New Historicism, 205n17
New Masses, 36, 37, 38, 48, 87, 97, 139; aesthetic standards in reviews, 41, 49, 60, 62, 160; "Author's Field Day," 38, 160, 190n16, 194n14; Cantwell as contributor to, 50, 106–7, 123, 160; Cantwell's critiques of, 57–8, 133–4, 160, 162; Cantwell's letters to, 78, 79–80, 82; critical style of, 161, 162; development of moderate tone, 121–2, 132–4, 135; and non-Party critics, 160–1; and Popular Front, 135; prize for best proletarian novel, 93, 94, 130; review of *The Land of Plenty*, 80, 84, 85; shift to weekly format, 107; and Writer's Congress manifesto, 120, 122. *See also* Freeman, Joseph; Gold, Mike; Hicks, Granville
New Outlook: Cantwell as book reviewer for, 49, 57, 107, 108–9
New Republic, 27, 35, 36, 43, 45, 137, 138, 146; Cantwell as book reviewer for, ix, 46, 49, 64, 98, 108, 130–2, 135–6, 201n30; Cantwell as contributor to, ix, 44, 111–17, 123, 125; review of *The Land of Plenty*, 81; review of *New American Caravan*, 188n26
Newsweek, 150; Cantwell as book reviewer for, 151, 152, 153, 181n8
New Yorker, 43; review of *The Land of Plenty*, 84
New York Times Book Review, ix; Cantwell letter to, 82; review of *The Land of Plenty*, 81, 85, 162; review of *Laugh and Lie Down*, 34; review of *Lumber* (Colman), 91

New York Tribune, 162
Night Riders in Gallup (pamphlet by Colman) (1935), 92

O

Obama, Barack, 177
Occupy Wall Street, 19, 172, 176–7
Olsen, Tillie Lerner, 7, 132, 168
Onalaska, WA, Cantwell youth there, 22

P

Partisan Review, 4, 42, 107–8, 134–5, 185n28, 199n54; anti-Stalinism of, 4, 137; Cantwell's views of, 127, 134, 160, 169; critical principles of, 133–5, 162, 163, 204n6; critical studies of, 181n3; "Proletarian Literature: A Political Autopsy" (Rahv), 4; review of *The Land of Plenty*, 81, 85, 195n41. *See also* Phelps, Wallace; Rahv, Philip
Paterson Strike Pageant, 89–90
People's Front. *See* Popular Front
Phelps, Wallace (a.k.a. William Philips), 41, 127; "Problems and Perspectives in Revolutionary Literature," 195n40
Phillips, William. *See* Phelps, Wallace
Popular Front, xvi, 15, 18, 69, 170, 177, 204n8; Cantwell response to, 121, 122, 123, 168–9; Denning on, xvi, 15, 18, 42, 118, 168, 185n28, 186n31; effect on literary left, 126, 135, 171; establishment of, 119–20; and music, 204n12; as response to Spanish Civil War, 137
Populist Party, 40, 89
Proletarian Literature in the United States, 195n40, 195n42, 198n38
proletarian literary movement, x, xiii, 36–41, 120, 161; and Aberdeen, 90, 92, 96, 130; and "bourgeois" aesthetics, 39–40, 43, 50, 60–1, 82–3, 127–8, 190n19; Cantwell's views on, xiv–xv, 53–8, 60–3, 64–5, 79, 111, 123–4, 125–35; "collective novel" variety of, 68, 82; critical study of, 174, 181n1,

189n8; decline of, 135, 173; as emergent literary form, 12, 16, 54, 56, 167; expansion of, 18; and gender, 60, 76, 193n83, 194n13; literary evaluation of, 161, 165–9; and modernism, 39–40, 180n7, 190n22; readership, 125–8; as a term, 36–7, 38, 189n8, 189n12; traditional criticism of, 4, 36–7. *See also The Land of Plenty*: as proletarian novel

Proletkult writers 37, 38

propaganda, 166; Cantwell's views on, 61, 63, 110–11, 164; *The Land of Plenty* as, 65, 78–9, 80–1, 82, 83, 84, 85, 86, 87, 88

Proust, Marcel, 39–40, 124, 163

R

Rabinowitz, Paula, 6, 16; on gender and the literary left, 7, 182n6, 185n28, 193n83, 194n13, 206n32; on *Marching! Marching!* (Weatherwax), 196n61

race and the literary left, 8–10, 76, 182n8

Rahv, Philip: and *Partisan Review*, 41, 127; "Problems and Perspectives in Revolutionary Literature," 195n40; "Proletarian Literature: A Political Autopsy," 4. *See also Partisan Review*

Rawling, Marjorie Kinnan, 56; Cantwell's views of, 57; *South Moon Under*, 56, 57

Red Scare, 28

Reed, John, 89–90; *Ten Days That Shook the World*, 89

"reworking" of American literature, xvii, xviii, 159, 174

Rideout, Walter, 5, 180n7; on *The Land of Plenty*, 65

Rivera, Diego, 93

Roosevelt, Franklin D., 47, 103, 107, 112, 113, 115. *See also* New Deal

Rosenberg case, 149

Roth, Henry, 39, 168

Rukeyser, Muriel, 7, 184n13

S

San Francisco General Strike (1934), xvi, 94, 107, 111–17, 121, 132, 199n51; Cantwell reportage on, 111–17, 199n54; and Popular Front movement, 118. *See also* Cantwell, Robert, unfinished manuscripts of: *Enchanted City*

San Juan, E., Jr., 9

Saturday Review, 83, 125; Cantwell as contributor, ix, 161, 175; Cantwell's views of, 60, 133, 162; review of *The Land of Plenty*, 195n32; review of *Marching! Marching!* (Weatherwax), 95. *See also* Canby, Henry Seidal

Saxon, Lyle, 30, 158

Schapiro, Meyer, 98

Schrecker, Ellen, 171

Scottsboro Boys case, 9, 92

Seaver, Edwin, 57

Sedgwick, Eve, 11

sexuality and the literary left, 10–11, 184n13

Seyersted, Per, 179n6

Sherman, John, 118, 143

Simmons, August, Cantwell's uncle, 29

Simmons, Katherine, Cantwell's grandmother, 21

Simmons, Michael Troutman, Cantwell's great-grandfather, 20–1

Simmons, Robert (Cantwell pseudonym). *See under* Cantwell, Robert

Sinclair, Upton, 40, 107, 121, 122; Cantwell's views of, 135–6, 202n42; End Poverty in California (EPIC), 121; *The Flivver King*, 135–6

Sleepy Lagoon case, 9

Sloan, John, 89

Smethurst, James, 8

Smith, Bernard, 162

Socialist Party, 40, 89

Sowinska, Suzanne, 10, 182n6

Spanish Civil War, 119, 137

Sports Illustrated, (Cantwell job with) 154, 181n8

232   INDEX

Stalin, Joseph, 4, 119, 137, 139–40
Stalinism, 4–5, 41, 42, 145, 171, 186n28
Stanton, Elizabeth Cady, 172
Steffens, Lincoln, 109, 114, 158; *The Autobiography of Lincoln Steffens*, 110; as figure in *The Enchanted City*, 132; friendship with Filene, 197n3; and *Merchant of Boston*, xv, 97–8, 99, 103, 104, 106, 108, 110; stroke suffered by, 99, 104; views of Filene, 101; views of *The Land of Plenty*, 110
Stein, Gertrude, 27; *Autobiography of Alice B. Toklas*, 158
Stolberg, Benjamin, 139
Stone, Geoffrey: review of *The Land of Plenty* (in *Commonweal*), 82
Strachey, John: Cantwell's views of, 109; *The Coming Struggle for Power*, 109
Strang, Gerald, 93
Strauss, Harold: on *Laugh and Lie Down*, 81; review of *The Land of Plenty* (in *New York Times Book Review*), 81–2, 84, 85, 162
Strong, Anna Louise, 89, 90; "The Trumpets of Freedom," 93
Student Nonviolent Coordinating Committee, 177
Symposium, 51, 163

T

Third International. *See* Communist International
Thoreau, Henry David, 177
Time: attribution of articles in, 200n14; Cantwell as writer for, xvii, 122–3, 138–9, 143–4, 145, 146, 147, 150, 151, 152, 181n8; Cantwell's severance package from, 149; employees subsequently joining CIA, 155–6; factionalism within staff, 138, 145, 147, 148, 150; Mary McCarthy's views of, 146; review of *The Land of Plenty*, 84. *See also* Luce, Henry
de Toledano, Ralph: letters exchanged with Chambers, 150–3; remarks on Cantwell, 152–3, 154

Townsend, Francis, 107
transition, 27
Trotsky, Leon, 3, 11, 119, 165, 186n28; *Literature and Revolution*, 41, 191n26; trial of, 137
Trotskyism, 40–1, 42, 137, 170
Truth, Sojourner, 172
Twentieth Century Club. *See under* Filene, E. A.

U

United Auto Workers, 135, 136

V

Vader, WA. *See* Little Falls, WA
Veblen, Thorstein, 36

W

Wald, Alan, xii, 14, 173, 180n7, 182n3; on race and the literary left, 8, 10, 182n8; on revisionist criticism, 17, 185n27; on sexuality and the literary left, 184n13
Walker, Margaret, 8
Wallis, Keene, 27, 187n19
Waltor, E. H.: review of *The Land of Plenty* (in *Forum*), 195n34
Warrior, Robert, 9
Weatherwax, Clara, 24, 91, 92–4; *Marching! Marching!*, xv, 90, 93–6, 130–1, 196n61, 201n30
Weatherwax, John ("Jack"), 93; "The Trumpets of Freedom," 93
West, Nathaniel, 15, 120, 168; Cantwell's views of, 109
Wilder, Thornton: Gold-Wilder controversy, 36, 42–3, 60, 190n20
Williams, Raymond, 11, 12–13, 168; and "emergent" cultural formations, 184n17, 204n10
Wilson, Edmund, x, 27, 39, 45, 50, 108, 169, 202n43; autobiographical writing of, 158; "The Economic Interpretation of Wilder" (in *New Republic*), 43, 191n29; and Gold-Wilder controversy, 43; and leftist literary criticism, 35–6, 40, 42, 43, 132–3, 160,

162; views of Cantwell, ix, 145; views of Moscow trials, 137
Winter, Ella, 114, 116, 132
Wixson, Douglas, 38, 39, 179n5, 185n28
Wobblies. *See* Industrial Workers of the World (IWW)
working-class studies, 174
Wright, Richard, 8, 39, 168, 182n8, 206n32
Writers' Congress of 1937, 202n43. *See also* First Writers' Congress

Y

Yellen, Samuel: *American Labor Struggles*, 131–2, 136

www.ingramcontent.com/pod-product-compliance
Lightning Source LLC
Chambersburg PA
CBHW020328240426
43665CB00044B/949